Awakening

—— THE ——

Leader Within

What People Are Saying About
Awakening the Leader Within . . .

Awakening the Leader Within is definitely a major breakthrough. Each chapter creates an engaging opportunity for personal introspection and professional breakthrough. The potential power to authentically link your personal values and beliefs to your leadership style is at your fingertips in this book.
— *Chuck Feltz, President, Deluxe Financial Services, Inc.*

Awakening the Leader Within's lessons on authenticity and leadership are outstanding. Cashman's pragmatic approach to helping leaders align with the principles of openness, honesty and integrity are worth the price of the book alone.
— *Rob Hawthorne, former President and CEO, OceanSpray; former President, The Pillsbury Company*

Awakening the Leader Within goes way beyond the typical business book focused on theory and concepts. It draws you into real-life situations and real-life business challenges and reveals the pathways to more authentic leadership.
— *Janet Fiola, Senior Vice President–Human Resources, Medtronic*

Awakening the Leader Within makes the critical connection between business conduct and personal authenticity. It also gives you great daily strategies you can use to immediately impact performance.
— *Gregg Vandesteeg, Executive Director–Research and Development, 3M Company*

Awakening the Leader Within is an exceptional and quite remarkable leadership book. It reads like a novel but has a practical power to change deeply those who have the courage to reassess their lives.
— *Norman Walker, Global Human Resources Head, Novartis*

Some of the world's great myths—the Grail King, Sleeping Beauty—teach that when the king or queen sleeps, those around them also sleep and the kingdom sleeps, but when they awaken, those around them also awaken and the kingdom flowers. Kevin Cashman's compelling and powerfully perceptive new book tells the story of how we as kings and queens can come to awaken, in the deepest sense, and by doing so can help the kingdom to flower. I recommend this book wholeheartedly.
— *Gregg Levoy, author of* Callings: Finding and Following an Authentic Life

Awakening the Leader Within will help you break free from being a captive of your own success. If you want to grow as a person and awaken deeper levels of authenticity and purpose, then this is the book!
— *James Behnke, former Chief Technology Officer, The Pillsbury Company,*
and President, International Life Sciences Institute

Awakening the Leader Within is engaging and thought-provoking. It's the type of book I read with a highlighter in hand, marking sections and dog-earing pages as I go along.
　—*Marti Morfitt, President and CEO, CNS, Inc., The Breathe Right® Company*

Awakening the Leader Within is an exceptional and rare business book! I was surprised how much I was drawn into the characters and equally shocked at how deeply it moved me. Once you take the transformative journey with Bensen and Kenji, you may awaken more than you expect.
　—*Jack Covert, President/Founder, 1-800-CEO-READ*

Far from the typical business book that is boring while it is informing, *Awakening the Leader Within* is engaging while it is inspiring. How Cashman leverages the power of a story to create a learning experience around enduring business and life principles is outstanding.
　—*William Scheurer, Director, Carlson School of Management, Executive Development Center*

Today's leaders are searching for a new sense of ethical consciousness. *Awakening the Leader Within* instills hope by showing us a way to live and lead that integrates authenticity with great business results. It does a great job sorting through the confusion about what is required for real leadership in these times of turmoil.
　—*Jim Secord, former CEO of Lakewood Publications, Publishers of* Training *Magazine*

Experiencing this book is equivalent to stepping into a clearing and seeing your shadows—your dark shadows and golden shadows—in a more enlightened perspective and then continuing your journey to authentic leadership.
　—*Cliff Eslinger, Senior Vice President, Spherion—Human Capital Consulting Group*

Awakening the Leader Within is an imaginative, soul-enriching book. It invites busy, successful people to connect with their own deepest purpose, enriching their work and every aspect of their life with the authentic, creative power at the core of their being. This book helps cultivate the habits and skills we all need in order to live good and decent lives in this time of great global change.
　—*Br. Dietrich Reinhart, OSB, President, Saint John's University, Collegeville, Minnesota*

After Enron and WorldCom, business leaders are challenged as never before to measure up. If you don't want to fall short, read *Awakening the Leader Within,* an essential, innovative guide to leading with responsibility and gaining authenticity, integrity and reassuring purpose in life.
　—*Stephen B. Young, Global Executive Director, The Caux Round Table*

Awakening the Leader Within is a real wake-up call to leaders at all levels. Whether you are a young, emerging leader or a more mature leader, use this book to find your purpose—it will transform how you lead and how you live.
　—*Kurt Mueller, President, Center for Entrepreneurial Leadership, Ewing Marion Kauffman Foundation*

Leading from the soul—read the story of Bensen and Kenji and you will never forget their lessons.

—*Judith S. Corson, Co-Founder and former President, Custom Research, Inc.,*
Malcolm Baldrige National Quality Award Winner

In this gripping story of an executive in crisis, Kevin Cashman uncovers and illustrates essential principles for long-lived effectiveness of leaders. Our world is in great need of leaders who lead from depth of character. *Awakening the Leader Within* will inform and encourage many.

—*David Wessner, President and CEO, Park Nicollet Health Services*

Whether you're a seasoned or an emerging leader, this book will speak to your soul. I guarantee you will be inspired!

—*Richard J. Leider, Founding Principal, The Inventure Group, and*
bestselling author of Repacking Your Bags *and* Whistle While You Work

Our professional work with executive coaching and employee engagement has taught us that coaching is indeed one of the most powerful ways to develop leaders. *Awakening the Leader Within*'s captivating story creates a living example of the transformational power of coaching and makes this book an essential tool for any business leader.

—*Cindy Rodahl, Vice President of Human Resources, Carlson Marketing Group*

Awakening the Leader Within is an engaging, riveting, impactful experience. It will take you on a personal journey to reconnect with what is really important in your work and in your life.

—*Scott Peterson, Senior Vice President, Life Time Fitness, Inc.*

Awakening the Leader Within put me in the most reflective place I've been in years! As Cashman weaves the story of Bensen Quinn, you will experience deeper levels of yourself and broader ways to contribute value. Whether you are an experienced executive or an up-and-coming manager, listen to the many "wake-up calls" in this book!

—*Richard Hynes, Senior Vice President, Alberto Personal Care Worldwide, Alberto-Culver*

Awakening the Leader Within is unlike typical business books, which engage the head, but miss the heart. It seeks deeper change, engaging you on an emotional level and making it impossible to ignore the personal implications of leadership.

—*Linda Sorrell, Senior Vice President, Talent Strategy, Diageo*

In today's pressure-charged, ever-changing world, the need to locate something deeper and more enduring has never been greater. *Awakening the Leader Within* will help you to navigate through this whitewater of change by applying principles that will guide your personal and professional journey.

—*Stephen Shank, CEO and Founder, Capella Education Company,*
and former Chairman and CEO, Tonka Corporation

Kevin Cashman is recognized as a leading authority on leadership. This book confirms why. *Awakening the Leader Within* is engaging and intriguing, but most importantly, it helps us to understand the significant contribution that each of us can make to the world.
   —*David McNally, bestselling author of* Even Eagles Need A Push *and coauthor of* Be Your Own Brand

In *Awakening the Leader Within*, Kevin Cashman doesn't just point us down a path to authentic leadership; he expertly navigates new and verdant terrain, while enticing us to do the same.
   —*Linda J. Page, President, Adler School of Professional Coaching, Inc.*

Awakening the Leader Within is a powerful and compelling story that forces readers to reevaluate their own personal and professional goals and priorities. Through the main character's search for authenticity and purpose and his eventual awakening, Kevin Cashman shares a simple yet complete blueprint for creating value in every facet of our lives.
   —*David Shadovitz, Editor in Chief,* Human Resource Executive *magazine*

In *Awakening the Leader Within*, Cashman challenges us to take an honest look into our hand mirror by reflecting on life's deepest questions. His book inspires authenticity as it integrates our hearts and heads as leaders.
   —*James Ehlen, M.D., Chief, Clinical Leadership, Humana*

Cultivating authentic leadership may be the most important component to create thriving, growing, sustainable organizations. *Awakening the Leader Within* gives you the practical tools to foster more genuine, purposeful leadership in your organization.
   —*Michael Howe, Executive Vice President and Chief Talent Officer, Allina Hospitals & Clinics*

Awakening the Leader Within is a powerful, spellbinding story that will inspire you to change your life as you read it. The few hours you spend reading it will be some of the best time you've ever spent. It offers you a path to a rich exploration of your own values in action and a way to make needed adjustments that will enable you to make a bigger difference to your family, your company and your world.
   —*Kate Ludeman, Ph.D., CEO, Worth Ethic Corporation, and coauthor of* Corporate Mystic

Awakening the Leader Within is an exceptional guide for exploring the essence of who you are and where you're going in life. It's especially valuable when you are navigating the truly challenging times.
   —*Dean Buresh, Executive Vice President, Bozell New York, an Interpublic Company*

Awakening the Leader Within is the highly anticipated follow-up to *Leadership from the Inside Out*. Cashman's masterful storytelling takes you on another journey to further deepen your authenticity and contributions in the world.
   —*Craig Neal, Co-Founder, Heartland Institute*

Awakening

—— T H E ——

Leader Within

A Story of Transformation

KEVIN CASHMAN

with Jack Forem

WILEY

JOHN WILEY & SONS, INC.

For general information on our other products and services please contact our Customer Care
Department within the U.S. at (800) 762-2974, outside the United States at (317) 572-3993 or
fax (317) 572-4002.

Wiley also publishes its books in a variety of electronic formats. Some content that appears in
print may not be available in electronic books. For more information about Wiley products,
visit our website at www.wiley.com.

ISBN 0-471-27319-8

Printed in the United States of America
10 9 8 7 6 5 4 3 2 1

Dedicated to the Awakened Leader
Who views leadership as a sacred calling
To make a life-enriching difference in the world.

Contents

The Journey to Awakening Starts Here . . .   1

One   Executive Suite   11

Two   Our Family . . . Our Town   20

Three   The Call of Awakening   29

Four   The End of the Fairy Tale   35

Five   Waiting for Awakening   39

Six   Dawn in the Garden   43

Seven   Awakening to Legacy   47

Eight   First Crossroads: Old Road or New Road?   50

Nine   Awakening to Purpose   60

Ten   Renewing a Vital Partnership   67

Eleven   The Strength of Vulnerability   73

Twelve   Awakening to Authenticity   81

Thirteen   Always Connected   88

Fourteen   Awakening to Essence   98

Fifteen   The Blossoming Bud   109

Sixteen   A Day of Decisions   120

Seventeen Heart to Heart   128

Eighteen	Piercing the Veil	132
Nineteen	Walking the Talk . . . with Baby Steps	151
Twenty	Awakening Together	168
Twenty-one	Facing the Demons of Doubt	173
Twenty-two	Passing on the Torch	192
Twenty-three	Gardener of Souls	211
Twenty-four	Purposeful Vision	223
Twenty-five	"Remember the Seeds. . . ."	239
Twenty-six	The New Gardener Begins His Work	244
Growth Guide	Awakening the Leader Within	260
	About the Author	315
	About LeaderSource®	317
	Bibliography and Recommended Reading	318
	Acknowledgments	321

The Journey to Awakening Starts Here . . .

For this is the journey that men make: to find themselves. If they fail to do this, it doesn't matter much what else they find.

—James Michener

Awakening the Leader Within chronicles a transformative journey to a new way of leading and a new way of living. It tells the story of the challenging odyssey we all travel as we attempt to bring together all the separate parts of our lives into a more meaningful whole. It is the hero's journey, an exploration into the wilderness of what is missing in our lives, followed by the triumphant return to all our life roles renewed with authenticity and purpose, prepared to make a genuine difference as a person, as a family member, and as a leader.

While the hero of our story, Bensen Quinn, is not a real person, *Awakening the Leader Within* is a true story. The journey Bensen makes is the journey *all* of us must make if we want to live a more meaningful life, a life that both is fulfilling to us and makes a substantial contribution to the wider communities in which we live.

The Crisis of Authenticity and Purpose

Many of the business, political, spiritual, and ethical dilemmas that we face today, in our personal and professional lives and as a nation, are symptomatic of a larger issue: a crisis of authenticity and purpose. The conspicuous absence of these qualities or principles leaves many of us craving more integrity, more substance, and more inspiration in our leaders . . . and in our own lives. In my 20-plus years of coaching senior executives, I have witnessed firsthand that being genuine, purposeful, and principled is the absolute bedrock on which character development, great leadership, and effective living rest.

Our main character, Bensen Quinn, painfully experiences the consequences of not authentically bringing forward all of who he is, and not fully living his values either at home or at work. Splitting off his behavior from what is important to him inevitably brings him down the road to career stagnation, disharmony and lack of fulfillment in his relationships, and a loss of meaningful contribution. Along with Bensen, you will take a new path, on the journey to awakening deeper dimensions of yourself and what you are passionate about.

Awakening the Leader Within closely examines the principles of authenticity and purpose, how they manifest themselves in the context of personal growth and leadership development, and why there is such a critical social need for more of these vital qualities. Bensen Quinn may be a fictitious character, but the experiences that he has on his journey to wholeness are drawn from countless similar experiences that I have seen real men and women undergo during personal coaching. When difficult and painful crises in his family and at work force him to look at his life—as we all must do in these challenging times—he finds himself facing his crisis of authenticity and purpose.

Like many people today, he is shocked to find that he cannot answer some of life's biggest and most important questions: Does my life have meaning? Am I truly making a difference? Is this the life I really want to live? Responding to his challenges and growing as a person, he also grows as a leader, becoming more authentic, more purposeful, more determined to add value to his community and to create a meaningful legacy.

Bensen is Everyman. His story is an inspiring portrayal of the great potential that so-called "ordinary" men and women have, to go way beyond what is, beyond "this is how we always do things," beyond "it's not our concern," to create entirely new possibilities for themselves, for their families, and for humankind.

Leadership from the Inside Out

For the past two decades, since I founded the leadership development and executive coaching consultancy LeaderSource, I have had the privilege of working with hundreds of Chief Executive Officers and other top leaders throughout the world as their executive coach. Unlike that of many other consultancies in the field, LeaderSource's work is not simply about skill building. It is about personal growth and transformation. As the title of my last book expressed, I have witnessed the power of *Leadership from the Inside Out.* I have found that to become a more effective leader—in every area of life, whether business or government, coaching Little League, guiding a family, teaching a class, or simply leading our own lives in the direction we want to go—the key is to grow: to become a more real, complete person.

In my own work, relationships, athletic endeavors, or spiritual development, a commitment to personal growth is first and foremost, and it's what I aim for when I am coaching. You might find this a bit strange. After all, the people I work with every day are already the cream of the crop: highly successful and effective individuals. Yet, like all of us, they face plenty of tests and challenges, both at work and at home. My task is to help them grow so they can master new responsibilities, communicate more honestly and effectively, infuse warmth and trust into their relationships, or transition comfortably to new career and life options—and, in the process, find their own answers to those critical, hard-to-answer questions about life's meaning.

Wrestling with these life questions puts us all on an equal footing. Whether we happen to be a CEO or a stock clerk, the fundamentals of life are virtually the same for all of us: daily triumphs and heartaches, the frustration of succeeding magnificently in one area while falling on our face in another, health concerns, problematic relationships, the necessity of coping with tragedy and loss, the desire to make sense of our life, to be a good person, to leave the world a little better by virtue of our work and our interactions than we found it. Like Bensen Quinn, we can avoid these questions and concerns only so long before life demands some answers. Our response, if we rise to the challenge, is our pathway to growth and transformation.

In our coaching at LeaderSource, I've noticed that exceptionally difficult or traumatic events tend more to reveal character than to build it. It is precisely this process of rising to the occasion that allows us to access the depths of who we are. As we do so, new potentialities, new energies, new passions are activated for us in all parts of our lives.

Fortunately, trauma is not the only pathway to this kind of growth. Skilled guidance and coaching can lead us to our deepest potentialities without our having to pass through painful difficulties to get there. *Awakening the Leader Within* is specifically designed as an interactive coaching experience to help awaken our latent capabilities, *before* life attempts to teach us these lessons in a much harsher manner.

Your Personal Coach

You are probably aware that coaching is an extremely fast-growing field. The benefits of working one on one with a qualified coach have become so apparent to leaders that it seems everyone who can afford it has a coach from time to time, or even a team of coaches: an athletic or physical trainer, a yoga teacher, a presentation or speaking consultant, and so on. Coaches help the excellent continue to excel. The top athletes in the world retain coaches to help them stay at the top of their game or pull out of a slump. Politicians and business leaders employ a bevy of consultants who advise them on everything, from policy to polls, from how to stand and move to the art of making eye contact, how to dress, and how to "hone their message." In a rapidly changing business climate, CEOs and other top executives routinely call upon coaches to help them fine-tune their interpersonal effectiveness, enhance their communication style, and become more effective, authentic leaders.

It's important to note that true leadership doesn't reside merely in techniques, or in manipulating the circumstances in order to persuade people. It's about showing up with our life story, with whatever the triumphs, sorrows, and joys in our lives have taught us is important, and integrating those experiences into our voice to serve others. When we speak from that authentic place in us, we will automatically touch the hearts and minds of people, remind them of what's important, and catalyze them toward enriched vision and action.

This book is not about buffing up our image to look like a leader, nor does it tout career techniques for ascending to leadership roles: *It's about truly being a leader, by becoming a person of vision, integrity, effectiveness, compassion, and courage capable of acting wisely and well in all circumstances.* As Ron James, CEO of the Center for Ethical Business Cultures and a former CEO at two major companies, put it, "Don't read *Awakening the Leader Within* if you are only concerned with your personal success. Read it if you are ready to begin the journey to a higher calling and really make a difference in the world."

New Leadership for a New World

In today's world, leaders are being pressed to answer deeper and more demanding questions than ever before. Instead of simply focusing on questions of profit and performance, we are now also being challenged to respond to questions of meaning and purpose, and not only for ourselves, but for our organizations. How can I bring my entire self into my work to make a bigger difference? Am I creating the legacy I want to be remembered for? Am I *really* living my values and purpose? What are the connections between personal growth and professional effectiveness? What is the purpose of business and its role in society? Are ethics just a nice thing to have if you can afford it, or are ethical behaviors essential for sustainable business performance?

Every day we see the devastating consequences of sacrificing character and principles on the altar of profit and results. They need to be brought together, and the point of intersection is the soul of the leader. Who is the *principal* in *principled* business leadership, anyway? This book will place you at the crossroads of business effectiveness, ethical dilemmas, and personal transformation, which all of us travel through each day. How well each of us navigates through that intersection will not only determine our quality of life, but it will eventually determine the quality of our organizations, our communities, and our world. As Mahatma Gandhi once said, "We must be the change we wish to see in the world." In order to solve the array of problems facing us today, we must be the ones to change, to grow, to develop. *We must be the leaders of character we wish to see in the world.*

Enter the Awakened Leader

The most awakened leaders that I have met—those who have, through heightened self-awareness, gained mastery over themselves and, therefore, over their behavior and actions—invariably function less in terms of narrow self interest and more in terms of serving the greater good. This is a natural and spontaneous by-product of personal growth. One's identity or sense of self expands to include a more intimate and sacred kinship with everyone and everything around.

When this quality emerges in powerful or influential leaders, the results can be phenomenal. Fired by their courage, capabilities, and principles, they aspire to produce more beneficial and evolutionary effects for the whole. They create new worlds. They do not live split lives, separating their personal life and their deepest values, desires, and beliefs from their professional or social lives, a split that will create painful dilemmas for themselves and for the people in their lives. Instead, they bring their whole, integrated selves forward in the service of others.

Truly visionary leaders, who at one swoop can change the destiny of humankind, are not common. Nor are the "born leaders" who seem able to guide and influence other people almost effortlessly. But not falling into either of these rather exceptional categories is not a reason to refrain from taking action to become a better leader in your own sphere or assuming more of a leadership role in some area of your work or social life. *Awakening the Leader Within* opens the door for *all* people, in all positions or walks in life, to begin to make a much greater contribution to society.

The Power of Stories

While my last book, *Leadership From the Inside Out,* influenced many people, I wanted my next book to have an even greater impact, even more closely simulating the transformation that can occur during an authentic coaching experience. As I searched for a way to do this, a faint but persistent voice within me kept whispering, "Write a story . . . write a story. . . ." At first, I just didn't listen. Then I dismissed the notion, saying to myself, "I've never written a story before." Later, in a self-coaching moment, I asked myself, "Well, if you did write a story, what would it be?" Responding to the challenge, I sequestered myself with my dear friend and collaborator Jack Forem for four solid days. What rolled out of us over these intense, inspiring days was the outline of the story you are about to read.

Leaders and teachers have always used stories to capture our interest and attention. Stories have been the principal communication and teaching tool in every culture throughout the ages. From small bands of tribal peoples sitting around their evening fire telling and retelling stories about how the world came to be, to the Greeks and Romans spinning myths about the gods and goddesses, to Jesus teaching with parables, stories have had a central role in human life.

Stories get us out of our heads and into our hearts. We let down our guard and relax—and in that quiet, receptive mode, we are able to listen and become open to insight. Stories plow the ground in preparation for the seed. They generate a wide range of emotions, and they inform and instruct us, often passing on dearly held values. Sometimes we tell stories to inspire others and to offer role models: "This is the way to live! Like the hero and heroine of this story: with courage, integrity, vision." Stories may leave us awed by the vast, unfathomable mystery of life; paradoxically, they often help us grasp, in direct, nonanalytic, nonconceptual ways, what life—particularly our own life—is all about.

We all know how deadly a presentation can be without stories to bring it alive. I remember one executive who stood up in front of a large group of managers and rolled out "The Five Key Values of Our Organization" in a deadpan, unexpressive manner, his voice as flat and unemotional as if he were reading a shopping list: "One, two, three, four, five . . ." When he saw the managers looking back at him with glazed eyes, he figured they were not getting the message. "I guess I need to go over this again," he said, and there was a nearly audible groan from the group. I could almost hear everyone's thoughts: "We've heard all this before!" "This is such a waste of time!"

Another kind of leader will stand up to go over the same points, but he or she will say, with passion and feeling, "Let me tell you about Value One. This is something that's become really important to me, but I didn't understand it until one day when I was . . ." Suddenly the entire room wakes up. The audience is alert, listening, wanting to hear, and as the leader speaks, they're projecting their own stories onto Value One, breathing more life into it.

Stories are the language of leadership. They touch the heart and help authentic leaders do what they do best: open up new possibilities, new visions and vistas, to help us go beyond what is. A good story, a compelling vision, awakens us to the possibility of being more of the person we know we can be and doing what we've never done before.

As stories are the language of leadership, *questions are the language of coaching.* By creating a pause—making us stop and think—questions require us to take a deeper look at ourselves and our lives. They help us to gain insights, make new commitments, and apply what we learn to our life and work. With stories and inquiry, both mind and heart are fully engaged, and transformation can begin. As the Irish poet and novelist James Stephens wrote, "I have learned that the head does not hear anything until the heart has listened, and what the heart knows today the head will understand tomorrow."

Don't Read—Interact

Using the power of stories to open the heart and the power of questions to deepen understanding and commitment, *Awakening the Leader Within* is unique. The main body of the book is a story, to which I've added components to make it interactive. First, I've woven in powerful coaching questions at particularly poignant moments, to help you look at your life and learn from it, as Bensen Quinn is learning from his.

Then there is the Growth Guide at the end of the book. As engaging as you might find reading the story and responding to the coaching questions, I strongly encourage you to continue on to the Growth Guide. This is a workbook that you can use to structure a personalized plan based on the "Six Seeds of Growth," the name I have given to the main principles revealed in the story. Spending a little time with these exercises will solidify the gains you achieve from reading the book in a reflective way and will accelerate and sustain your progress. This completes the coaching experience.

The result: *This book is as close as you can get to a comprehensive personal coaching experience.* When I asked an executive coaching client of mine to read a draft of the manuscript and comment on it, he said, "It was less like a book and more like watching a film. I would get pulled into the story and then, at just the precise moment, you would come into the scene and ask me the perfect question to get me to make it real and relevant to my life."

We all have the noblest of intentions whenever we buy a book seeking to hone our skills or enhance our life in some way. But it usually requires tremendous motivation and self-discipline—and an abundance of time—to study and absorb the principles and, most importantly, to apply them all to our daily lives. The problem for most of us, most of the time, is that whatever inspired us to buy the book doesn't last; the energy to take our life to a higher level isn't sustained.

Awakening the Leader Within is different. By utilizing the interactive process—combining a meaningful and inspirational story with questions, reflections, and brief exercises—the book offers a chance to sustain the enthusiasm *and* do the work of applying it, in one easy and enjoyable flow.

Author Your Own Story

As you begin your journey through this book and beyond, I want to make clear that the story of Bensen Quinn is *one example* of the growth to greater authenticity and purpose. The last thing I want to do is to convey the message "This is the only way to do it" or "You should make the same decisions or follow the same path as Bensen in *your* life." Bensen could have made other choices and found other ways to add value to his life, and still have aligned with his deeper truth.

Deeper than the story, then, the real message of this book is this: Take your own journey to authenticity and purpose, consistent with your values, principles, and life circumstances.

CEO for Life

Often when I speak, coach, or write about leadership, people assume that what I have to say is only directed at or applicable to the obvious leaders of the pack, the key or most senior players, the "bosses." And yet many less senior employees often come up to me and say how much my book or my presentation spoke to them about their own need for greater authenticity and purpose in their private lives, their careers, or both. My response: "Regardless of your particular career role, you are the CEO of your life."

Every decision or choice we make, as our own personal Chief Executive Officer, builds and creates our life and our legacy. At any moment, our life is the sum total of all the choices we've made. The joy and challenge of being the CEO of your life is that right now, at this moment, you have the power to make a choice that could change your life, and possibly the lives of many others, from this point forward. Of course, that choice would be different for each person. It might be about a relationship, your career, or self care. It might be a spiritual choice. But if you come from a place of greater authenticity, your choice will have a deeper, more positive, and perhaps even far-reaching impact.

Ashleigh Brilliant once wrote, "At any moment I could choose to be a better person—but which moment should I choose?" *Awakening the Leader Within* will give you many moments to choose a new way and forge a new path, to bring your whole self into your work and into your life. Choose well as you take your journey to a more authentic, purposeful life.

———

If you would like to receive a *free* Awakening the Leader Within Discussion Group Guide to facilitate team building or general discussion groups, you can access it at www.leadersource.com. Just click on "books" and go to "Awakening the Leader Within" to download this helpful guide.

Executive Suite

At a quarter past four on Friday, Bensen Quinn, chairman and CEO of High-Quest, finally breaks free from putting out fires long enough to hold his twice-rescheduled Monday morning meeting with his top executives. Talk among the officers assembled in the boardroom ceases as Bensen steps through the double oak doors and takes his place at the head of the conference table.

"Gentlemen, Anne," Bensen says matter-of-factly, greeting them all with a quick glance. "Shall we start by watching the video segment? I haven't seen it yet."

"I've got it queued up," says Joe Northrup, VP for marketing.

"Roll it," Bensen directs. "When did it run?" he asks as they all shift in their chairs to view the large screen.

"Yesterday morning. The stock price, as you probably know, is up about fourteen percent since then."

"All right!" one of the execs calls out as they all applaud.

The lights dim and in a moment one of afternoon television's leading financial pundits appears, with stock market tickers running along the bottom of the screen.

"Today's edition of Corporate Profiles spotlights HighQuest," says the talking head, with a quick cut to the HighQuest logo followed by a pan of the buildings at corporate headquarters. "The Connecticut-based sports apparel company has shown remarkable growth even through the recent sluggish economy and the epidemic of corporate accounting scandals. CEO Bensen Quinn:

"'When I came to HighQuest about eighteen years ago as a young executive,'" says the TV Bensen, "'it was a small, specialty, niche company that made outdoor apparel for hikers and campers. I felt we had a shot at a much broader market, and I pushed hard to expand the product line to include clothing with wide market appeal at a reasonable price. At the same time, through R&D, we perfected our high-end products.'"

Amused at watching himself on screen, Bensen stretches his six-foot frame and relaxes into the big chair. "Do I look that old?" he wonders aloud, speaking over his own voice. The others laugh.

"Quinn's double-barreled approach vastly increased the company's visibility and market reach," the commentator continues. "The high-end garments soon became known worldwide as *the* products for serious hikers and climbers. The company's popular lines are displayed in sporting goods chains and apparel retailers, and last year's models fill the racks at the big discount stores."

As the broadcaster speaks, the onscreen visuals show several athletes, models, and a popular female entertainer dressed in HighQuest clothing and outdoor gear.

"Capitalizing on endorsements by high-profile athletes and projecting an image of clean living," the voice continues, "HighQuest products have gained increasing favor with young consumers as well as health-conscious boomers. The innovative young executive quickly moved to the presidency, and four years ago, at the age of forty-six, was also named CEO. Now let's take a look at the company's numbers. . . ."

Bensen smiles with pride as the company's success story flashes on the screen. When the segment concludes, another round of applause fills the room as the lights come back up.

"Great, that's great," Bensen says. "Can we get some more light in here now?" Another exec stands and works the control panel, sliding back the louvered vertical blinds. Bensen takes a moment to look out across the wooded corporate campus to the gently rolling hills.

"They did a good job on that," Bensen remarks. "And I'm glad it encouraged investors to check us out. But what we need is increased growth. We've got to keep producing the numbers." He glances around the table. No one is looking at him.

"All right, let's hear your reports."

It's an important meeting, to go over preliminary second-quarter results. One by one the executives read key numbers from their reports, and then summarize. "Sales volume in our U.S. market is up three percent over second quarter last year," says the VP for sales. "We're hitting our top-line revenue goals. Actually, we've exceeded them by almost one percent. And Latin America is really exploding for us. Up seventeen percent in sales, and our market share is growing every month."

Bensen breaks in. "Phil, I thought you said last month that we could expect a four percent increase in sales volume. Or am I not remembering correctly?"

A little flustered, Phil drops his eyes, then replies, "No, you're right, that's what I said. And it may still come in at four, these are preliminary numbers. But it looks like three."

"All right," Bensen says. "Let's move on. Joe?"

"Product development on the new Sierra line is moving ahead well," the marketing VP reports. "Market tests and focus groups for Sierra are coming up very positive; people like the design and the comfort. It looks like a winner, and I'd like to get the new ad firm we've been trying out to come in for a meeting to show some ideas."

"Just schedule it," Bensen says.

Next the vice president for operations reports that, thanks to the closing of another North American factory and the continuing shift of production to Asian and Latin American facilities, costs have come down for the sixth straight quarter.

Summarizing, COO Bob Barnett tells Bensen, "We're on plan. We hit our profit goals for the quarter, and then some. And we're on target to continue. Our Six Sigma process improvements are kicking into gear and producing some great returns."

The executives are feeling good about their results, but they're also a little nervous and fidgety. They know that despite their having modestly surpassed their goals, Bensen will not be content. Even as they go through the motions of making their reports, they know that at the end, the CEO will raise the bar and press them to jump higher.

True to form, when the reports are finished Bensen says, "I know you're all satisfied with your achievements, but let me tell you, I'm not satisfied. In today's world of business, you can't be satisfied; that would be the end of us.

"Okay," he continues. "Fine, we're meeting our profit goals. But we've got to push harder. The upcoming quarter is crucial. There's tremendous volatility in the market; no one knows how it's going to shake out. Consumer confidence is down, so we need to work a little harder and a little smarter to get our message across. We need to grow sales, expand the top line, and in case the economic uncertainty makes people slow their buying, we've got to maximize production efficiency and keep costs controlled.

"I'm counting on the Sierra line to make a big impact; I want you to do everything possible to get those products in the stores well before Christmas.

Let's build on our success. I want to see profits four points better than what we've planned for the next quarter."

As he speaks, the joyful air produced by the upbeat video report and their success at beating their own goals is quickly smothered by the force of Bensen's demands. Privately, though the execs may grumble a little behind the CEO's back, they all acknowledge that it's his job to set the goals and drive their performance, and they respect him; they know it's because of his relentless achievement drive that the company is doing so well at a tough time. But they would appreciate a little recognition from their boss. A heavy silence fills the room as Bensen continues to speak, and then suddenly Joe Northrup interrupts him in midsentence:

"I hesitate to say this, Bensen, but we're on target, and in this marketplace, to be on target is practically a miracle. Give us a little credit! The results I heard in here today are pretty damn good. It's Friday, we're tired, we've worked hard this week as we always do, and we're exceeding our goals. 'Congratulations, gentlemen, well done' would mean a lot to us."

"*Well done?*" Bensen explodes. "We don't have time for 'well done.' We only have time to get to the next level. We're all grownups here, we don't need that kind of reinforcement. We need to excel. In the marketplace our competitors aren't going to pat us on the back, they're going to kick us in the butt."

As usual, Bensen does little to foster a spirit of partnership beyond the quest for results. He maintains the distance between himself and the others. It's clear: He's the boss, and they are the employees. He calls the tune; they dance. He is in control, and they are not. For them, a moment's pause to appreciate themselves and be appreciated is important. For Bensen, what is important is profit and achievement.

———

The silence in the room lasts a long time. Finally Bensen asks, "Okay, what else? I know it's getting late. Anything else that can't wait till Monday?"

"There *is* something," one of the VPs says.

"What?"

"What do you want to do about the call regarding Jim Morris?"

"What call?" Bensen asks.

"I left a memo for you. Maybe you didn't see it yet. A reporter called looking for a comment from you. There was a story in Mexico City. They claim Jim's been giving bribes to develop business."

Bensen laughs. "That's how business is done down there, isn't it?"

"Bensen, you can't say that. 'Down there'—that's pretty judgmental."

"Well, it's true, isn't it?"

"It may be true for some companies there, but we have Arthur Andersen and Enron and WorldCom—does that mean we sit here and cook our books and say, 'That's how business is done around here'?"

"True. So . . . ?"

"So you can't just brush it off," the executive insists.

"What does Jim say?" Bensen asks.

"We haven't talked to him yet. We thought maybe . . ."

"Maybe I'd want to handle it."

"Right."

"So what exactly did the reporter want to know?"

"If there's any truth to the allegations. We told him we're looking into it. But if it comes out in the New York media . . ."

". . . it will not look good for HighQuest." Bensen completes the sentence.

"It won't exactly be a great follow-up to the story we just saw."

"Okay. I'll give him a call. I'm gonna be really pissed if he's done something to put us in jeopardy."

"It's more than that, I think," says Joe Northup. "If it's true, and it breaks in the media, you're probably going to have to let him go."

Bensen pauses, holds back. "Well, we know he's your good friend," Northup says. "And we know how successful the division has been. But bribery *is* illegal. Not to speak of being strictly against company policy."

"Well, this is a great finale to a great week," Bensen says, beginning to gather his papers. "At least we got a little good press on the tube."

Then the lone woman in the room, Anne Holmes—HighQuest's Chief Financial Officer, someone Bensen has been mentoring for several years as his potential successor—speaks up. "Wait a minute, Bensen, gentlemen. We don't know who or what is behind this accusation."

"Are you talking corporate sabotage?" Bensen asks quickly.

"I don't know. I've only met Jim a couple of times, briefly, but he doesn't seem to me like the kind of guy who would do something really wrong."

But nobody supports her. Instead, Bob Barnett says, "Well, suppose it is illegal. Is it really *wrong,* if it's standard business practice?"

"I don't know," Anne replies. "I'd say it merits some thought, and some discussion. I wouldn't jump to the conclusion that you need to fire him, without looking more deeply." After a moment she adds, "And I wouldn't be so quick to fire him just to protect the HighQuest image, either. He's been doing a great job."

"I'll go for that," Bensen says. "And I'll call him. Then we'll see." He stands up. "Okay everyone, have a good weekend." Then, with a little grin, he adds, "But come in here Monday morning with your guns blazing: I want those four more points of profit!"

As he's about to go out the door he turns and says, "I *am* going to call Jim, but I'd like somebody here to take charge of investigating from our side. Put somebody on it; find out what happened. Anyone?"

"I'll take care of it," says Northrup.

"Thanks, Joe. Keep me posted."

———

Bensen feels uncharacteristically eager to get out of the building, but he knows he's got to call Jim and deal with it, and he's not happy about the prospect.

"Mr. Quinn, can you sign those letters now?" his assistant calls out as he swings past the door of her office.

"Not now, Marie. I'm busy."

"If you sign them, I can drop them at the post office on my way home."

"If they're that urgent, why didn't you sign for me and get them out with the office mail?"

"But you . . . um . . . well . . ."

"Never mind," Bensen snaps. "Where are they?"

"On your desk. Center left. Where I always leave them."

———

The letters signed, Bensen takes a deep breath and thinks for a moment before calling Jim's direct line. He had brought Jim into the company just over five years ago and named him Director of Operations for Latin America. Hiring an old friend for a key position is always risky, and some eyebrows were raised. But it had been a good decision. A go-getter, Jim opened an office in Mexico City and promptly put the new division on the map, steadily and substantially generating new business and overseeing production at the factories there.

They had never talked about *how* the new business was generated. Bribery? That was too strong a word for what was probably just some well-placed gift-giving.

"And maybe Anne is right," he thinks. "Maybe this supposed information came from a competing company wanting to get rid of a highly successful executive and throw a negative light on the HighQuest name, all in one stroke." He's known Jim since their college days as a genuinely religious man who would not do anything he felt was unethical; if he did offer "incentives" in order to land contracts, it would only have been in situations where that was how business is done. "But it still won't look good," Bensen admits to himself. "And it's explicitly against company policy."

He taps out the numbers, and when Jim picks up, he wastes no time. "Jim? Bensen. Listen, what the hell's going on? I'm getting calls from the media about some bribery charges. What's it all about?"

"Oh Jeez, Bensen, there's this disgruntled employee who's been running all over town trying to give me a black eye. He thought he was up for promotion, but instead I let him go, and he's been trying to get back at me."

"You're saying it's just a guy spreading rumors?"

"Essentially, yes."

"And there's no truth to it? There's no problem?"

"Well, there *are* problems down here, but this situation is because of this one guy. I didn't pay anybody off."

Bensen presses. "I've got to know the truth."

"That could take a long conversation."

"I don't have time for a long conversation right now. It's been a tough week, I've had a lot of hard decisions to make, we're in the middle of closing another plant and acquiring SportCo—yeah, the sweatshirt and uniform outfit—so just tell me whether you did or did not pay anybody off to get a contract."

"No money changed hands. I assure you."

"Good, that's all I need to hear. I trust your word on this."

"Bensen . . ."

"Yeah?"

"It's a little more complicated. There *is* an angry former employee, trying to get back at me. . . ."

"It's not a problem with a woman, is it? You didn't do something stupid. . . ."

"No! Nothing like that. It's like I said. An executive I fired for performance reasons. But—I have been giving out some gifts."

"I thought you said—"

"I said no money changed hands. There hasn't been any money. But there have been some nice presents. An expense-paid weekend, a case of good wine, stuff like that. One car. To open some doors, cement some accounts. Nothing more than that. What I *am* surprised about is that the media are giving it any play time here. Everybody does it—even to get a good ticket to a soccer game you have to pay the piper."

The line is silent for a while. Then Jim says, "Bensen, I'm really sorry that you have to deal with this."

"*You're* sorry? Hell, I may have to fire you."

"Come on, Bensen, there's got to be some way to work around this. I mean, it's just this one angry guy creating an uproar; I'm really not doing anything that wrong, and you know it. I've been busting my butt not only to build the company, but also to make life a little better for our people down here, to improve working conditions, pay them a little more. This situation is not a big deal. We've got to find a way to get past it."

"You want to deny it?" Bensen asks.

"Yeah, deny it. We can do that."

"Does this guy have anything on you? Does he have any proof?"

"I don't know," Jim says slowly, searching his memory. "He's been around. He may have seen something. But whether he has actual proof—I don't know."

"Well, can you take charge of this? Can you find out whether he has anything concrete? Because if he does . . . it could be bad."

"Dammit, Bensen, you know I'll always be grateful to you for taking a chance on me for a position my background didn't qualify me for. But you know who I am, what my values are. You know I gave up a vice presidency in advertising because I couldn't stand to hawk products I don't believe in."

"I know, I know . . . listen, just tell me you'll look into it."

"I'll look into it."

"And before we come out with anything that ramps up the controversy, let's wait and see if it comes out in the U.S. media. If it's only down there, maybe we can just let it drop."

"That would be great."

"Now, what is this about working conditions? Why do you keep bringing this up? You've called me two or three times about it, and I keep telling you I can't afford to allocate resources to improve conditions there. We need to stay lean now."

"Bensen, it may not be good for the quarterly report, but you've got to start thinking more long-term. This will come back to you. I hate to use such strong language, but some day you're going to regret being so stubborn about this."

"Hell, man, look who's talking."

"Well, I guess we're all human. We all make mistakes."

"Give me a break," Bensen snaps. "Listen, I can't talk about this any more right now. Think it through, will you? And find out if that guy has anything solid."

2 Our Family
. . . Our Town

Around seven o'clock—earlier than usual but later than he wanted—Bensen leaves his top-floor office. In the empty parking lot he listens for a moment to the wind rustling the big leaves of the sycamore and maple trees. Taking a deep breath of the late-spring air, he notices with pleasure that the days are growing longer.

The brief respite ends as he begins his homeward drive, agitated by the emerging situation with Jim. "He's been one of my best friends for more than two decades. I thought I knew him, and could trust him." Now he wonders whether Jim is telling the truth. "What if something else is going on, some worse scandal. Maybe money did change hands . . . and if it's serious, then he's not only made the company look bad, he's made *me* look even worse. I hired a guy whose previous experience didn't qualify him for the position, a personal friend—who turns out to be a crook!"

The ring of his cell phone brings him back to the moment; it's Emily's pre-programmed signal, and he takes the call, glad to hear from her.

"Hi!" he says, "I'm on my way home."

"Ben, hi. Listen, I told Katie I would pick her up after her play rehearsal but I'm running late in an important meeting and I'd hate to have to ditch it. Any chance you could go get her?"

"Why? Where's her car?"

"It's in the shop longer than we expected."

"So I have to be the chauffeur? We could have a driver, if you weren't so damn adamant about that."

"Ben, now's not the time to go over that again."

"Well, I've had a really tough day, and I have to work out some numbers tonight, too."

Emily is silent for a few seconds, then she says, "Bensen, I've been working all day, too. I'm still in a meeting. And I hardly ever ask you to do anything."

When he doesn't respond immediately she adds, "She's your daughter too, you know. This would be a way for you to spend a little time with her."

"All right, you're right. Where is she?"

"In the theater, at the high school."

"Where's that?"

"Bensen, you don't know where the theater is at the high school? We've seen her in plays there."

"Oh yeah, right, okay. Big parking lot, in the back."

"Right. She's supposed to be done at seven thirty, but sometimes they run a little later."

He looks at his watch. "It's only five after. What am I going to do until then?"

"Bensen, you can figure that out. I'll see you at home."

"All right, all right. Hey, what play is she in?"

"*Our Town.* Remember? That sweet play about a small town at the beginning of the twentieth century? Grover's Corners? She's playing me."

"What do you mean, she's playing you?"

"I thought you might remember. Her character's name is Emily. We saw the play together, but it was a long time ago."

"Sorry, I guess I don't remember. Okay, see you later. Oh, Em? Got another minute?"

"I suppose. I *am* in a meeting."

"I had a disturbing call today about Jim. There are allegations that he's been making bribes to get contracts."

"Jim Morris?"

"Yeah, Jim."

"Are you sure?"

"Well, no, not exactly."

"That doesn't sound like the Jim I know. You'd better look into it carefully. But I gotta go now."

"Okay, see you later. Will you be home for dinner?"

"I'll whip something together. Or, if you want to pick something up . . ."

"Never mind. Go back to your meeting. We can talk later."

———

The back doors of the theater are wide open when Bensen pulls into the parking lot, and he walks in and makes his way in the semidarkness to a seat in the rear of the auditorium. The stage is bright and the house lights are low; it's a dress rehearsal. Katie and a boy are seated at a makeshift soda fountain counter, in the midst of a conversation. All Bensen can make out, at first, is that they are in love, or falling in love . . . then the scene ends, and abruptly the stage is rearranged to simulate a wedding chapel. The "parents" and "relatives" of the young couple sit with their backs to the audience, and on a pedestal at center stage, the preacher waits to conduct the marriage ceremony. Suddenly Katie, standing near the footlights at the edge of the stage, calls out, "Papa, Papa!" and one of the "parents" jumps up from his chair.

Father: Emily! Now, don't get upset . . .

Emily/Katie: But, Papa—I don't want to get married . . .

Father: Sh-sh, Emily. Everything's all right.

Emily/Katie: Why can't I stay for a while just as I am? Let's go away . . .

Father: No, no, Emily. Now stop and think a minute.

Emily/Katie: Don't you remember that you used to say—all the time you used to say—that I was *your* girl! There must be lots of places we can go to. I'll work for you. I could keep house. . . .

As he watches his daughter, Bensen realizes with a shock how grown up she is. Before long, he'll be standing beside her at *her* wedding! God, how could it be? "In another year she'll be off to college. It's unbelievable how quickly the years have gone by."

After the wedding, the director takes the actors into the next scene. For a few minutes Bensen is swept up in the play. He feels very proud of Katie, for her acting skill and for the beautiful young woman she has become. Yet at the back of his mind he remains uncomfortably aware of how little time they've spent together lately and the distance that has sprouted between them. "I've got to schedule some time to spend with her every week," he vows, "even if it's only an hour. I'll have to block it out on my calendar, or it won't happen."

The scene ends and the bright stage lights dim. "All right, people," the director says, "that was great, really excellent. I'll see you all on Monday. We're getting close, you guys are doing a great job. John, Jason, I'd like to see you for a few minutes. Katie, Jessica, everyone else, you can go home."

As the house lights go on, Bensen stands and walks toward the front of the auditorium. Katie doesn't see him yet; she's busy at the edge of the stage talking with her friends. Released from her role, she's just being herself, a laughing, playful teenager.

Bensen walks toward her, his heart warm with love and pride. He's almost at the foot of the stage before she notices him.

"What'd I do to deserve this honor?" she says, looking at him with an almost blank expression.

"Whaddaya mean?" he recoils.

"Where'd you find time to show up here?"

He feels his heart sink. "Don't be so smart," he fires back. Then, in a quieter voice, still trying to connect, he says, "You were really great! I didn't know you were such a good actress."

"There's a lot of things you don't know about me," she responds, the sharpness in her tone mixed with a hint of sadness.

"All right, all right," Bensen says. "How soon will you be ready to leave?"

"I just need to pick up my stuff."

She disappears offstage, then reappears carrying a fat backpack. As they settle into the car he says, "Your mom's not home, do you want to stop and pick up some Thai take-out? I know you like that."

"No," Katie replies, "I'm going out with some friends."

"But you do like Thai, right?" Bensen asks.

"Yeah, yeah, I like Thai," she says, trying to keep her voice noncommittal. But she's feeling his effort to connect with her, and turns toward the window to hide her small, grudging smile.

———

At home, Katie dashes upstairs to shower and dress for the evening. Bensen goes into the kitchen to pour himself a glass of wine and to unwind a little from the day. He almost drops the glass as the stereo abruptly goes on upstairs and loud music starts to rock the house. "Hey," he shouts, intending to ask her to lower the volume a little, but then decides to let it go.

He thinks about having a bite to eat, opens the refrigerator door, looks in, and shuts it again. Sitting down at the table, he looks idly through the stack of mail piled on the table. He hears Emily's car pull into the garage, and soon she comes in through the kitchen door carrying her briefcase.

Almost simultaneously, Katie comes thumping down the stairs.

"Where are you going?" he asks.

"I told you before. I'm going out with some friends."

He senses that she's hiding something, and asks, as nonchalantly as he can, "What're you gonna do?"

"Oh, we're just going out. Maybe have something to eat."

"You're not going to one of those rallies, are you?"

"What if I am?"

This had been a hot-button issue in their home for several weeks. Katie had already attended a couple of talks critical of working conditions and labor practices in overseas factories run by American corporations. "They say some of the worst ones are operated by your company, Dad," she had said after the first meeting. "I can't believe it!"

"You shouldn't believe it!" he had shot back. "They don't know what they're talking about. I thought you were brighter than that. A bunch of bleeding hearts come to your school and fill your mind with rubbish about 'sweatshops,' and you buy into it. Who do you think would know better, the head of the corporation, or them?"

"They had a lot of facts. And photographs . . ."

"Well, it wasn't any of our plants," he had insisted, but let the matter drop. Tonight he's in no mood to compromise.

"Katie, I don't want you going to these rallies. It's not right for the daughter of the Chairman of HighQuest to be seen at something like that. Don't you understand?"

"Sure I understand," his daughter responds passionately. "I understand that you're more interested in yourself and your career than in the people who are struggling and suffering in the world. I understand that you care more about your image than you care about me—or about what's right!"

At that moment a car horn honks outside. "That's Jessica," she says, and starts for the door.

"Katie!" her father calls out in a loud voice. "You're not listening to me!"

"Well, you're not listening to *me*!" she shouts back. "Mom, help me out here," she pleads. "Tell him to lay off."

"Oh no. This is between you and your father," Emily says, making an attempt at maintaining neutrality.

"Mom, please . . ."

"Okay, if you're going to force me to get involved . . . I think your father is right, that it *will* look bad for you to be there."

"Thanks a lot, Mom."

"But if this is really important to you, I wouldn't want to stop you."

Katie steps lightly across the kitchen, gives her mother a quick hug, and with barely a glance at Bensen, runs out the door. A moment later she opens it, leans her head in and says, "*I* don't just care about my image, *I* care about people."

Bensen feels an arrow in his heart at these words, and has no answer. A second goes by, another second, and she is gone.

———

"You could have backed me up, you know," he says to Emily when they are alone. "She's so damn stubborn!" He shakes his head, annoyed.

"Are you still angry?" Emily asks.

"No, that's not it. The irony is, when I was watching her rehearse, I felt so proud of her, and so much . . . *awe* at how she is growing up. And then I end up yelling at her! It's the last thing I wanted to do."

Emily sits down across the table and gives him a sympathetic look, but says nothing.

Then, his irritation melting, he starts to laugh. "Well, I guess it's not really that serious, is it? Her going to that meeting, I mean."

"I don't think so," Emily replies. "But she does needs your support right now, not your opposition. She adores you, you know; and she looks up to you. This business about the sweatshops—she's terrified that you might turn out to be like one of those people from Enron or WorldCom—it's confusing her, shaking her faith. If it turns out to be true . . ."

Bensen ignores the implicit question. Instead he says, "If she loves me and respects me, why doesn't she listen to what I say?"

"Because she's herself, and she's trying to find her own way. I would think you'd be proud of her for that."

When he doesn't respond she adds, "The truth is, Bensen, you don't spend much time with her. She might be more willing to listen to you if she knew you cared about her."

"But of course I care about her!"

"How's she supposed to know it if you don't talk with her or do anything with her? You didn't even know she was in a play."

The truth of that hits home. "She's a lot like you, in case you haven't noticed," his wife tells him.

"You think so?"

"Yeah! Have you totally forgotten your youth? She's just as strong-willed and determined as you are when she believes she's right about something. She's got your spirit. It's just that she's engaged with people and social causes right now, and you're engaged with your business."

———

"It's been quite a week," Emily sighs. They are sitting across from one another at the dining room table after a quick supper. "How about a movie or something for fun?"

"That sounds great, but I've got to go over some numbers."

Disappointed, Emily says, "Well, I guess I'll finish writing my speech for the women's organization dinner."

"How's that going?" Bensen asks, his attention already moving away from her toward the work he is going to do tonight.

"I'm making progress," she says, sensing that he is not really there.

A few minutes later, Bensen is upstairs in his office, connected to the firm's network, studying financial reports for HighQuest's European operations.

By nine thirty, Emily has completed all the work she can manage for the evening. She powers down her office in the west wing of the house, shuts off some lights, and goes upstairs. Outside Bensen's door she pauses and looks in, wanting to at least say goodnight, but he is so absorbed he doesn't hear her or sense her presence.

Not wanting to break his concentration, for a long while she stands in the doorway, looking at the back of her husband's head as he stares at the screen, seemingly mesmerized by the rows and columns of figures on colorful spreadsheets. Dozens of images rise up in her memory from the early days of their marriage, when they could hardly wait to get home to each other in the evening, and spent as many hours together as they could, sharing their stories of the day, going out, staying up late, entirely forgetting about work. Looking back, it seems to Emily that they were always laughing, always holding hands when they walked, always in love.

But then Bensen withdrew more and more into his work. On the fast track in a rapidly expanding company, he became entirely caught up in the business. He seemed to forget about their life together; personal advancement and the company's bottom line drove his every waking hour. It was clear that he was a business genius—he almost single-handedly formulated the vision for HighQuest's expansion, and piloted its growth from a small national company to a multinational organization with tens of thousands of employees and dozens of factories throughout the world. Emily knew from watching him grow through each step how much responsibility and power he wielded, and how high the stakes were; she understood that he had to be on his toes every day, studying the market and the competition, building teams, creating new products, schmoozing investment bankers and fund managers. She was happy for him—he loved what he did—but she was not happy about the cost.

She also knew that he felt he was working for the good of his family, to provide her and Katie with opportunities he never had. From a material standpoint, it was certainly true. She had all she could ever want and more, and Katie would never have to worry about money for the rest of her life. She would go to the college of her choice, travel the world. . . .

But Emily had made very different decisions. Her own career had gotten off to an auspicious start, but when she became pregnant, after a short but intense period of soul-searching she decided to quit the job to take care of their child full time. Bensen had been entirely supportive, even happy with her decision. He was doing so well that they didn't need her financial contribution; what he needed was her insight and good judgment, as well as her loving support, and she had given those in full measure.

When Katie was born, Emily enjoyed being a mother so much she knew it would be a long while before she went back to a "job." Yet her creative energy and strong spiritual and social values prompted her to volunteer for community organizations—primarily as a fund-raiser and advisor—and as time went by she quietly created her own career as a consultant, helping to guide community and not-for-profit organizations. She ran the business from home, first from one room; then, when they bought the old estate and began to renovate it, she converted an entire wing to a suite of offices. People looked up to her, and she became a force in the community, occasionally writing a piece for the local paper or speaking on issues of common concern.

She was so good at what she did that she repeatedly had to decide whether to allow her business to expand or to apply the brakes to its growth in order to maintain her chosen focus on her home and family. "Until Katie goes off to college," she determined early on, she would work only part-time and limit her staff to one assistant and a secretary, "and then we'll see." Now that decision was only one year away!

Somehow, despite her loneliness and her disappointment that the intimacy and fun of the early years of their marriage had considerably dimmed, Emily never gave in to bitterness. Either it was foreign to her nature, or she was wise enough to grasp that Bensen, despite his complete absorption in work, really did love her. He just wasn't able, most of the time, to show it.

And tonight, she realizes, will hold no departure from the norm; all she will get is a view of the back of his head. With an inward shrug she brushes away the rising resentment, then turns and goes to their bedroom.

The Call of Awakening 3

Sometime before midnight, Bensen grows too drowsy to concentrate and shuts off the computer. He glances at the clock, thinking about Katie, but it's too soon to worry about her; chances are slim that she'd be home this early on a Friday night. He feels a twinge of guilt about their argument and apprehension about the sequel he anticipates may arise tomorrow; he tries to summon up a strategy to prevent it, but is too exhausted to think clearly.

Yet he's not ready to go to bed. He's upset and perplexed by what happened with his daughter—how his feelings of love and appreciation turned uncontrollably to anger—and by what he senses as an impending confrontation with his old friend Jim. He knows he'd just toss in bed and probably disturb Emily with his restless energy. Instead, he goes downstairs, opens his modest but well-stocked wine cellar, pours himself a glass of merlot, and stretches out on the living room couch, leaning against a pile of silk-covered pillows.

Something Emily said this evening had crept into the edge of his awareness several times while he was working, and now it surfaces again: "Have you totally forgotten what you were like when you were young? When you were as passionate about your principles as Katie is now?"

The truth is, he hasn't thought about that era of his life for a long time. It was a part of his past that didn't matter anymore, didn't fit with the business world and the corporate life he was living. And he had rarely, since his mother's death, revisited any of his childhood. But all of a sudden his wife's words have opened up a Pandora's box of memories.

Even with his eyes open he can clearly see the working-class section of Brooklyn where he grew up surrounded by dilapidated row houses and nondescript five- and six-story brick walk-up apartment buildings. It was the era when the neighborhood had as many candy stores as bars, and you could get a coke for a nickel or a dime. He can see the vacant lot next to Sully's grocery store, where the neighborhood kids played baseball with a taped-up ball, using jackets, shirts, or rocks for bases, and the narrow streets where they played hide and seek among the parked cars when they were little, then, later, stickball with a broom handle and a rubber ball.

He had always had enough to eat, a shirt on his back, and a coat in winter, but beyond that, nothing was handed to him; from the beginning, he had to fight hard for every step he took beyond the rough streets and alleys of his childhood. Even his father, despite apparently good intentions, was more of an obstacle than a support. A strong, stocky Irishman, Jimmy Quinn went straight from high school into professional baseball. A powerful slugger, he had set the Class AA season record for runs batted in and seemed destined for big-league stardom, when the Korean War snatched him up and sent him overseas in a different kind of uniform. When he came back, shrapnel lodged in his legs and near his spine made it impossible to resume the career that was his passion.

Jimmy Quinn never recovered, either from the trauma of war, which haunted his dreams for the rest of his life, or from seeing the door to his expected future slam suddenly and irrevocably shut. When he first came back he told friends and family, "I'm lucky to be alive. So many of my buddies didn't make it." But those fine Hollywood-like sentiments soon eroded, to be replaced by a bitterness that could not be assuaged, no matter how hard he tried to drown it in every variety of cheap alcoholic beverage. Morose and resentful, unable to do what he loved most, with no education beyond high school and no vision of possibilities for himself other than the now-impossible dream of baseball, he gave up on life before he was thirty. Bensen's dominant memory of his father was of an unshaved man with unruly hair, wearing a sleeveless white undershirt, seated alone at the kitchen table with a cup of coffee or a bottle of beer, poring over the sports pages.

By nature, Jimmy Quinn was not a loud or violent person. "Before the war," Bensen's mother said more than once, "he was a cheerful, optimistic sort of fella." But over time, as his anger and frustration grew, he would yell uncontrollably at his little family. Now, reclining on his soft leather couch, Bensen can hear his father's voice and see their fourth-floor apartment, with its bedroom windows looking across an inner court at other windows, and the yellow-walled kitchen, the metal table with its plastic tablecloth, the chrome-legged chairs with bright red plastic seats and backs. Late at night—or so it seemed to him when he was a boy—he would stand guard just inside his slightly open bedroom door, watching his father shouting and gesturing at his mother, prepared to rush in to try to stop him if the words turned to physical violence. Luckily, there never was a need for him to try.

From time to time, faced with the reality of being a husband and father, James Quinn tried to make a go of it at various jobs, but he inevitably drank his way back to the ranks of the unemployed. He was, Bensen had long ago decided, essentially a good-hearted man, shattered by his experiences and unable to put the pieces back together in working order.

"Shine it up any way you like," Bensen says to himself, refilling his glass halfway, "he was still a drunk and a failure. There's no getting around that." As a boy, he had felt ashamed of his father's behavior, and angry at him for failing to overcome his weakness and take care of the family. Deep in his child's soul he committed himself to being a responsible, successful adult, in control of his life and his destiny.

Thus it fell to Bensen's mother to support the family. A gentle soul, Judith Quinn was unsuited for grappling with the harsh economic realities of city life. Minimally educated like her husband, she found a job as a checkout clerk when the first supermarket opened in their neighborhood, which turned out to pay better than she anticipated. But standing on her feet all day, dealing with an endless river of often-impatient customers, then going home to cook, wash, counsel, and cajole a very reluctant student, to say nothing of the demands of dealing with an alcoholic and depressed husband—these things would have flattened a hardier woman, and they exacted a heavy price from her rather delicate constitution.

Growing up with his mother gone all day and his father conspicuously inattentive, Bensen might have fallen into the kind of trouble that was increasingly a cause for sorrow in his neighborhood. But somehow he avoided it. Strong like his father, bullheaded, energetic, and competitive, he lived for years in an underachiever's paradise of sports, games, and fun. Then, one gray winter afternoon when he was about twelve, he noticed his mother walking home from the market clutching two heavy bags of groceries to her chest, her step slowed by fatigue. Unexpectedly granted a vision of the living daily sacrifice she was making, he rushed to help her.

"Mom, I'm going to get a job," he said impetuously, removing one of the bundles from her arms as they walked toward the apartment. "To help out."

Anticipating gratitude, he was unprepared for her response. "Don't you think of it, Bensen Quinn. Leave that to me and your father." Her blue eyes flashed and her voice rose in pitch. "You study hard in school and make something of yourself! You've got all that it takes."

"But you're working so hard!"

"Don't worry about me. I'm doing what I want to do. If you want to help me, make something of yourself, and take care of me when I get old." Then she paused, and in a softer tone she said, "And if you make a lot of money, don't forget where you came from; be sure to give something back to others, to people in the community. It's very important."

Bensen cherished his mother, and saw, even at twelve, that these words came from a generous and devoted spirit—and that there would be no arguing with her. He took her words to heart, and truly did look forward to caring for her in old age, in a way that he could see his father would not be able to do. Sadly, those later years never arrived. Judith watched with pleasure and pride as her son grew into a young man of character and launched what promised to be a successful career, but before his daughter was born, and long before he could pay back the debt he felt he owed her, she passed away. This always remained a source of deep sadness for Bensen.

He did embrace his mother's lovingly assigned commission, to make something of himself, although for what seemed the longest time he didn't know what that something would be. He channeled his abundant energy into his schoolwork, and began to earn top grades. In high school, he played both football and baseball—and, because he was so competitive and self-assured, was generally asked to be team captain—but he kept his focus on academics, with an eye toward the future. His tenacity paid off when he received academic scholarship offers from half a dozen colleges and universities.

A natural leader, Bensen was also an idealistic young man, with a strong sense of justice and fair play. These values made him burn with indignation if he felt he, or someone he cared about, had been wronged. As his experience broadened, he began to see some of the many injustices built into his culture, and these perceptions, combined with a naturally compassionate heart, led him to a short but fiery period as a student activist. He worked intermittently during his undergraduate career as a volunteer for an antihunger organization and another that built homes for the poor. Once he was nearly arrested for leading a protest against his university's investments in South Africa, long before international pressure forced that country to abandon its practice of apartheid. Having grown up in a poor family in the heart of a city, he felt a kinship with people who were struggling against the odds.

———

Bensen arrived at college at the tail end of the social and political reform efforts of the sixties. The war in Vietnam was beginning to wind down, the Civil Rights movement was floundering without its leader, but he caught a whiff of the intoxicating perfume of those idealistic times.

Vietnam was not a burning personal issue for Bensen. He felt fortunate to have received a high draft number, and was aware that he could get a student deferment if he needed it. He knew he didn't have to worry about military service disrupting his plans and goals, and that unless the fighting dragged on for a very long time, he wouldn't be called.

Nor, being a white male at a good college, was civil rights a burning personal issue. But on principle he strongly believed in equal rights for all people, whatever color they happened to be, and he did oppose his country's involvement in a war that had already killed hundreds of thousands of people halfway across the globe, where American interests were not threatened and American lives did not need to be at stake. Though the fervor of the previous few years was fading as the troops started to come home, he felt an inward pull to participate in public demonstrations to stand up for these values he cared deeply about, and from time to time, he did. Yet, as meaningful as these actions were to him, he did not let them distract him from his chief goal—to make something of himself.

"Bensen," he remembers his friends urging him one morning, when half a dozen of them had gathered in his room, "all this important stuff is going on, and you're sitting here studying. Take your nose out of the books and get out there and make a difference. You're a natural leader; we need your help. Nothing's more important than this. Don't you care?"

"Of course I care," he answered. "But I need to study. I need to make good grades." He wanted to help out, but more than that, he wanted to succeed.

Bensen's passion to succeed, to move steadfastly forward, was unrelenting. He felt that he had a long road to walk to achieve the level of attainment he dreamed of and that he didn't have a moment to waste.

He followed up a high-achieving college career with an MBA from one of the most prestigious programs in the country. Toward the end, when the corporate recruiters came around to pluck the finest fruit of his graduating class, he landed exactly the job he desired.

From a difficult childhood beset by the twin land mines of alcoholism and economic affliction, his hard work and perseverance had delivered him into a new world. With a high-paying job about to begin in a few days, he splurged and flew his mother into town for the graduation ceremony. His father, despite the offer of a ticket, wasn't there.

Once out of school, Bensen quickly forgot both his idealism and the world he had emerged from, and became entirely caught up in a corporate lifestyle. Promotions came quickly, and finally—after 20 years of 60- to 70-hour work-weeks—he achieved the goal he had emblazoned on his mind two decades before and moved into the CEO's office of the multinational corporation he had helped to create.

———

Sitting on his couch in the late-night stillness, Bensen feels pleasure and pride in his extraordinary success. Not only has he put his difficult and unhappy childhood completely behind him, he has also emerged into a fairy-tale hap-pily ever after, filled with material comfort, privileged contacts, and a warm and lively family life he never could have envisioned as he climbed the stairs of the walk-up apartment, dreading his father's alcoholic rage and dreaming of a better life.

Yawning and feeling the heaviness that will allow him to relax and sleep, Bensen walks through the kitchen, deposits his wine glass on the counter, glances at the clock, and heads upstairs. It's now after one o'clock, and he's a bit more anxious about Katie, but he shrugs it off.

He finds Emily sound asleep, a book next to her pillow, her reading light still on. As quietly as he can he switches off the light, then crawls in and settles himself on the opposite side of the bed so as not to disturb her. Within minutes, his tired brain stops spinning and he drifts into a fitful slumber.

———

Late that night, the insistent ring of the phone in the quiet house rouses him from a heavy sleep. Suddenly afraid, he reaches for the phone and lifts it from its cradle. Moments later he and Emily are racing down the stairs for the hos-pital.

The End of the Fairy Tale 4

"My God, how pale she looks," Emily whispers, clinging to Bensen's arm as they stand beside their daughter's bed.

Katie's face—what they can see of it through the bandages—is already turning purple from the bruises. Both her legs are in casts, a thin tube carries oxygen to her nostrils, and another slowly drips a nutrient solution through an IV into her right arm.

Driving home in a light rain and fog, she and her friends were hit broadside by a driver who skidded through a stop sign. The others suffered only bruises and cuts and one slight concussion, but Katie, who was in the direct path of the oncoming car, is in a coma, completely unmoving and expressionless; the doctors have cautiously said they do not know if she will recover. Monitors glow eerily in the semilit room, pulsing with secret messages: her heartbeat, her breathing, the rhythms of life, Katie's life, now hanging in an uncertain balance between her bright future and oblivion.

Bensen is doubly distressed. The situation is horrible enough, but he's also confused by a flood of powerful emotions.

"I want to kill the bastard that ran into them," he whispers hoarsely.

"That would solve a lot of problems," Emily says without looking up.

A few moments later he says, "It's my fault. I shouldn't have let her go. I shouldn't have yelled at her."

"No," Emily whispers back. "Don't blame yourself. There's nothing we could have done."

"You heard how I talked to her. She had every right to be upset."

"Ben, it doesn't matter," she says, impatient with his self-concern. "This is not about you. All that matters now is to help her get well."

True, he tells himself. True. But he can't free himself from the swarm of turbulent feelings. He still feels accountable for what happened, and remorseful for the rough way he spoke to his daughter. He's enraged at the driver who ran the stop sign and is barely restraining himself from leaving Katie's bedside and contacting his lawyer about a suit.

But mostly he's frightened. He's accustomed to being in control of things and firmly in command of his own feelings. Now, without any warning, his comfortable sense of dominion over his life is shattered. And his *daughter's* life—

"My God," he says aloud, "you never know, do you?"

Wake-Up Call . . .

Personal leadership involves going beyond what is—sometimes intentionally, sometimes unexpectedly.

When in your life have you had to leave familiar ground and step into the unknown?

_____

_____

_____

For example: *After a serious illness; after the loss of a loved one; when terminated from a longtime job; when starting a new job that stretched you in a new skill area; when creating a new business.*

*What lessons did you learn?*_____

_____

_____

_____

_____

For example: *I learned perseverance; with the death of a loved one I realized I had a depth of inner resources that I didn't know I had; when I lost my job and started my own business, I learned how I could overcome my need for security and create my own life.*

Reminder: Don't just accept these examples; look for your own authentic response.

The parents sit by their daughter's bedside, settling in for what they know might be a long vigil. Too tired and anxious to speak, they sit mostly in silence, absorbed in their own thoughts and feelings.

Emily cries softly, crushing a wad of moist tissues in her hand, watching her child's face for a sign of life. Bensen doesn't cry, but his heart aches for his daughter, and for himself.

From the moment, sixteen years ago, that the nurse placed his tiny daughter in his arms, being a father had brought a profound and entirely unanticipated joy to Bensen. As a young man he had read that children of alcoholic or abusive parents tend to repeat the pattern and, acutely aware of his childhood, held back from fatherhood for fear of perpetuating the pain he had felt as a boy. But with Katie's appearance in his life, his heart burst open and a new tenderness was born—though it lived in a realm entirely distinct from his persona at work, where he was known for his toughness. The deep bonding, and the almost instantaneous sense of sacred responsibility that he felt, came as a complete surprise, and they came full blown: before he had a chance to question his new role or back away, he was hooked.

Remembering the intensity of love that he had felt for that little girl, how much he delighted in her company and in her growth, and realizing how little time he has spent with her in recent years, he wonders with amazement, "What could have happened to make me neglect her? Have I really let myself forget how important she is to me?"

"Nothing happened," he perceives as quickly as he asks the question. "I just drifted away."

A picture jumps into his awareness: She was three years old and he was returning from a long business trip. His heart filled with joy as he turned into the driveway, and there she was! He practically flew from the car, eager to scoop her up in his arms. But he had been away so often and so long that she didn't recognize him; frightened, she turned away and ran into the house screaming for her mother. Hadn't that been enough of a wake-up call?

With or without her father's attention, Katie Quinn grew up. She was bright and fun loving, and blessed with some of the best qualities of both her parents. A good student like both of them, she had her dad's natural athletic ability and outgoing nature, and her mom's sincere concern for others. She made friends easily, excelled in dance and soccer, had a finely tuned ear for music and foreign languages, and seemed to be navigating the treacherous seas of adolescence without undo trauma. No one could have had a brighter future.

And now, this.

All the problems of his business, the decisions and corporate strategizing that dominate his attention for 14 or 15 hours day after day, no longer seem so compelling. Right now, his life and happiness revolve around whether his daughter is going to wake up or not.

"Damn!" he shouts inside his brain, standing and pacing the room. "I always say my family is most important to me, but where have I put my time and energy? The truth is, my career has been my priority. By far."

Not ordinarily a praying man, Bensen shuts his eyes and utters a silent plea for his daughter's recovery.

Emily has pulled her chair closer to the bed and is leaning forward, her head in her hands, quietly sobbing. Looking at her, Bensen now feels the loss of something else precious to him: the sweetness, intimacy, and joy he and Emily once shared in their marriage. He stands next to her, puts a hand on her shoulder. Immediately she reaches up a hand to grasp his. After a while he draws a chair up next to hers. Exhausted but too traumatized even to doze, the distraught parents sit side by side in silence. Nurses come and go; loudspeakers call out names and codes; the monitors blink and pulse. The long night passes, and their daughter does not move.

Waiting for Awakening 5

In the morning, Emily steps completely away from her business to focus full attention on her daughter. She instructs her assistants to tell her clients about the accident and that she will be unavailable until further notice. Bensen does not feel he can cut himself off from the company. With the hospital's cooperation—no doubt facilitated by his hospital board directorship and philanthropy over the years—he commandeers a small glass-enclosed waiting area as his temporary headquarters and arranges for his administrative assistant and a secretary to bring cell phones and laptops so they can work with him.

For the next three days and nights, Emily and Bensen hover in the vicinity of Katie's bed. She is still in the intensive care unit, where after the first night, when the nurses generously stretched the rules, visits are limited in length even for CEOs who demand continuous access. For as many hours in the day as they are allowed in, they sit with her, either together or in shifts.

Each day, feeling the pressure of responsibility building, Bensen struggles with his need to go to the office and carry out his corporate duties and the need to stay in the hospital with his wife and daughter. One afternoon when his assistants are taking a break, he steps into the small waiting room where Emily is resting. Pacing the floor, he says aloud, "I've *got* to get to the office." But a moment later he answers himself, "How can I go?"

"Oh, Bensen, just go if you have to," Emily responds.

"What if she wakes up?"

"Well, I'll be right here. And I'll call you."

Bensen doesn't say what is really troubling him: What if she *doesn't* wake up? He can't believe, and can barely bring himself to consider, that she may not emerge from the coma, yet he knows it is possible. If she does awaken, he feels he must be there for her; if she doesn't—if she dies, if her system just shuts down completely—he has to be there for Emily.

As the hours turn into days and Katie remains locked in her strange sleep, he acknowledges that he needs Emily as much as she needs him.

Late the third night, when the secretaries are long gone, few visitors are around, and a welcome quiet descends on the hospital, Bensen persuades Emily to let him turn down the bright overhead fixture in their waiting room in favor of a table lamp; in the subdued lighting, curled up on a couch and covered with a hospital blanket, she lets herself fall into a deep sleep, and Bensen goes alone to be with his daughter.

"It's been so many years since I've sat with her like this," he thinks as he settles into a chair beside her bed, remembering the nights he would read her to sleep with a storybook.

"Read it again!" she would squeal, delighted with some story or other about talking pigs or a honey-loving bear caught in a tree trunk. And then, in a soft, sleepy voice, hugging her pillow or a teddy bear, "Again." And he would oblige.

"What was the name of that book you used to love?" he says aloud. "*Goodnight, Moon*. Yes. I remember feeling you drifting off, and I'd read, more and more softly, 'Goodnight trees . . . goodnight birds . . . goodnight sky . . . goodnight moon,' and then I'd say as softly as I could, 'Goodnight Katie Quinn,' and in the tiniest, sleepiest voice you would say, 'Goodnight, Daddy.'"

Then, Bensen remembers, he would often sit for a few more minutes, simply gazing at her with an almost unbearable tenderness. "I thought I could protect you from all evil, all harm. And look at you. Look what's happened."

———

On the morning of the fourth day, as a faint glow of light appears outside the window, Dr. Schmidt, the lead physician on Katie's case, arrives on his morning rounds. He scans through the waiting stack of charts, examines the silent girl, and tells them, "Her condition seems to be stable. There may not be any change for some time. You're both exhausted. Why don't you go home and get some rest, and come back later."

"I can't leave her alone!" Emily protests as Bensen begins to stand up. "You go, if you have to," she says to him. "I need to stay with her."

"It *would* be good for me to go to the office for a few hours," he says. "All kinds of things have been piling up that demand my attention, that I really can't handle here." He looks at her closely and sees the dark circles under her eyes, her disheveled hair and rumpled clothing. "Why don't you drive home with me," he says softly, "take a nap and a shower, then come back?"

"We'll call immediately if there's any news, any change," Dr. Schmidt assures them. "We have all your numbers—home, office, cell," he adds, glancing at the top of the charts.

"They'll let us know if there's anything we can do," Bensen presses, gently insistent.

Reluctantly, Emily agrees. Husband and wife leave the hospital together, and they remain quiet as they drop their weary bodies onto the front seat of the Mercedes and start the drive home.

Within minutes, Bensen's car phone rings. They flash each other a hopeful look, and he grabs the phone. "This is Bensen," he says, then angles it away from his mouth to tell her, "It's the office."

When he hangs up, Emily sees the pained expression on his face. "What now?" she asks.

"It's about Jim. It seems he *has* been making illegal—or at the least, very questionable—transactions. The story is getting a lot of media attention in Mexico City, and it looks like it'll be breaking here, too."

Emily sighs and closes her eyes. "I'm sorry," she says, too tired to ask him about it. Jim is one of their oldest and closest friends, and they are both stunned by the news. But his people have left him with the question, "How do you want us to handle it?" and soon he will have to answer.

Back home, Bensen pulls into the circular drive and they enter the big house. Emily moves toward the stairway to the bedrooms. "I'll try to get a little sleep," she says, then stops and reaches out to him. "Won't you come up with me? You've slept less than I have these last seventy-two hours, or whatever it's been."

Bensen stands for a moment looking at her. "No, Em," he replies quietly. "I'm sorry. I can't. I have to go to work, and I've got to get myself together to deal with this Jim situation and a thousand other things. I'll just shower and change my clothes. Maybe I'll rest a few minutes in the garden before I go."

Emily nods in acknowledgment, but her expression barely conceals her disappointment. She realizes, as she remains facing him for a few seconds before going up the stairs, that she has been alone for a long time, and she is conscious of a familiar empty feeling that has been there since long before Katie's accident. Usually, she can set aside her emotional needs by focusing on her work and the demands and gratifications of parenting, but today she yearns to intimately connect with this man she still deeply loves.

But there's nothing more to be done or said; she has asked, and he, not understanding—or perhaps unwilling to choose her over his work—has said no.

A few minutes later, Bensen, wearing a beautifully tailored suit and bright silk tie, sits in his garden on the hand-carved wooden bench near the stream, his heart heavy. He too feels terribly alone, disconnected from Emily, pressured about his business, and worried about his daughter. All of a sudden the whole ship has sprung leaks, the crew is racing about, frantic—and he is supposed to be the captain!

Now the sun is rising over the treetops, and their longtime gardener, Kenji Ueki, pulls up in the driveway in his old Toyota truck. Bensen hears the engine shut down, the door slam shut, and the slow footsteps of the old man as he approaches on the gravel path. When he sees Bensen sitting on the bench, Kenji's serene, ancient face breaks into a smile. Eyes sparkling, he calls out a greeting:

"Good morning, Mr. Quinn."

Dawn in the Garden 6

Reluctant to move, Bensen lingers in the garden, trying to gear up for the day. He's so absorbed in the many problems awaiting his attention and in anxious thoughts about Katie and his friend Jim that he's oblivious to his surroundings until Kenji's voice, humming a lovely, plaintive melody, breaks in on his deliberations. Only then does he look around and take in the beauty of the garden, with its many varieties of flowers and plants, the curving footpaths surfaced with fragrant cedar chips, a small wooden bridge arching over the stream, the pond where multicolored fish lazily glide. How wild and overgrown it was when they purchased the long-neglected estate and began slowly rebuilding and refurbishing it. And now Kenji, who has supervised the landscape design and done most of the labor from the beginning, is working away, tending to everything. At least here, all is in order, all is in its place.

For a minute or two, Bensen observes Kenji with admiration, noticing that he works with economy, grace, and ease. He thinks, "The peace of the garden and the peace of the gardener are similar; look how he moves." He is struck by the contrast between his own inner turmoil, his agitated state, and the harmony and peacefulness of the garden and the gardener. He senses that Kenji's inner and outer aspects—his character and his works, who he is and the beautiful garden he has created—are aligned.

And just at that moment, Kenji looks up and gives him a knowing smile.

"Wouldn't it be nice to have such a simple, uncomplicated life, like him, and not feel all these responsibilities weighing on me?" Bensen muses as he watches Kenji at work. "What if I only had to take care of this little garden, and not be concerned with problems at dozens of production facilities, employee demands, marketing decisions, finances in the billions of dollars, endless crises to handle every day?" Then, noticing Kenji's calm and happy state, he thinks, "What is it about this guy?"

Very tired, and momentarily more relaxed than he's felt in days, he closes his eyes and drifts in a half-sleep back to an earlier time. A twenty-one-year-old college senior, he was sitting in the office of the university president with ten other students. They had walked in early in the morning, when the executive's office was empty, and announced that they would not leave until the school negotiated with them about liquidating its investments in countries with unacceptable human rights policies, especially South Africa.

Bensen had been entirely unaware of apartheid until William Jordan, an African American MBA student he had befriended, urged him to learn about it. Appalled by what he discovered, Bensen gathered a few interested students around him and planned a protest.

They had been in the office less than an hour when President Reynolds surprised them by appearing in person. A tall, dignified man with a trim gray mustache, he calmly asked if they would allow him to sit and discuss it with them. When they agreed, he closed the door, sat on an unoccupied chair, and listened carefully to their views. Bensen made an impassioned plea for the university to drop the investments, to signal its disapproval—"its twelve-million-dollar disapproval," he said, holding up an accounting sheet—"of a minority regime that uses its power to imprison, torture, and exploit the majority of people. This is wrong. We shouldn't support it."

To Bensen's surprise, the president had nodded thoughtfully. "I couldn't agree with you more, Mr. Quinn." Looking around at the others, he added, "Thank you for coming here. Someday you may understand that it would have been politically difficult for me to advocate the changes you are asking for, without jeopardizing the institution and my own position here. The publicity you are generating with your protest will put public pressure on the trustees, and I may now be able to accomplish this."

The students were speechless. "This is bullshit," one of them muttered. "You're just trying to get rid of us."

"Oh no, Ms. Garboni. Definitely not. I promise you." There was something about his unruffled manner that convinced them; their angry energy subsided. This was not what they had anticipated. They had gathered with visions of policemen dragging them down the halls, of masses of students outside the window holding up placards and chanting in support of their cause—and instead, in a matter of a couple of hours, they were accomplishing their objective.

The impromptu meeting came to an end and the students began to file out of the office, bearing a signed statement from the president agreeing to take their grievances to the Board of Regents. As Bensen reached the door,

Reynolds said, "Mr. Quinn, if you have a minute, I'd like to speak with you. Please sit down."

This time the president took his own chair, and Bensen sat facing him. "Mr. Quinn, you are a fine student and sincere about your beliefs. I know you didn't come here looking for advice from someone you think is perpetuating an evil— but I am going to give you some anyhow, which I do hope you'll take seriously.

"I've seen several demonstrations over the years. In fact, I sympathized with the students' positions on a number of those issues, or at least I admired their passion and conviction, something I don't see enough of these days. But I can tell you that in this country, very little change can be made from outside the system. A lot can be accomplished from inside it. For example, your protest has put pressure on the university. There are many ways we could deal with it. We could have you arrested. We could make promises that we would never keep. Essentially, we are in power, and you are not. You are fortunate, Mr. Quinn, that I happen to agree with what you want to achieve. So as you see, I am not going to have you arrested, and I am going to work to change the university's policies. In fact, I am going to invite you, personally, to present your case to the Board of Regents, and if you will permit me, I will help you prepare your talk so it will be most persuasive and effective."

Here President Reynolds paused and regarded Bensen with what felt like sincere warmth. "Now," he continued, "here is my advice. You are clearly someone who can rise to the top. You are bright, ambitious; people like you, trust you, follow you. And I believe you are something of a visionary in your own way. So I advise you not to waste your time and energy butting your head against the wall. Some walls might buckle or crack; a few might even fall. But if you get *inside* the walls, you will be the one in power, and what you can achieve will multiply exponentially. I urge you to choose a field you're passionate about— government, business, science, whatever it is you are drawn to—and go into it with your whole heart. Allow yourself the pleasure of excelling in it, and the joy of taking it in a direction that's meaningful to you. But, Mr. Quinn—don't lose sight of your goals, your vision. Be sure to dedicate your energies to fighting *for* something, don't get lost in resisting and battling *against* things. . . ."

Slipping out of his reverie and back into the garden, Bensen has a hazy awareness of how much President Reynolds's long-forgotten words had affected him. To make a difference, to change things, was precisely what he wanted. He wanted to change his father from a bitter and disillusioned drunk to a loving, participating dad. He wanted to free his mother from the weight of those grocery parcels that symbolized for him the heavy burden she had chosen to take on. Looking around the world as he grew into young manhood, he saw much—and ever more—that he wanted to change and fix: poverty, domestic violence, blatant racial prejudice and discrimination, men working at jobs they hated, women working at the same or even less-satisfying jobs for substantially less money, the wars that blazed around the world, genocide in the name of religious belief—the list was endless. Bensen's childhood had attuned him to suffering and unhappiness, and he cared about it.

> ### Wake-Up Call . . .
>
> Managers enhance existing systems; leaders transform them. Inside the "walls" in which you reside (your company; your family; your church, temple, or mosque) what would you like to transform? _____
> _____
> _____
> _____
>
> For example: I would like to transform the team dynamics at work; I would like to create more openness and communication in my family . . .

But somehow, President Reynolds's words, "Get inside the walls," which meant to him, "Get yourself into a position of power," resonated less with his passion for social justice than with his need to feel in control of his life. So he had redoubled his already strong efforts to excel, put his idealism on hold ("until I can really do something with it") and devoted himself single-mindedly to success. "And here I am," he muses, "inside the walls. . . ."

Suddenly he feels a presence. He opens his eyes, and the gardener is standing next to him. Startled, he looks up into that lined face, with its kind, steady gaze, and immediately feels calmed.

"Are you all right, Mr. Quinn?" Kenji asks.

"I'm fine," Bensen replies. And then he adds: "I think I've been asleep. In more ways than one."

"If you want to wake up," Kenji says, "I have something I'd like to show you."

Awakening to Legacy 7

The gardener fumbles in the pocket of his faded denim shirt. "I wanted you to see this picture." He takes out an old newspaper photograph, torn at the creases with age, carefully unfolds it, and hands it to Bensen. It's a tiny premature baby, curled up in the palm of a hand. "This is my granddaughter," he says.

Bensen's eyes tear up. He holds himself back, not wanting to show his vulnerability in front of the gardener.

"I'm sorry," says Kenji. "Is there something about this picture . . . ?"

"It reminds me of my daughter."

"Is she all right, sir?"

"No, actually she's not. She's in the hospital. She's been in an accident."

"I'm so sorry."

"I just came from there. I was sitting with her, next to her bed, remembering when she was born. . . ." His voice trails off. "But why did you show me the picture?"

"I thought the story might interest you."

Tempted to say, "What possible interest could I have in this, right now?" Bensen politely replies, "Tell me."

"When my granddaughter was born, she weighed eighteen ounces. She was so small that I could take off my wedding ring, slip it over her hand and slide it all the way up to her shoulder. That's how delicate, how tiny she was. But they took good care of her. She was in an incubator, of course, and while she was in the hospital, they played classical music for her twenty-four hours a day, and our family took turns gently massaging her to comfort her and keep her stimulated. She grew beautifully.

"One day," Kenji continues, "when she was seven or eight years old, she came home from school and some music was playing in the house. She stopped abruptly and said to her mother, 'This is the music you played when I was in the box!' Her mother dropped the dish she was holding onto the floor and stared at her.

"'What did you say?' she said.

"'This is the music you played when I was in the box.' Her mother turned pale and said, 'My God, you remember that?'

"My granddaughter became quiet and reflective, and said, 'Yes, I remember. This is the music you played when you massaged me.'"

"That's an amazing story!" Bensen exclaims.

"Yes, isn't it?" Kenji replies. "Each time I think of it, I ask myself, 'What music will *I* be remembered for? Am I touching people's lives, right now, in a way they are going to remember?'" He pauses and adds, "My granddaughter is seventeen now."

"Just about Katie's age," Bensen says. "She's sixteen." He looks once again at the picture, then hands it back.

"And she is so precious to all of us," Kenji adds quietly, taking the picture and fixing Bensen with a penetrating look. "Even more so, because we didn't know how long she would be with us." Again powerful emotions well up in Bensen. Kenji regards him a moment longer, his dark eyes set in hundreds of tiny wrinkles. Then, in a lighter tone, he says, "Well, I'd best get back to work."

"Yes, I have to go to work, too," Bensen says, standing up.

Kenji folds the dry, yellowing newspaper photo with a care bordering on reverence and puts it back into his pocket. Half turned to go, he pauses, looks Bensen directly in the eyes, and says with conviction and a piercing presence, "Your daughter will be all right."

As Kenji speaks those words, Bensen feels a charge of energy surge through his body, and for a moment,

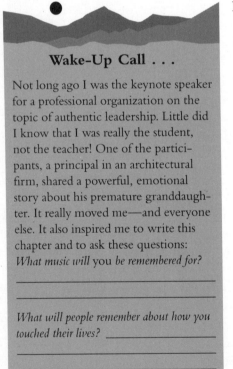

Wake-Up Call . . .

Not long ago I was the keynote speaker for a professional organization on the topic of authentic leadership. Little did I know that I was really the student, not the teacher! One of the participants, a principal in an architectural firm, shared a powerful, emotional story about his premature granddaughter. It really moved me—and everyone else. It also inspired me to write this chapter and to ask these questions:

What music will you be remembered for?

_____

_____

What will people remember about how you touched their lives? _____

_____

_____

his awareness shifts; he feels a sense of peace that lingers briefly, and then dissolves.

"What was *that?*" he wonders. Slightly dazed, he says, "It's kind of you to say so," as if the gardener has simply made a polite remark.

Then Kenji adds, speaking slowly but with even more force, "And *you* . . . will be all right . . . too."

8 First Crossroads: Old Road or New Road?

At corporate headquarters, Bensen steps into a manic atmosphere buzzing with activity. Even before he gets to his office, people are running next to him in the hallway holding memos and files and asking about one crisis or another:

"The media are calling and want a statement about Jim Morris. What are you going to say?"

"CNN analysts are predicting the stock price will plummet if there's a scandal."

"You've got to do something fast."

The company is also in the midst of the SportCo acquisition, and negotiations have stalled; they need his input, *now*!

Exhausted from lack of sleep, his heart at his daughter's bedside, Bensen wants to turn around, go home, and crawl into bed rather than face the onslaught. But after a minute or two he kicks into gear and finds he's able to go through the motions and get things done. Even working at reduced capacity, he's still the corporate Superman:"Do this, do that, call so-and-so, set up a press conference!" Though his feelings are subdued, he barks out orders like a drill sergeant. Things are happening, he's in control again, and it feels good.

"Thank God I have my work," he thinks, settling behind his desk. The tall stack of letters, memos, and reports awaiting his attention; back-to-back appointments and meetings throughout the day; dozens of e-mails waiting on-screen—this is home base. Momentarily distracted from the pain and worry about Katie and his ruminations about his life, he plunges into action.

Later in the morning, in the midst of all the frenzied activity, Joe Northrup comes to the door, waits for Bensen to finish a phone call, then leans in. "Sorry to disturb you. Here's the press release we've prepared about Jim and the Mexico situation, and a background memo detailing what happened."

"Thanks. Shut the door on your way out, will you, Joe?"

Staring at the press release, he knows that whatever it says—if he allows it to go out at all—will affect his friend's life as well as the company. A quick read through the memo convinces him that the evidence is irrefutable. Against company policy and a growing international consensus, Jim had indeed given expensive gifts to obtain contracts for HighQuest products. "If the company denies it and backs Jim," he concludes, "we would take a second hit for covering up—and by implication, condoning—unethical and possibly illegal behavior." Turning to the press release, he sees that his corporate communications people are trying to put a positive spin on the situation, but he knows in his heart that what they're saying isn't true.

Wake-Up Call . . .

Work can be an expression of purpose and creativity, but it can also be used as an escape. As an escape, work is a convenient sanctuary from personal, family, or other problems and difficulties in our lives. Neglected health, neglected relationships, and lack of personal satisfaction can be the eventual results.

When have you used work as an escape?

_____

_____

Can you recognize the signs that you are using work this way? (for example, working long hours and avoiding difficult conversations at home, feeling relief and a greater sense of control at work, being more relaxed at work than at home) _____

_____

With his door shut, he has a moment of quiet and takes a deep breath. An image of Kenji in the garden flashes before his eyes, and the picture of the tiny baby. "What an incredible story," he thinks. He looks down at the press release and wonders, "Is this the music that resonates with me, the music I want to be remembered for? Is this how I want to touch people?" And his struggle begins.

———

Later, in a meeting with a few key executives, COO Bob Barnett asks if he's gotten behind the decision to close yet another North American plant. This action will mean laying off nearly 3,000 people and moving the operation offshore.

"Not yet," Bensen replies.

Barnett presses him. "Then let me run the numbers by you again. It looks like a no-brainer to me." Powering on the computer, he projects several graphics on the screen detailing the financial benefit to the corporate bottom line from moving production to Latin America, where costs will be about 50 percent lower than in the United States.

"I see your point," Bensen says, then falls silent.

"Am I missing something?" Barnett asks.

"No," says Bensen. "We've done this so many times, we ought to be able to do it in our sleep. But . . . something's holding me back."

Then Anne Holmes, the CFO, chimes in. "You know I always play by the numbers, Bensen. But I've been thinking about it, too. As you all probably know," she says, looking around the room, "many of these people have worked for us for fifteen or twenty years. Moving operations offshore and closing the plant will lower our costs, sure—but it will devastate the economy of an entire town. I made some phone calls: There's not much else going on out there, job-wise. A few people will find decent work. But it looks to me like a bunch of loyal, hardworking people will end up on unemployment, trying to feed their families on a fraction of their salary; some may lose their homes. What will happen to their kids? I don't like it. Isn't there a better way to handle this?"

For a moment the room is silent. Then the executive who's been pressing for the plant closing replies, his tone softer now, "I'm sure we all share your sentiments. We know it's going to be a difficult time for them, and we'll do our best to ease the transition. But don't you think it's better to pare down costs, so we can strengthen the company and stay competitive? A thriving company means jobs. . . . The numbers are compelling. . . ."

As the conversation shifts to the arithmetic justifying the plant closure, Bensen uncharacteristically loses focus and drifts off. Anne's angle happens to be in line with his own thoughts, and he's inclined to support her and extend the discussion—but something else is bothering him. One of the memos on his desk this morning is from a human rights group that monitors working conditions in production facilities worldwide. Despite assurances from contract factory owners and managers, when HighQuest's offshore facilities in Asia and Latin America were being set up, that workers would be paid a decent wage and their hours regulated fairly, he repeatedly hears from groups like this with accusations of deplorable working conditions. Substantial changes must be made, these groups insisted, not only in the factories HighQuest hires to produce their products, but also in their own, corporate-owned plants. With pain in his heart Bensen remembers the first time Katie asked him about it, innocently trusting.

"Dad, none of your factories are like that, are they?" she had asked. "You wouldn't let that happen, would you?"

He had brushed her off, assuring her that everything was fine. "But what if it's *not* fine?" he muses now. "Should I look into it? Is this what Jim's been bugging me about?"

He feels the moment, the possibility of walking a different road, then he lets it go. The room has become quiet and everyone is looking at him. One of them says, "It's Katie, isn't it, Ben? You're not yourself today."

Snapping back into the moment, Bensen feels a rush of heat to his face. "Of course it's Katie!" he shouts. "My daughter is fighting for her life!" He wants to add, "How do you expect me to focus on these things?" But he knows he *has* to focus on them, so he says nothing; the others back off and give him space to cool down. "What *is* wrong with me?" he thinks. "Whatever may be going on in my personal life, I can't think about continuing production in a factory that costs us fifty percent more to run! I'm the CEO, I'm responsible to my shareholders. I may not like putting people out of work, but it's my job to make the tough decisions. If I keep that plant open it will cost us millions. And if I don't authorize the press package about Jim, the stock price may not come back up for months." He knows that in order to protect the company and the shareholders, he's got to sign off on the press release. He knows he has to close the plant.

"Okay, Bob," he tells the executive with the computer graphics, "start the steps to close the plant! Send out the damn pink slips." And turning to another: "Go ahead with the press release about Jim."

On the way out the door as the meeting ends, Anne corners him. "I'm not sure we should blame it on Katie," she says quietly. "Maybe keeping that plant open would be the right thing to do."

"Anne," he replies, feeling weary but keeping his voice upbeat, "the numbers are there. And that's what it's all about."

"Is it?" she asks, as they start walking together down the corridor.

"You know it."

"You're heartless," she replies in a bantering tone. Bensen is too tired to notice that only the smallest of smiles curves her lips.

"Gotta be," he says; "that's my job."

"Ben," she begins, but doesn't continue.

"What?"

"I took a pretty big risk in there, saying I thought we could do things differently. . . . I was hoping you'd support me. I felt that we were on the same wavelength."

"We were," Bensen admits. "You were right about that part. But I can't go that way. I was having some personal feelings about the situation, but that's not appropriate; it's not relevant to the decision. People lose jobs. They figure something out. They get by."

"I know," she replies. "I understand. I do."

After a short, awkward silence, Anne asks, "How is she?"

"The same. The doctors said they'd notify me if there was any news, but I haven't heard from them. I've been calling the nurse's station more often than they want, and Emily's there, she's been calling me. There's no change, nothing new."

"She'll be okay."

"I hope so, Anne," Quinn says, stopping and turning to face her. "I feel so damn frustrated that I can't just *fix* it, make it turn out the way I want. Hoping is not my usual way of dealing with things."

——

The day goes by. Bensen, who had planned to put in a few hours and return to the hospital, finally walks out the door after six o'clock. Driving the short road that curves through the business campus to the highway, he calls Emily at the hospital.

"Hi Em; I'm on my way."

"I'm okay by myself for now," she says. "I got a little rest this morning. Go home and get some sleep. Nothing's changed in the last hour. You can come later."

He hasn't slept more than seven or eight hours in the last three and a half days, and he's feeling it. "All right," he says. "But call me right away if there's any news."

"Of course, what do you think?" she answers.

——

Feeling wound into a tight coil by the tough decisions of the day, added onto the three terrible days and nights in the hospital, Bensen decides to give himself a few minutes in the garden to unwind before going inside. Walking from his car to the bench by the stream, he notices, for a moment, that the sky is turning lovely pastel colors; then his attention becomes absorbed in reviewing the day's developments and prioritizing tomorrow's tasks. As he recalls his decision to authorize the factory closing, a fragment of his conversation with Kenji early in the morning flashes through his awareness and he thinks, "It wouldn't hurt to take a look at the kind of music I'm playing in my life, as he put it—the influence I'm having, how people will remember me. . . ." He's startled to hear footsteps coming his way, and then Kenji, tools in hand, emerges from the trees.

"What are you doing here at this time of day?" Bensen asks. "I was just thinking about you."

"I started something this morning," the gardener replies, his eyes sparkling; "I wanted to do a little more with it." He walks to a half-dug plot nearby, and begins working the ground with a hoe. Once again Bensen observes Kenji with fascination. There is something about his movements that impresses him, something indefinable but very satisfying to observe, like the performance of a dancer or a fine athlete.

Kenji looks up, and when he sees that Bensen is looking at him he asks, "What was it you were thinking, when you were thinking of me?"

"About what you said this morning, that we'll be remembered for the music we played, after we're gone. I have to admit that my music may be a little dissonant. I can be pretty demanding or overbearing at times, I'm told."

"Do you think so?" Kenji asks.

"I'm afraid it's true," Bensen says with a smile. "But, you know, it's worked for me. I doubt that I would have achieved what I have without being so aggressive. And I think I kind of like it!"

Kenji stops digging, walks a few paces toward where Bensen is sitting, and stands leaning on his hoe. "With weeds, with insects that are damaging your flowers, you have to be tough," he says. "Sometimes it's necessary." Then he adds, "But not always."

Bensen looks thoughtful. "Yes," he says. "Today, there were a few moments when I became aware that maybe, if I wanted to, I could change the rules. Do something different, something that might be better. But I didn't. I did things my usual way."

Kenji turns and leans the hoe against a nearby tree, where he had placed a small brown paper bag. He removes an apple from the bag and walks back toward the bench. "Do you mind if I sit down, Mr. Quinn?" he asks.

Bensen shifts to one end of the bench, and the gardener takes a pocket knife from his overalls—a very nice Swiss army knife, Bensen observes—and sits next to him. Slowly and meticulously in the deepening twilight, he peels the apple, concentrating on each motion of the knife. Watching, Bensen perceives how completely present and focused Kenji is on the task of the moment. "That's it!" he says to himself. "That's what I was observing about his work in the garden, but I couldn't put my finger on it." And he realizes in that same instant that when Kenji speaks to him, he is also fully present, his eyes steady, his attention apparently unwavering.

The gardener finishes peeling the apple, cuts off a slice and offers it to Bensen, then cuts a piece for himself. Together, the two men silently eat. When only the core remains, Kenji breaks it open, revealing the dark oval seeds. "The seed is the concentrated essence of the tree," he says, turning to Bensen. "If you want an apple tree in the garden that will be beautiful and strong and yield sweet fruit, Mr. Quinn, you have to have the right seed. If you want dahlias, you can't plant tulip bulbs. Be clear about what you want, and then plant the proper seed. Nurture it, guard it, and care for it."

"That sounds like solid advice," Bensen comments. "It's like what I do with an important business idea: define what I want to achieve—whether tulips or dahlias—then commit to it and persevere with whatever's required to make it grow."

"Yes," says Kenji. "It's true in all parts of one's life. I think like a gardener, so I look at what I do as sowing seeds for the future. Every thought, every word, and every action is a seed. I always ask myself, 'Are the seeds of your thoughts, words, and actions creating the garden you want, or not?' If I say a kind word, or do something helpful for someone, I know it will take root and grow into goodness. But what will happen if I speak harshly, or ignore someone's need? The consequences will come."

He pauses to let Bensen take that in, then continues, "So, if you don't mind my asking, do you think the seeds you are planting now will create the trees and flowers you intend? What is it that you want to grow?"

When Bensen does not reply, he adds, "You said there were moments today when you could have done something different. Those could have been times to plant a new seed. Only a new seed will yield a new crop."

"That's so true!" Bensen exclaims. "With one word, I could have saved hundreds of families from economic hardship. Something in me wanted to, but I didn't do it. I couldn't. All that I've ever learned about business stood in the way." He turns to face Kenji. "I'm not saying I did the wrong thing, mind you—I did what I had to. But I know those people will not appreciate the music I played for them, and that makes me a little sad."

"Play the music that comes from your heart, Mr. Quinn," Kenji immediately responds. "Attune to that music—to what you care about, what is meaningful to you—and express it. Then you will touch others in a way they will remember with gratitude." He gives Bensen a kindly smile.

Despite his habitual caution, Bensen can't help a momentary feeling that this man not only knows what is good for him, but that he cares, like an old and trusted friend. "But that's absurd," he thinks. "Ever since our planning sessions, years ago when we discussed the layout of the gardens, we've done little more than exchange polite hellos and goodbyes. Why should he care about me, or have any idea of what I need?"

The Seed of Purpose: Play the Music In Your Heart

Yet the feeling persists, and it creates an atmosphere of trust in which Bensen feels free to express his thoughts. "What you suggested raises an important question," he says. "Do I care about the people whose lives I influence, or only about getting things done? Do I want to create some life-enriching value in the world . . . ?" Inwardly, he completes the question: ". . . or is my daughter right: that I only care about myself and my career?"

Almost as if responding to Bensen's thoughts, Kenji says, "When I was a much younger man—perhaps about your age, Mr. Quinn—I decided that whatever I did with my life, whatever I left behind, must be something I could be proud of. I come from a culture that values the long term: Some companies have hundred-year plans. . . ."

"Yes, I remember that from business school," Bensen interrupts. "It seemed almost unfathomable to me."

"I'm afraid it may no longer be true today, when conditions are changing so fast," Kenji says. "But the principle behind it—that remains important."

"What principle is that, do you suppose?" Bensen asks.

"That we need to pay attention to the impact of our lives, our decisions and actions, on the men and women coming after us. I was pleased to learn that your Native American peoples taught their children to consider the effects of their behavior on the next seven generations. And to take into account the good of the whole, beyond the moment."

"I didn't know that," Bensen says. "People don't think that way these days. I certainly haven't."

"I believe it's important to work for future generations, not only for ourselves," Kenji says, and Bensen nods in agreement, although he hadn't thought much about it before, beyond his almost instinctive desire to provide well for Katie. Looking at the gardener, he admires what he perceives as the old man's integrity, clarity of mind, and openness of heart. By contrast, he senses that his own life may not be so congruent; it may be lacking alignment with his deepest values, values he's not even sure he could define.

"Well," Kenji says, standing up and stretching, "it's too dark to work any longer today. I'll just put the tools back in the shed, and go on home."

"Yes, I guess I'd better go inside," Bensen says.

"Good night, Mr. Quinn. I'm enjoying talking with you, after all these years."

"Yes," says Bensen, "I'm enjoying it very much too."

Wake-Up Call . . .

As important as the act of leadership are the seeds the leader will sow. Within a few decades, you will die; within two or three generations, memory of you will be mostly lost. Your true legacy will be the seeds you have planted, the contributions you have made, the music you will be remembered for.

What music do you want to be remembered for? _____

_____

_____

What seeds—what life-enriching principles—are you planting now in your relationships and in your work? _____

_____

_____

_____

What new seeds do you need to plant to more deeply root the living legacy you intend?

_____

_____

_____

For a few minutes after Kenji departs, Bensen continues to sit, reacting to their conversation. "I'm not sure I know how I'd like people to remember me," he muses. "Do I want them to respect me and be able to rattle off a list of things I accomplished? Or would I prefer to be remembered with fondness for the way I treated them? And if I do aspire to create some value in the world, to make the world a little better for future generations, what exactly does that mean? Make quality products? Provide jobs for families? Help my daughter grow up to be the best person she can be? If I can't define what legacy I want to leave behind, I have no way to gauge the appropriateness of my actions. Like Kenji said, if I don't know whether I want dahlias or tulips, how do I know how much to water them, how to care for them?

"I'm so good at this when it comes to business. If we want to produce four-hundred thousand sweatshirts and make a profit of fourteen percent, I can figure out how to organize each step, what works and what doesn't work, what's cost effective and what's too expensive. I'm not so good when it comes to personal goals, the 'product' I'm producing with my life. I've poured all I had into creating a legacy at HighQuest, growing a company I could be proud of, that others could look at and say, 'Bensen Quinn built that.' But what have I done about building Bensen Quinn himself?"

As darkness descends, a brooding Bensen hears the engine of the gardener's old truck start up in the driveway. Soon he, too, leaves the garden and goes inside. His feelings stirred up by questions of meaning and purpose, he is clearly at a crossroads: between his old road, which seemed so ideal but is now beginning to reveal its hidden bumps and crevasses, and a new road, which has yet to be built.

9 Awakening to Purpose

"I wish I had better news," Dr. Peter Schmidt tells Bensen early the next morning during their daily update on Katie's condition. "There's no immediate crisis, but there are no signs of improvement, either."

Bensen has persuaded a weary Emily to stay home awhile and rest, then driven alone to the hospital to see Katie and speak with her physician before going to work. "Basically," the doctor explains, "her condition is unchanged. That's not unusual, though to be frank, the longer it continues like this, the worse the chances are that she will come out of it."

Bensen is discouraged and deeply upset, but sits on his true emotions and says nothing. Schmidt is the best specialist he and Emily could find, and he has quickly assembled a team of top doctors. Today, they will conduct a further round of tests: a blood chemistry workup, an EEG to study her brain waves, another MRI, and tomorrow another CT scan. Then he will hear their recommendations and decide whether to stick with Schmidt and his team or seek other help.

After speaking with the doctor, Bensen takes the elevator to Katie's room in the intensive care unit, circles around her bed, gazes at her, kisses her forehead, sits a few minutes by her bedside, then stands and restlessly paces the room again. She is much the same as she was yesterday and the day before. But *he* is not the same. More troubled and agitated each day, he desperately wishes he could wake up his daughter and take her home. "How is it," he thinks, "that I can have so much power and control over one area of my life, at work, and so little power and control over something so important to me?"

He looks up at the big clock on the wall and thinks, "I've got to get to the office," though he's not at all sure he can put his mind on his work. "What else can I do?" he asks himself. "Just sit here with her? What would that accomplish?"

Yet he does sit down again, and looking at his daughter's bandaged face he feels an almost unendurable longing. Without warning, a surge of feeling rises up from his gut, a mass of grief and pain, and for the first time since his mother died, nearly twenty years ago, he begins to cry. He feels self-conscious and tries to stifle the sound, leaning forward and covering his face with his hands, but the deep sobs convulse his body and emerge from his throat despite his efforts. A nurse passing in the corridor pauses at the door to look in, nods her head, and moves on.

When the storm of emotions subsides, Bensen pulls a handful of tissues from the box near the bed and blows his nose. His turbulent mind grows more settled and clear. He rises from the chair and stands peering down at his daughter, wondering if there is any possibility that her energy and joy in living will ever return.

———

The major event of the business day is a lengthy staff meeting—planned many months in advance—facilitated by a team of consultants Bensen has brought in to help the key executives clarify HighQuest's "mission and vision." They are set up in the board room, with its plush chairs, elaborate audiovisual capabilities, and giant-size action photos on the walls of the company's top endorsers—prominent sports figures, mountain climbers, and other famous adventurers—clad in HighQuest garments.

The facilitators, a man and woman in their late thirties or early forties, bright, well-groomed, and articulate, lead his people smoothly through a carefully prepared sequence of presentations, discussions, and exercises. Less than an hour into the program Bensen becomes aware that he's not participating with his characteristic passion and engagement. He barely hears the presentations and squirms through the brainstorming session, in which ideas about the corporate mission and identity are put forward and written on the board:

"Be the best company in the sports apparel industry."

"Respond quickly to market changes."

"Be results oriented."

"Serve the customer with quality and value."

None of it seems particularly fresh, exciting, or significant, and later in the day, when the discussion shifts to strategies for expanding sales, increasing profitability each quarter, and coming up with new product ideas, he is equally uninspired. Worse, he finds himself hypercritical of the consultants and their relentlessly upbeat presentation style, dissatisfied with the ideas his people are generating, and annoyed at himself for giving his okay to what now seems like a wasted day. His mind repeatedly drifts off, not only to anxious thoughts about Katie, but also to the people who are right now opening their pink slips in the factory that he decided to close, and to the morality and consequences of his friend Jim's behavior. He keeps wanting to bring these points up for discussion, but is not sure how they would fit. When he leaves after the day and heads home, he's feeling restless and more than a little annoyed.

A light spring rain had fallen in the late afternoon. The sidewalks are dark with the moisture, and small puddles gather along the curbs. Climbing out of the car at home, Bensen notices how sweet and fresh the air feels, breathes it in deeply, and decides to walk off some of the day's stress with a turn around the garden before going in the house. Unexpectedly, he finds Kenji at work.

"Here again in the evening, Kenji?" he calls out.

"Yes," the gardener replies, "the rain softens the ground. It does some of my work for me."

Looking around and feeling the tranquility of the garden, Bensen lets out a sigh. "Tough day today, Mr. Quinn?" Kenji asks.

"In a way, yes," Bensen says, and describes the meeting with the consultants and his own unenthusiastic reactions. "I couldn't get myself to focus on it," he confesses.

"Maybe what you were talking about wasn't meaningful to you," Kenji proposes.

"Of course it's meaningful!" Bensen counters. "It's important. It's about the company's future. And my future, too."

"Is it *really* important?"

"How important does it have to be, to be important?" Bensen snaps, irritated.

"Do those phrases you mentioned express what *you* stand for, Mr. Quinn?" Kenji replies calmly. "To be results oriented? To increase profits? Is that why you got into business? Is that what you want to be remembered for? Is that your legacy?"

Bensen laughs abruptly, realizing that this is precisely why he was upset. "Oh, you mean *important* important!"

Kenji gives him a moment, then asks, "When was the last time you thought about what is meaningful to *you?*"

"Well, I hadn't for a long time. It seems that when I decided to go to business school, I set my life on a course and then went along on autopilot. Just lately, I've started to think about it again."

"What have you decided?"

Bensen laughs again. "I've only started to think about it," he says.

"What meaningful possibilities do you see at this point?"

"A number of things," Bensen replies vaguely, hoping the gardener will let it drop. But Kenji is waiting expectantly, so he tosses out a quick list: "Serving people—the community, my family. Working hard. Accomplishing something worthwhile. Making a difference."

"Those are all honorable goals," Kenji says. "Many people share them. But what has your life taught you about what is meaningful?"

Bensen doesn't quite know how to answer. Feeling pressured to respond, and remembering the intensity of his emotions as he sat at his daughter's hospital bed early in the morning, he says, "To make every minute with the people in your life count—connecting with them, showing them that you love them and care about them."

"And you live by those values?"

"Well, I try," he says defensively.

"Let me ask this," Kenji says. "According to my understanding, you've spent most of the last twenty years of your life concerned with your business. What does this ideal of love and connection have to do with your work?"

"Not much!"

"So in practice, it hasn't been that important to you."

"Well . . . I'd have to say so."

Kenji pursues the question. "What do you think *is* meaningful to you—at work, which has been the center of your life?"

Bensen sits silently, and Kenji tries another angle. "When you tried to focus on your company's mission statement today, you felt restless. Perhaps it's time to look at your own mission statement, for your own life."

Bensen nods in assent, but this kind of introspection is difficult for him, and his mind keeps wandering off. Once again he finds himself becoming annoyed: "Why am I sitting here letting my gardener quiz me on my values? Is this the best use of my time right now?" Yet the dialogue is compelling. "As much as I'd like to brush off these questions," he thinks, "what he's asking does seem important."

"I'm sorry," he says aloud. "My attention keeps drifting away."

"You're tired, I'm sure," Kenji responds. "And you have so much on your mind."

"Yes, I do."

"We can talk about this some other time. Or not at all, if you prefer."

"No," Bensen says. "It seems worthwhile to look at these issues. I just haven't had the time, or so it seems."

"Most people don't take the time."

"So what is it you were asking?"

"About what motivates you, and gives your life meaning."

"Yes, I'd say that's worth considering," Bensen replies in a tone half earnest, half self-mocking. But he's truly unable to answer, and instead throws the question back at Kenji.

"You're asking me to define my life purpose, my guiding motivation," he says. "What is yours?"

"I am *kyosei*," Kenji says earnestly, pronouncing the Japanese word with deep feeling.

"I thought you were Kenji!"

"*Kyosei* means *living and working together for the common good,*" the gardener says. "That is what I am, that is what I do, and that is what I seek to do in all parts of my life." He leans forward, picks up a twig, and draws a character in the earth.

"This is the symbol for *kyosei*, Mr. Quinn. It is the symbol for living and growing. As a gardener, I am *kyosei,* and I strive to make my entire life embody this principle."

Bensen is stunned by this profound self-definition. "It will be hard to top that, Kenji!"

"No need to top it, Mr. Quinn. This isn't a contest. But perhaps what I have said may help you define your own core purpose."

When Bensen does not attempt an answer, Kenji pursues. "Let me ask it this way. What do you feel is the essential contribution you're trying to make? Do you think you could sum up in a few words how you'd like to be remembered by others?"

"Right now, people at work would probably write on my tombstone, '*Here lies Bensen Quinn. He got things done.*'"

Kenji chuckles. "Not as flattering as you might desire?"

"At one point I might have been pleased with that. Not any more."

"So then, what is it about you that distinguishes you? After all, you're a respected leader. What is it that expresses your inner core, that engages your deepest talents and capabilities? When you're feeling a flow of energy and essence coming through you, and you know you're making a difference—can you recall any times like that?"

"Yes, of course," says Bensen, remembering the energy and fulfillment of the many peak experiences in his life, like the instant synergy he felt with Emily when they met, and the moment he was offered the chairmanship of High-Quest in recognition for all he had done to help the company grow. "Those are my best moments."

"And in those moments do you sense what your meaningful contribution is?"

"I'm sorry, I'm still drawing a blank."

"If you look at your past," Kenji offers, "do you see any pattern that reveals what you've cared most about?"

A series of thoughts and images flash quickly on Bensen's screen of consciousness: growing the business, expanding and improving the product lines, and mentoring key people like Anne Holmes—the excellence of their strategy and their image in the community.

"If I had to put into words what I do best at HighQuest, and what I want to do with my life," he says with some conviction, "I think it would be this: growing excellence."

Kenji again chuckles. "So, Mr. Quinn, you're really a gardener at heart, just like me." Then he probes more deeply. "That may be true in your business. It shows up there. How about growing excellence in your relationship with your family?"

Bensen again faces the truth. "Okay. I see it. I've been out of synch with my purpose there. But it *is* important to me!"

"How about growing excellence in your community?"

"Oh God," says Bensen, sounding increasingly disconcerted, "you know, every year I try to do some nonprofit board work or community service of some kind, but there never seems to be enough time. . . . Besides, Emily does a lot."

"And you think that takes care of your responsibility?" Kenji asks.

"Well . . . I can't do everything."

"What about growing the excellence of Bensen Quinn?

Bensen manages a sardonic laugh. "You mean, you don't think I'm perfect as I am? A couple of months ago, even last week, before my daughter's accident, I might have gotten offended if someone suggested that I had any growing to do. I *did* think I was damn near perfect! My life seemed to be going so well. . . ."

"And now?"

"Now . . . there's a lot I'm not sure of any more."

Bensen is now sounding quite dejected, and he is leaning forward, elbows on his knees, resting his head on his hands, staring at the ground. Gently, Kenji says, "Perhaps we've talked enough for one day." But then, as if summing up the conversation, he adds, "If growing excellence is your purpose, then your challenge is to align with it—in all parts of your life. Seek integration, Mr. Quinn, and *be* the growing excellence you wish to bring to others. Live a life of wholeness!"

"That's quite an assignment!" Bensen replies, sitting up straight.

Kenji laughs and says quietly, "Sometimes friends have to help by challenging. Your Ralph Waldo Emerson said he'd rather have a friend who's a thorn in his side than one who's merely an echo."

"You read *Emerson?*" Bensen exclaims, his voice rising in pitch with incredulity.

Kenji chuckles. "There are many things you don't know about me, Mr. Quinn. Many things."

Wake-Up Call . . .

Truly heroic leaders throughout the ages have taught us that it is better to die pursuing one's core purpose than to live disconnected from it. *What are you willing to die for?*

_____

_____

_____

What is your core purpose: the gifts you have that make a meaningful, life-enriching contribution to serving the needs of others? _____

_____

_____

How aligned or misaligned is your core purpose to your work . . . to your relationships . . . to your community . . . to yourself? _____

_____

_____

The following morning, Bensen again opts to spend a few hours at the office before resuming his vigil at the hospital. When he pulls up his calendar on his computer screen, he sees that this is the night Emily is to be honored by United Women's Groups of Connecticut for her "outstanding service to the community."

"I hope she hasn't cancelled," he thinks. "That kind of affirmation could be very healing for her, and maybe for both of us, right now." He immediately phones her.

"Hi, it's me," he announces. "Are you planning to go to the banquet tonight?"

"Oh my God, the Women's Groups. I forgot all about it!"

"Good, that means it's still on. Do you think we should go?"

"Bensen, I can't do something like that *now*."

"I think it wouldn't do Katie any harm if we went away for a few hours. I can practically hear her voice, can't you? 'Mom, don't sit around in the hospital. . . .'"

"Ben, please don't push. I really don't want to do it."

"Well, of course, it's your choice. But you know, since you didn't cancel, everyone will be expecting you," he says.

"They'll all understand if I don't show up. I'll call now and let them know; they'll have time to organize something."

"But it would only be a couple of hours at the most," he persists. "We don't have to stay for the whole thing. Just accept your award, give your talk, and we'll go. You've already written the speech, right?"

"It's basically finished, but . . ."

"But?"

"I look terrible. I'm exhausted. I'll be incoherent."

"You'll look beautiful, as you always do. And you're never incoherent."

"Well, they *have* gone to a lot of trouble. . . ."

"Yes, they have. Emily, I promise, I'll leave work early and take over at the hospital so you can go home to grab a little rest and get ready."

"Well, maybe it won't be so bad," she says.

———

The evening starts with a spontaneous outpouring that really moves Bensen. When Emily enters the banquet room, the entire group—hundreds of highly successful, prominent women—rise up in one motion and give her a standing ovation. They have heard about the accident, and this is their way of telling her right from the start that they are with her.

And that's just the beginning.

"Those of us who have been fortunate to know Emily Cavallo Quinn," the woman introducing Emily says, "know her not only as a dynamic high achiever who has helped dozens of organizations and countless individuals in the community, but as an outstanding, genuine human being. Many of us have fallen under the spell of that magnetism she has that draws people to her and instantly wins them over. She is self-contained, yet she exudes a warmth and radiance that go out to all around her. She is smart, and funny, and deep. And perhaps most striking of all, she is authentic. There is nothing 'put on' about Emily Quinn, no false persona that she hides behind. She's one of those wonderful people about whom we say, 'What you see is what you get,' and what you see is magnificent."

Listening to this praise, Bensen recognizes the truth of it, and he glows with pleasure and pride in this woman who has been his life partner for more than two decades. When she steps to the podium to receive her award and deliver her speech, his feelings grow even stronger. He has accompanied her many times in recent years to fund-raisers or other community events where she was the keynote speaker, as she has so often accompanied him, yet tonight he's particularly struck by the eloquence of her speech, and by her beauty and charisma, just as he had been taken with her when they first met. And even as his eyes remain riveted on her, Bensen's mind drifts to an earlier time. . . .

He was walking through campus on a breezy spring morning during his junior year at college. At the south end of the quad, he came upon a large crowd gathered around a makeshift platform and heard a woman's voice speaking passionately about civil rights. Although he had intended to spend a couple of hours in the library researching a paper, the topic was something he cared about; he stopped to listen, and was moved by the eloquent way she encouraged people not to abandon the struggle, but to persist in the ongoing battle for racial equality and human dignity.

As he listened, gradually working his way to the front of the crowd, Bensen was captivated as much by her energy and appearance as by her message. She was animated and charismatic, and beautiful to look at, with the kind of beauty that attracted him: not the polished, pampered features of a fashion magazine cover girl, but more natural and earthy, with dark hair and intelligent, sparkling eyes. He was immediately and strongly interested in more than the message, and he asked a woman standing next to him who the speaker was.

"It's Emily Cavallo," she replied, as if that was all that needed to be said.

"Am I supposed to know who she is?" Bensen asked, with the characteristic bluntness that took him years to temper.

"She's student body president," came the reply.

When the talk ended, Bensen found himself drawn to the knot of people that gathered around Emily. He was impressed by how energized they appeared to be by her talk, eager to help her and to do their part. He was also impressed by how she related to them: honestly and simply, with no show of self-importance, even though people were thronging around seeking her attention.

He stayed till the crowd thinned out. Then, hearing the carillon bells start to ring, she glanced at her watch and said, "I'd better get to the library."

"I'm headed there myself," he volunteered, realizing that he probably would have said so even if it hadn't been true.

But they never reached their destination that morning, nor that afternoon. Within minutes they were engrossed in a conversation about civil rights, Vietnam, and Emily's commitment to taking a stand for what she believed.

"I couldn't agree more," Bensen said, "but sometimes it's complicated. There are a lot of things I care about and would love to get involved in, but I kind of pledged when I was a kid that I'd work hard and 'make something of myself,' as my mom put it." He told her a little about his childhood, his father's lost baseball career and his drinking, how hard his mother worked to support the family, and the fateful moment when he offered to get a job and his mother urged him to concentrate instead on his school work. Despite his deep commitment to honoring her request, as he spoke he feared that Emily might mock him and wonder what kind of man he was for putting so much energy into pleasing his mother!

Instead, she looked at him and said, "That's a beautiful story. I admire her for what she did, and I understand how you must feel about honoring her wishes."

Pleased, Bensen said nothing for the moment, and Emily continued in a reflective tone, "I feel like I understand your background, Bensen, but my life was very, very different. My parents are both professionals—my mom's a doctor and my dad's a law professor—and I guess I was pretty spoiled growing up. We had plenty of money and all that."

When Bensen heard those words, he was surprised to feel a chill of fear go through him, which later turned out to be prescient. He knew he was destined for something substantial in life, but he guessed that her parents wouldn't believe it; they would view him as a kid from the wrong side of the tracks, and he was certain they would discourage their daughter from what he already saw as an important relationship. He could only hope that Emily would see the truth of who he was.

All this took place before they reached the bottom of the library steps. By this time, the feeling between them was so intimate and compelling that they stopped and looked at each other.

"Library?" Bensen asked.

"Maybe later," Emily replied.

"Great. How about some coffee, or an early lunch?"

"Sounds good to me," she said. And for the rest of the morning, and long into the afternoon and evening, they walked and talked, strolling through the campus and along the river, sitting under a tree with the sandwiches and drinks they bought at the Italian deli . . . sharing everything, feeling as if they'd always known each other and were just catching up, like old friends.

———

Brought back to the present by the applause at the end of his wife's speech, Bensen stands and claps with the rest of the audience, and is pleased that she looks over at him with a smile. In moments, a crowd gathers around her just like the crowd on campus—eager to connect with her, to share in her energy, and in this case to offer their support for the difficult time she is going through.

Bensen had promised to rescue her from just this situation, so after a couple of minutes he walks to the front, and as people turn to him, he says, gently but definitively, "I'm sure you'll understand: We've got to get back to our daughter now. I'm afraid I'm going to have to steal away your guest of honor."

———

In the car, Emily continues to glow. "That was nice, Bensen. Thank you for urging me to go." But a few seconds later she adds, "I do feel guilty for leaving her."

"I'm sure it's okay," Bensen says, attempting to reassure her, but she cuts him off.

"You know, Bensen, it makes me realize, I am proud of my career and my community service. It's important to me. But Katie is really important. I'd drop all that in a minute if I had to make a choice."

"You did choose, Em."

"You mean by limiting my career so I could be with her?"

"Yeah. And this is the moment of truth, when you can see that it was the right choice for you."

"I do see that, Bensen," she says softly, tears welling up in her eyes.

"Good." After another minute he adds, "This was a good thing, tonight. I think it will give you more strength to go through whatever we have to go through. And for me—in case you're interested . . ." She pokes him gently in the ribs. "For me, it was great to see how much people love and respect you, and that they recognize what a magnificent human being you are. . . ."

Caught up in renewed worries about her daughter, Emily does not really take in Bensen's sentiments. She has already extracted her phone from her purse and called the hospital. A minute later she reports, "They say there's no change, her condition is 'stable.' I hate when they say that, it's so impersonal, like she's some kind of chemical compound."

"But you want to stop there anyway, don't you?" he asks.

"I do. Don't you?"

"I do," he says, reaching over and taking her hand.

———

It requires only a few minutes at their daughter's bedside, a close look at her face, and a few words with the nurse on duty to persuade them that indeed nothing has changed. Trusting that Katie is being carefully looked after and that there is nothing they can do for her tonight, Emily and Bensen go home to rest and prepare themselves for another day of heartrending uncertainty.

Bensen, remembering the stack of memos and reports he had carried home, goes to his office. Emily, exhausted, goes to their bedroom.

But Bensen cannot focus on the paperwork. The powerful feelings stirred up during the past few days—from the crisis with Katie to his unsettling conversations with Kenji in the garden and the questions they brought up about the direction and meaning of his life, his anxiety about confronting his friend Jim, and even the sweet, rich feelings of the evening—all contribute to an unfamiliar mix of emotions that keeps his mind in turmoil. Finally, he gives up, shuts off the light, and walks quietly to the bedroom.

The Strength of Vulnerability 11

Emily's reading light is still on, although she's curled up under her favorite afghan quilt with her back to the door, seemingly asleep, a book lying next to her pillow. He stands silently in the doorway for a moment.

"I tried to read but I couldn't," she says without looking up. "I don't think I can stand not being there with her."

She rolls over to face him. "It's so strange, how peaceful she looks," she says. "I mean, she's so banged up, but she doesn't look like she's in pain."

"No, thank God for that, at least," he says.

"The house is so quiet."

"I know. I miss her laughter, the telephone calls—even that music!"

Emily starts to cry. "It's unbearable! I'm trying to be brave, but I don't have any words for how much I miss her, how scared I am."

"I know," Bensen says.

"What do you mean, *I know?*" Emily snaps, sitting up, her mood suddenly shifting. "Where were you all day? I feel like I've been carrying the whole load of this. You're hardly ever around!"

Bensen feels unjustly accused, and strikes back. "I can't just drop all my responsibilities! What do you want from me?"

"I want to know that you care about your daughter. And what about me?"

"Emily . . ." Bensen breaks off, holds back. She's accused him many times of not being around enough, but this time it just isn't true. "I'm sorry if you feel I'm not doing my part here," he says.

Seeing that he means it, Emily softens. "I'm sorry I snapped at you. Actually, you *have* been around, ever since the accident. It's just that I'm so worried. I keep thinking, what if there's brain damage from the concussion? She may have to live the rest of her life in bed, or in a wheelchair. Maybe she won't recognize us, maybe she won't remember anything about her life. It's not fair! She has so much to live for!"

Then she looks at Bensen and says, "Deep down, I feel she's all right. That she'll be all right, she'll be home. Or is that just wishful thinking?"

Bensen sits on the bed next to his wife, puts his arms around her and softly says, "I don't know, Em. You know how I am: I always think things are going to work out. But this seems to be out of our hands."

"The hardest thing for me," he continues, his voice faltering, "is . . . I just can't accept the possibility that she might not make it, that she might . . . die. I can hardly use words like that, about Katie. But we have to face it." He continues to hold her for another minute or so, then finds his mind leaping uncontrollably from problem to problem. He stares blankly ahead.

"What are you thinking, Ben?" Emily asks, sensing his attention move away from her.

Startled, he replies, "Oh, you don't need to hear it. I've got a lot on my mind."

"I *want* to hear it," she says, leaning back against a pillow.

He hesitates. Then, deciding to unburden himself, he's not sure where to begin: He's seeing difficulties and shadows everywhere.

"Well," he says, looking down at the floor, "to start with the obvious, I can't stop thinking about Katie—especially about how close our relationship was when she was little." He pauses a moment as a memory surfaces. "Remember the time we bought her that little western getup?"

"The Annie Oakley outfit?"

"Yeah. How old was she? She couldn't have been more than three."

"I had forgotten that," Emily says softly. "She was so crazy about that little outfit, I couldn't get it off her. I think she slept in it!"

"There was so much like that," Bensen continues. "Holding her, laughing with her, reading to her, playing together—*you* know. My God, for every hour I spent with her like that, you must have spent a hundred or a thousand. And now I don't know if I'll have another chance to be a good father again, to help her with things, to let her know how much I love her.

"I was so proud of myself for all the wonderful opportunities I was providing for her," he continues. "A beautiful home, a good school, classes she was interested in—all the stuff my dad never gave me."

"You *do* give her all that, Ben. Don't take it away from yourself."

"Okay. But what has happened to me? I was behaving as if material things were more important than love, attention, and my presence in her life. Did I actually believe that buying her a flashy car when she turned sixteen was what she needed? She needed more time with her father.

"And," he adds after a moment, "I needed *her,* too. The bottom line is, we both lost out, and we may never have another chance. And that's what I want more than anything now—another chance. What does it mean to love someone, if you don't share yourself with them?"

Shifting his weight on the bed and looking directly at Emily, he tells her, "When people have asked me about what's important to me, I've always said, 'my family,' the way everyone does. But like you said before, I haven't been around much, and I didn't realize it, till this happened."

"You've been great in these last days, Ben," she says softly.

"Well, I'm glad. But now I can see why you've complained, or, to be more fair, tried to get me to see how little attention I was paying to her. And . . . to you."

Emily can hardly believe she is hearing these words; they are loaded with meaning for her, and she reaches out a hand, which he takes in his.

"It's making me think about my life in a different way, Emily. About what's important to me and what isn't. Even about my own death, and what I want to accomplish before that time comes."

She squeezes his hand tightly. He studies her face for more of a reaction to his words, but when she says nothing, he continues. "And then Kenji—we happened to talk for a few minutes yesterday, and he asked me what legacy I want to leave behind, what music I want to be remembered for, as he put it. It's got me wondering if my life has expressed who I really am, or who I always thought I was, anyway. . . ." Again he pauses, and Emily remains still, letting him talk. "I've been haunted lately by so many questions."

"Such as?" she asks, adjusting the pillows behind her.

"Such as, have I lost touch with myself, with who I am? Tell me—did I turn out to be the kind of man you thought I would be? Aren't you a little disappointed in me?"

Bensen's question shocks her, and touches a tightly guarded, sensitive place in her feelings, but she tries not to show it. She *has* felt disappointed about his total absorption in the business, to the virtual exclusion of everything and everyone else, and sad that he had moved so far away from the values that forged their initial bond. "I used to see you more driven by your beliefs and ideals than you are these days," she says, choosing her words carefully.

"I don't know what I believe in any more," he admits, then says tenderly, "On the other hand, *you* are definitely the woman I thought you'd be, the one I admired and fell in love with. The banquet tonight proved it yet again. You didn't abandon *your* ideals."

Emily's face glows. "Thank you," she says. "It means a lot to me, that you feel that way. That you care about that."

"How could I not? It's obviously true," he says. "You've continued all along to work for what you believe in. Whereas I . . ."

"You've chosen a different path, Bensen. We each followed our passion. And you've certainly proved the distinguished Drs. Cavallo wrong!" Indeed, as Bensen had feared, Emily's parents had done all they could to dissuade her from marrying the son of an alcoholic ex-baseball player and a supermarket clerk.

"Yes," Bensen says with a smile, "I can't really complain about my career. I've helped grow a successful company. I've received a lot of recognition. And we've got all we'll ever need financially. But I don't know if I believe that the business is more than just a good job now. It's *not* a passion any more, the way it was when I had the challenge of building it into a success. Now that I've achieved that, I'm wanting it to be something else, something more."

"Well, maybe it's time to do something new. Or to rekindle some of the ideals you felt strongly about. They haven't seemed important to you for a long time."

"That's what I'm starting to see," says Bensen. "When we met, I thought I knew what was important. And unless I'm kidding myself, I did live more in synch with what I believed, even if I didn't get as involved as you did. Where did all that go? Don't I care about people any more, and about the world outside HighQuest?"

"It happens to a lot of people, Ben. I see it every day in my work with the foundations and nonprofits. People in midlife start volunteering, or they may even set up a new organization to accomplish something they care about. Sometimes they feel they've abandoned part of themselves, and they want to get back to it, honor it."

"Do you think it's because I've been so totally immersed in the business?"

"Well, sure, that's one reason," Emily replies. "But it happens to people who aren't CEOs, and people who don't even go to work—it's just the demands of life, I think. All the countless tasks and chores you have to do to keep things going. The pressures of life overtake us and we forget."

"That's so true," Bensen says. "I've found myself wondering if what I'm doing is really *my* life, what I want to do from inside myself, or whether I've just been successfully responding to a series of circumstances."

She looks at him fondly. "You really do have a lot on your mind! And not just business, for a change."

"Oh, that's not all of it," he replies. "I've been realizing that I've made decisions I'm not proud of. I've hurt people, I've okayed a cover-up for Jim even though I knew in my gut that he's been doing some questionable things but I didn't want to look at it, I haven't been spending enough time with my daughter, my wife is distant. . . ."

"I'm not distant, Ben," his wife says softly. "I'm lonely. When is the last time we talked this way together? Do you remember how it used to be with us, how we talked all the time, about everything? How much do I see you, really?"

"Not enough," he answers. "Not enough." He reaches for her and pulls her close, and she responds eagerly. They hold each other with an intensity they haven't shared in months . . . or years.

———

A few minutes later, Emily whispers, "I've been waiting for you."

"Oh?" says Bensen, "I was sure you were asleep."

She glares at him. "I've been waiting for you for a *long time,* Bensen Quinn!"

He leans his head back to read her expression, and as he understands her message, his emotions well up and he says, "I'm so sorry, Emily." Then, moving a little bit away from her, "I've got to pull myself together."

"I think you *are* pulling yourself together. I know you, Ben. You're strongest when you let yourself be open."

"How can that be? I feel weak like this."

"No. When you're like this, you *are* the man I married."

"What do you mean?"

"This is when you're in your power. When you face yourself squarely, when you're connecting to the totality of who you are—that's when I feel your strength, your integrity. When you think you're 'strong,' no one feels that you need them or even want them around." She lets these words linger in the air a few seconds, then says, "We'd all like to be one hundred percent together and in control, but you know, nobody is. Not even you."

While Bensen is considering this, she adds, "You know, Ben, I've never said this to you, but I've always believed that if you had the courage to bring forward the whole person that I know you to be, you would become a much more powerful leader. A great leader. Instead of being the driven, successful man that you are, you'd be someone who could truly inspire people's hearts and minds and take them to a higher level. You would move from being the leader you are now to being a truly great leader."

"It sounds good, but I'm not really following you," he says.

"It seems to me," she explains, "that accepting our vulnerabilities—our weaknesses, if you will—is part of being an authentic person. If you want to be a complete, integrated human being, you've got to look at the entire picture. Not just the good stuff."

"I'm not sure I buy that," Bensen says, starting to squirm a bit. "And even if it makes me a more integrated human being, as you put it, how does that make me a better leader?"

"Think about it," she urges. "What are the consequences of not facing the places where you're not strong?"

"Sorry, it must be getting late; I'm still not sure what you're getting at."

She looks at the clock. "Well, it is after midnight. But let's give this five more minutes, okay? I think it's important."

"Whatever you say. You're the woman with the award."

She looks up and sees him smiling. "You're just jealous," she playfully shoots back.

"Hey, I've got more than you do."

"Always a competition, isn't it?"

"It's a male thing."

"Okay, Mr. Man, let's say that intuition isn't a strong area for you. Or, even better, maybe it *is* developed but you don't trust it. What's the result?"

"If I don't trust myself enough to move on an intuitive hunch . . . I may blow an opportunity." He pauses a moment, then, catching on, he adds, "And if I'm too arrogant and self-assured to ask for expert opinions, I'm limiting my knowledge. If I don't acknowledge where I need to grow, or something I ought to learn, then I can't stay ahead of the flow of change. I see now where you're going with this. I have to admit the places I'm not strong, so I can strengthen them. Otherwise, I'm susceptible there."

"Yes, that's true," Emily says. "But I think there's a certain strength in *not* doing anything about it, too. Just being ourselves, acknowledging the entirety of who we are—warts and all, as the saying goes. I think it's important to admit that we have weaknesses and underdeveloped parts."

"And blow my image?" Bensen quips, starting to grasp her point.

"Yes, exactly. Blow your *image*—and be *yourself*! If you refuse to look at those places and try to paint a rosy picture of yourself, don't you think other people will notice anyway? They'll see that you're hiding something, and you'll lose credibility as a leader."

A dozen examples of the truth of what Emily is telling him flash across his mind. Executives who were insecure in their position and compensated with arrogance or bravado; others who exaggerated facts about their company to impress or persuade; leaders who hid their weaknesses behind their image, position, or achievements. People like this *do* lose credibility, he reflects. They lose the respect of their peers and the allegiance of their employees.

"If you can accept yourself as you are," Emily says, "if you're not afraid to be open and honest and you can even laugh at yourself a little, people will trust

Wake–Up Call . . .

"I thought my power was being right; now I know my power is being real!" This is how, at the moment of insight, a highly effective leader framed it for me. It was a breakthrough moment for him. The credibility of leaders is directly proportional to how well they understand and acknowledge their true strengths and vulnerabilities. Letting go of the facade of "having it all together" is the first step to authentic leadership. It is also the first step to gaining credibility and committed followers and partners.

What are your strengths? _____

_____

_____

*What are your vulnerabilities?*_____

_____

_____

Where can you begin "showing up" as a whole person to practice more authentic living and leading? _____

_____

you, and they'll follow you without being told. Authenticity carries a lot of power."

Noticing her husband stifling a yawn, Emily breaks into laughter.

"What's so funny?" he asks.

"It's tiring, listening to your wife go on and on, isn't it?"

"Hey! Tell me we're not both totally exhausted."

"Ben," she says softly, "I'm not sure you really know what I've just been talking about, and I want you to. The thing is, the way I see it, you're an extremely effective leader. You didn't get where you are by accident. You have an energy, a drive, that's irresistible, that won't take no for an answer. But that's only part of you. You have a tender side, too, and there are things that hurt you, things you're not sure about. And you have secret dreams, dreams I know about, that I dreamt with you—dreams you'd like to live out, but you're not, and whenever you think about them, it distresses you. That's what I'm talking about."

"How do you know so much?" he asks her, only half kidding, "about me, and about life?"

Awakening to Authenticity 12

For the first time in many months, Emily and Bensen wake up in each other's arms, relieved and happy to feel their love flowing more freely.

"Let's stay together a little longer," Emily says, snuggling closer. "Do you have time?"

"I think my boss might let me take some time off," Bensen replies with a smile.

"How about if we go to the hospital together," Emily proposes. "Then you can drop me at home on your way to work. If they're really going to move her out of the ICU to a quieter room," she says, sitting up and reaching for the phone, "I want to be there for that."

Bensen sits up next to her while she speaks to the nurse and receives the latest update about Katie: the recurring yet somehow reassuring "her condition is stable." Then, after a quick shower, he leaves his wife to dress and heads downstairs to make coffee. It's a morning ritual he enjoys; even when Katie was small and the family had a live-in housekeeper, he retained that task for himself whenever he was home.

He carries his coffee mug to the kitchen table and looks out through the sliding glass doors at the garden. For the moment, his problems have receded to the background of awareness. In the foreground, a glorious, late-spring day is starting to unfold. He hears the cooing of doves and spies a pair of them sitting together on a high branch, surveying the scene.

Kenji, who likes to work early in the morning before the heat starts to build, is whistling somewhere in the garden. Bensen slides open the doors to listen, then goes outside. He finds the gardener with his arms full of flowers, bending and snipping more to add to the already large bouquet.

"Good morning, Kenji," Bensen calls out as he approaches. "I enjoyed our talk yesterday."

"I'm glad," Kenji replies, straightening up. "I thought maybe I asked you too many questions."

"No, it was good for me," Bensen says.

Kenji smiles, then holds out the flowers. "Here. Take these to your daughter's room. I haven't had time to arrange them properly, but you can see to that."

"Thank you," says Bensen, touched by this gesture of kindness. "It turns out that we're going over there right now." Kenji looks at him and nods; it occurs to Bensen that—somehow—this man already knew.

Over Kenji's left shoulder, across from his favorite bench by the stream, Bensen sees what looks like a small, half-completed shrine. Among the wildflowers and tall, waving grass on the far side of the water, some artfully arranged stones form an archway, with an open space in the center.

"What is that?" he asks.

"A surprise," Kenji says.

Bensen laughs. "Okay! No questions. Whatever you create here is always beautiful; I am willing to wait and see."

Kenji looks at him warmly. "I'm pleased that you enjoy the garden."

"I certainly do," Bensen says. "Ever since I was a boy living in the city, I've had a love for plants and flowers, things that grew. This garden is one of the main reasons I bought this place!"

Kenji listens attentively, then stands unmoving, without replying or turning to go to work. It makes Bensen a little uncomfortable, and he says, "After our conversation last night, Emily and I had a long talk, and she helped me see something important."

"She is a very wise woman."

"Yes," Bensen says. "Sometimes I forget that."

"You mustn't forget, Mr. Quinn! My wife has been my greatest friend and teacher, for almost fifty years now."

"How wonderful, Kenji. I'll remember what you said. And speaking of friends—I feel that you and I are becoming friends, and it's starting to bother me that I call you 'Kenji' and you call me 'Mister Quinn.' I know I'm your employer . . ."

"And in my country, it's proper to address one's employer in a respectful way."

"Yes, but if we go by that standard, I should address you as 'Mister' too—you're my elder."

Kenji smiles. "Yes, that would be correct."

"So why don't we just do as we do in America, and call each other by our first names. If that would be all right with you."

"It might take some getting used to, after all these years. But it would be fine."

"Good. Then, getting back to what I was saying, Emily helped me see the value of being more self-accepting—acknowledging all aspects of myself, even things I'm not so proud of. I think what she said will help me be more patient with the confusion I've been feeling about my life since Katie's accident."

Kenji seems delighted at these words, and he leads Bensen a few steps over to the roses, which are blossoming in a profusion of yellow, apricot, pink, white, and red. "Even the most exquisite roses in the garden have thorns," he says. "It's the way of life, the way of wholeness. I can remember my grandmother saying to me, when I was a boy, 'Some people will say the flowers are good and the thorns are bad, Kenji, but they are all part of the whole.'" He carefully takes hold of the stem of a yellow rose and lifts the blossom toward Bensen. "The true story of the rose is about both blossom and briar, Mr. Quinn . . . Bensen. The lovely petals, the tender green leaves—*and* the sharp and painful thorns. If you truly love the rose, you have to love all of it."

"Because if you love only the flower . . . you aren't appreciating the whole?" Bensen says, grasping for the principle.

"Yes, that. And also, the thorns make the branch strong. They protect the flower from harm. They go together. It's a—what was that expression?—*a package deal!*" He laughs, enjoying his own joke. His laughter rolls out like a waterfall; it is contagious, and Bensen joins in.

"I think you're saying what Emily was getting at," Bensen tentatively offers, "that if I don't acknowledge both my strengths and my weaknesses, if I don't use my abilities and strong qualities, as well as look honestly at the things in myself and in my life that are painful or difficult—the thorns, so to speak— then what? That I'm not being true to who I am? Is that what you're saying?"

"Everyone has a hidden side, like the roots invisible under the ground. For most people that unseen part is something they're ashamed of, or something they fear. We all try to display our flower and hide away our thorns. But you, Bensen, you have done almost the reverse."

"What do you mean?"

"You've hidden part of your nature that is admirable and worthwhile. Locking it away limits you; it restricts your power, your creativity, and your joy."

Bensen does not know what to say. "I think that what is hidden away in your soul is a great compassion, a deep caring," the gardener continues, his dark eyes fixed on Bensen.

Bensen knows that Kenji has put his finger on a very real but latent place within him, yet he resists accepting it. "Kenji, I'm afraid that caring is not part of the job description of a CEO!"

Kenji chuckles. "Most people fear their hidden side because they feel it contains the seeds of personal destruction. That's why many people try to conceal their weak spots. You, Bensen, even though your unexpressed side is something positive, you fear it, too."

"Why would I fear something positive? That doesn't make sense."

"Because to honor it, to express it, would require change. A different kind of behavior. A different kind of leadership."

Bensen feels a chill run along his spine and tingle his scalp. He knows it is true. In these past few days, he *has* become increasingly aware of a part of himself that is far more human, humble, and caring than he ever allows himself to feel or express, especially at work. Katie's accident has shown him how little he is actually in control of his life. And it has helped him grasp how important it is—to him, Bensen Quinn—to be a more caring person. Taking in Kenji's words, he sees that if he is going to be true to himself as the coming weeks, months, and years unfold, he will have to honor that wellspring of caring and allow it to overflow to the people around him. That, indeed, will be a different kind of leadership.

"As you can see, Kenji," Bensen says, drawing a wide circle in the air in a gesture that takes in the big house, the rambling lawns and gardens, "I've been very successful. And I don't believe it's been an accident. I was born with some positive qualities, but nothing was given to me. My parents were actually quite poor. I've worked hard since I was a young boy, and done my best to take advantage of every opportunity that came my way. But I've made plenty of mistakes, too, and I see now that I haven't always been faithful to who I thought I was, to my deeper values, as you pointed out yesterday."

"I was suggesting . . ."

"No, you were absolutely right. I've failed to do that, and I intend to do better. I've grown the most, as a leader and as a person, from meeting challenges and working through difficult situations. I believe that what you said about me just now is correct. I don't know at this moment what I am going to do about it—but I will do my best to bring that side of myself into my life.

"And you're right," he continues. "I am afraid of it. I don't know how it will play out in the corporate world. But I'm willing to face it. I know that obstacles and problems can ultimately be helpful."

"You will find a way," Kenji states.

"I suspect I will."

For a long moment, neither speaks. Then Bensen says, "So, Kenji—the flower and the thorn . . . ?"

"Yes," Kenji replies. "They go together. Life is very big. It is not all sweetness and light, as some might wish, nor is it all bitterness and struggle. It welcomes both night and day, positive and negative, creation and destruction. Joy and sorrow, birth and death are part of its eternal dance."

"But what about my daughter?" Bensen interjects. "I've never had anything more difficult to deal with. Never!"

"Is nothing good coming to you from her accident?"

"What good could there possibly be?" Bensen says, flaring up defensively. "She's in a coma. She may die."

"Your heart, Bensen. You are remembering how much you love her."

"What good will that do, if she dies?"

"Whether she lives or dies, my friend, is not up to you. But with an open heart you can do many things."

Suddenly Bensen becomes aware of how late it is getting. "We've got to get to the hospital!" he says, glancing at his watch. "And I've got to get to work!" But then he stands absolutely still, looks intently at Kenji and says, "So—be like the rose. Enjoy the greatness and the good times, and accept the hard times too. They're all part of the whole."

Kenji smiles broadly. "Yes," he says. "And the whole is good. Embrace the flower, embrace the thorn."

Just at that moment, a hummingbird darts overhead, the whir of its wings delighting both of them. Bensen notices the sun, warm on his face as it climbs over the

The Seed of Authenticity: Embrace the Flower, Embrace the Thorn

treetops, and the layers of sweet and pungent scents rising from the freshly cut flowers in his arms. In a moment of quiet communion with each other and the forces of nature awakening in the garden, the two men fall silent, watching and listening.

"Ben, are you ready?" Emily's voice from a side door breaks the spell.

"Time to leave," Bensen says. "I hope your work goes well today. I will see you next time you are here."

"Yes," says Kenji. "I will be here."

———

In the hospital, the bouquet of flowers from their garden brightening Katie's new room with color and fragrance, Emily and Bensen sit side by side next to their daughter's bed, holding hands and talking quietly, sharing memories and stories, poignantly aware of how much promise there is in her young life, how deeply and tenderly they love her, and how passionately they want her to live.

"Do you remember," Bensen asks, watching a scene unfold in his mind, "how she used to go around the neighborhood with that scruffy dog we rescued from the animal shelter, raising money? God!"

"You didn't want her to do it, as I recall," Emily says.

"Probably not," Bensen admits. "She was just a little girl."

"And you were a pretty protective father."

"Yes, I guess I was. I remember keeping my eye on her from across the street. That mutt would sit next to her when she rang the doorbell. Someone would come to the door and say, 'Yes? What can I do for you?' They probably thought she was selling lemonade or something. Then she'd pull out her jar with the animal shelter fund-raising label. They'd take a look at that dog, and at that earnest little face of hers; I don't think anyone ever turned her down."

"Then she'd bring her jar to the animal shelter," Emily says, "and empty it on the counter."

"She was so proud of being able to help," Bensen says. "She really cared."

"She really cares now," Emily says. "That's what's behind her interest in the sweatshops and all that, you know."

"Caring?"

"Of course. And a sense of justice. And protectiveness. Only this time it's for people, not just puppies."

They sit quietly for a while. Then Bensen says, "She's just getting started, isn't she? Just beginning to figure out who she is, what she believes in, what she cares about."

As he says that, he catches a faint glimpse of the fact that, in an odd sort of way, he's doing the same thing.

———

The parents take turns holding their daughter's cool, limp hand. At one moment, Emily cries out, "Ben! She just squeezed my hand!" He leaps up and looks down at Katie's face. She remains expressionless, and nothing else happens: no change in breathing, no beeping on the monitors, no open eyes. "Well, it was a light squeeze," Emily admits. "But I felt it. I'm sure I did." After a while, another faint pressure, and again the parents feel a surge of hope. "Maybe she's coming back," Emily says, a hint of exhilaration in her voice.

"Maybe we're coming back, too," Bensen replies, looking tenderly at his wife. They press each other's hand tightly, their hearts full of hope.

13 Always Connected

Later that morning, Bensen arrives at corporate headquarters without switching gears. He's still moving in the world of feelings, sensitized by renewed intimacy with his wife and their emotional visit to the hospital. Walking past his administrative assistant to his office, he notices that her "Good morning" greeting doesn't ring with its usual buoyancy. He stops and turns to face her. "Are you okay today, Marie?"

She doesn't quite know how to respond. "He never notices personal things," she thinks. "Why is he asking? Is he going to criticize me for something?"

But she sees kindness in his eyes and takes a chance. "My son has a high fever," she tells her boss. "I'm worried about him."

Without hesitation Bensen offers, "Do you need to take some time off to deal with it?"

"I think he'll be all right. They have my phone number if they need me. But thank you so much for asking." He feels a surge of energy.

An hour later, a young staff support person hand delivers a memo he had asked for, summarizing a recently completed employee survey. "Have you read it?" Bensen asks.

"Yes, I helped compile it."

"What do you think of it? Is there anything you feel we should take action on around here?"

The young man stares at him. This is the first time he has been face to face with the CEO. A little in awe of Bensen and his powerful presence, he's saying to himself, "This guy *never* asks what we think; he always has the answer. He must be upset about his daughter." So he holds back, afraid to say something stupid.

But Bensen continues to look at him, without picking up another piece of paper or punching a number on his speakerphone, and finally he musters the courage to say, "I'll tell you the one thing that surprised me, sir. There was a question on the survey that asked us to rank the importance of four items: compensation, sense of mission and purpose, life/work balance, and participation in company decisions. Well, money came in dead last."

"I've read that kind of thing before," Bensen says. "I didn't know if I could believe that people truly feel that way. Do you? Do you think it accurately represents people's attitudes here?"

"I do," the young man replies. "I mean—we all value money. Especially a guy like me, I'm new, I don't make much, but . . ."

"How did you rank compensation?" Bensen interrupts.

"Third. After mission and participation in decisions." He pauses a moment, groping for an idea. Bensen glances down, scans the first page of the report, then continues listening. "See, the thing is," the man continues, "those are the factors that would make a job, any job, really meaningful and exciting."

Bensen nods in agreement. "Absolutely," he says.

"So, if I don't have a sense of involvement, if I'm just given a job description and told what to do, well, then money becomes more important."

"To compensate—so to speak—for the satisfaction you would have if your job were more meaningful," Bensen says.

"Right, exactly."

"So you're saying these results express an ideal, the way people would like things to be, rather than how they actually are."

"When it comes to this question, yes," the young man says.

"Do you think people have clear, or even partially clear, ideas about what would make them more satisfied here, what would give them more of a sense of meaning and participation? Realistic ideas, things that could be implemented?"

"Yes, I'm sure they do. And if they were asked to think about it, they'd certainly come up with answers."

"Okay, here's what we're going to do. Who's your supervisor?"

"Sylvie Marceau."

"She's the one behind this report, right?"

"Yeah, she guided the creation of the survey."

"And your name is?"

"Hari Rao."

"Well Hari, from what you're saying, I think we should consider a follow-up survey—you may want to write this down; here's a pad—asking people for tangible, viable ideas on how their job could be more meaningful to them, and in what ways they believe they could contribute to decision making in their department and in the company as a whole. Would you speak to Sylvie and ask her what she thinks about it?"

Still writing, Hari nods.

"Good. I may have some ideas for your second survey as soon as I look over the first, so make sure I get a draft before it goes out."

"I will, Mr. Quinn."

"Good! I'll be eager to read this now," Bensen declares and looks down, turning his attention to the next task. But as the young man moves toward the door, Bensen obeys a sudden impulse to look up again. "Thanks, Hari, for your work on this," he says. "And for your input."

"Thank *you,* Mr. Quinn," Hari replies, a bit stunned by the unexpected attention.

Bensen smiles. "And you thought you were simply dropping off a few papers, right? It's dangerous to walk into this office!"

"Oh no, sir. This is more than I could hope for."

Again Bensen feels a wave of satisfaction, the opposite of the drained feeling he often gets when he's too controlling or overbearing. For a split second he feels, "*This* is the music I want to play."

Of course, during most of the day he's in his usual, take-charge work mode. But in his weekly staff meeting with his vice presidents and senior executives—minus CFO Anne Holmes, who is out of town at a conference—his new, more open approach manifests itself a third time. Following the usual format, the VPs of marketing and manufacturing, the COO, and several other executives spread out around the conference table and take turns reporting to him about achievements and challenges in their sphere of responsibility.

From the outset, he feels more receptive to the others, more willing to pay attention and less in need of taking control. Listening to the executives recount their accomplishments—"We're on target," "We're going to hit sales this month," "We're on top of it"—Bensen perceives that they are living the rules and values with which he has indoctrinated them. When they are finished, he sits back in his chair at the head of the table and surprises them by calmly saying, "This is terrific. You're all achieving the goals we set, and I thank you for it." He looks around, smiles, and then he adds, "Now let me put a different kind of question to you: What's really important around here?"

"Getting results!" they respond, as if to say, "We know, boss, you've taught us over the years, you've set the example." They are anticipating his usual demanding send-off, challenging them to go out and do more.

Instead, Bensen leans forward and addresses them in a tone more personal than they are accustomed to. "Is that enough to keep this place going? To keep us all here? Is it enough for our employees? Just results?" After a pause, he pushes them one notch higher: "Is it enough for *you*?"

His people don't know what he's looking for; unsure of how to respond, they sit in stone-cold silence. But Bensen, feeling less guarded and cautious, tells them, "I've started to do some thinking lately, about what goes on here. I think all of us in this room might profit from looking more closely at what we're all about." The room remains quiet. Sensing their discomfort, Bensen laughs. "Okay, that's it! No more philosophizing! What else have we got?"

Bob Barnett, the Chief Operating Officer, asks, "You all know about the *New York Times* article, right?"

"Damn!" Bensen says. "Not the Jim Morris story?"

"Worse," Bob replies.

"Tell us!" Bensen snaps, coming back into a more familiar mode.

"Well, it seems the shit's about to hit the fan. You remember that a plant manager alerted us a while back that a *Times* reporter was snooping around, researching one of our offshore facilities."

"Where?" Bensen asks.

"El Salvador," Bob replies. "but he started at some plants—not ours—in China. Apparently he's got a travel budget; we've been told that he's found some pretty questionable conditions in several other factories, and . . ."

"How questionable?" Bensen interrupts.

"Here's what I've been able to learn," Bob says, looking down at his notes. "He's writing a series of articles about the downside of globalization. The first is an investigative piece about what he calls sweatshops, mostly labor-intensive factories that make shoes, toys, and—you guessed it—textiles. We're the lead story in the first article. He'll be talking, I understand, mostly about one facility. One of ours. It's got twenty-seven hundred employees, nearly all of them young women, and according to him, some children as young as nine. He claims the average pay is twenty-five cents an hour. Apparently he's going to open the piece by saying that the plant looks more like a prison than a factory—barbed wire fences, dictatorial management, half the workers living inside the facility in dormitories above the factory floor, ten or a dozen to a room. According to him, there's no medical care; the plant is blazing hot, and there's no air conditioning and poor ventilation; the workers have to ask permission to go to the bathroom, and on and on. Oh, and allegations of verbal abuse and sexual harassment by male managers. Not a pretty picture."

"And he claims this is *typical,* not an isolated instance?" one exec asks.

"The bastard's trying to win a Pulitzer at our expense," another mutters, expressing the consternation of the group. But Bensen has momentarily tuned out. His immediate thought, like when he first heard the accusation that Jim was offering incentives to win contracts, is to blame a competitor. "Someone's trying to bloody our reputation by telling exaggerated stories to the press," he thinks. "It might hurt us momentarily, but we'll get through it. We've got a name people trust, and we've worked hard to earn it."

But listening to Bob's recital of horrors, he is appalled and once again mindful of his daughter's trusting eyes when he assured her that such things would never happen at one of his factories—and her anger when she had information to suggest that what he was telling her was not the truth. "Have I had my head in the sand?" he finally asks himself. "Why would I expect the factories to pay a decent wage, or to provide reasonable conditions and benefits, when our demand to them has always been, 'Drive production and keep costs down'? I just didn't want to look at it. I kept telling myself that we're paying more than they could get picking tomatoes or working the rice paddies. That may be true, but so what? Maybe it's not good enough."

He hears Bob asking, "What kind of spin should we put on this, Bensen? Should we make an outright rebuttal, or say we're looking into it, or what? We need to put someone on it right away."

After a long moment, Bensen replies, "Maybe we shouldn't put *any* spin on it. Maybe we should deal with it. Is spin what's called for here? Are the accusations true? Isn't it our responsibility to look into them? We're the employers. Maybe we should take this seriously."

Bob responds, his voice rising, "Excuse me, Bensen, but what the hell are you talking about? We can't afford to pay more. We can't throw money out the window for medical care or to install air conditioning in those huge plants. We've struggled for years to get the edge on costs, and we've finally got it." After a pause he adds, more matter-of-factly, "Besides, those people are used to the heat. And no one else is offering more than we are."

"Well, maybe we should set a higher standard," Bensen puts forward. "Maybe we should take a new, longer view. I know I've set the agenda the way it is. But is it in our best interest, long-term, to be known for running facilities like that? And even if nobody finds out, is it the right thing?"

"People are going to know, Bensen. The first article is coming out any day. The question for us is, how are we going to respond?"

"I don't know, Bob. I need to think about it a little more."

At the end of the meeting, when he goes back to his office, he feels a calm energy, despite the fact that he's not at all sure that the new direction he's thinking about is appropriate. It seems risky for HighQuest, even dangerous. Yet something about it feels right, and he wants to give it a chance to unfold. Within himself, he definitely notices a difference between his habitual, results-driven, "I'm in charge and I know what I'm doing" mode, and this more open approach in which he's genuinely concerned with doing the right thing. He's surprised that the energy lasts through the afternoon and continues even after he leaves work.

———

"Please sit in the waiting room, Mr. Quinn," a nurse directs. "The doctors will be with you in a few minutes." He has arrived early for the conference he had insisted upon, with Dr. Schmidt and the team of specialists treating his daughter. Frustrated by Katie's apparent lack of progress, he is determined to have them sit together and agree on a new and perhaps more aggressive treatment plan.

He cannot bear to face the alternative: that the longer Katie's condition continues unchanged, the greater the likelihood that she may never come out of her coma. His daughter may die. Extremely agitated and unable to sit quietly for more than a few seconds with this awareness, he paces the room until Emily arrives.

"How is she?" he asks as she walks in the door. "Anything new?"

"Nothing," she replies. "Nothing at all."

A minute or two later they are ushered in for the meeting.

Just like in his executive meetings, the doctors begin by taking turns, each one reporting on test results, examinations, or observations and weighing in with recommendations for treatment. Their reports seem to Bensen overly detailed and laden with an alphabet soup of jargon and abbreviations that he doesn't fully understand—NG feeding, CT scan, CBC, MRI, ECG, and EEG—and eventually his frustration and fear burst out.

"Can we skip the details and cut to the chase, doctor?" he practically shouts, interrupting Dr. Schmidt in midsentence. "What are you going to do for my daughter? How are you going to bring her out of this? You've got to do everything you can!"

Dr. Hirschman, a neurologist and an acquaintance of Bensen's, stands up, puts his hand on Bensen's shoulder, and says, rather calmly in the face of his hostility, "Ben, we are doing everything we possibly can."

The doctor's quiet conviction is like a mirror, in which Bensen sees that his attitude and behavior are insensitive and offensive to these experts, who are working hard to save his daughter. Embarrassed, he backs off and relaxes. "I'm sorry," he says. "I know you're doing all you can. I'm just so worried."

When he shows his vulnerability, the doctors relax too. "We understand, Bensen," says the neurologist. "We can all imagine what it would be like if it were one of our kids. We will continue to do everything possible for her."

"Other than what you're proposing, is there anything more Bensen and I can do, from our side?" Emily asks.

"Just what you're doing. Come see her. Sit with her. Be with her. Maybe even talk to her. There's no logical reason for that, but most of us feel it's the right thing, that it might help." A comradely feeling fills the room; they are no longer adversaries, but members of a team.

———

In the elevator on the way downstairs, Bensen says quietly to his wife, "I hope I didn't embarrass you in there. I'm sorry if I did."

"I'm sure they understand," Emily responds. "We're not the first frightened, anxious parents they've had to deal with."

"Thanks," he says, looking a little sheepish.

She laughs and takes his hand. "How many years have we been married now?"

He smiles, warmed by her acceptance. Then she asks, "Did you happen to notice the difference between how they responded to you when you were angry, and how their attitude changed when you calmed down and admitted how you were feeling?"

"I certainly did," he replies. "It's been happening a lot, lately—that I seem to be acting in two different modes."

"What do you mean?"

"Well, I spend most of my time being Bensen Quinn, CEO, and in that role, I feel like I have to exert my will, push hard to make things happen. That's what I've always believed being a leader requires. Or maybe that's how I rationalize being an aggressive, obnoxious person!"

She squeezes his hand. "Don't get carried away here!"

"The problem with acting that way," Bensen continues, "is that the results I'm looking for don't always show up. And even when they do, more often than not I feel tired, stressed out."

"And the other mode?" Emily asks as they work their way through the maze of corridors toward the parking lot.

"It's when I feel more centered—just as purposeful, but less driven and less pushy."

"And how does that work out?"

"It seems to me that I can get good results just as often, and I don't feel drained, I feel energized. And people seem to respond positively."

"That doesn't sound so bad."

"It's not bad, but it's confusing. It's a different approach from what I'm used to."

By now they have reached Emily's car. "Talking with the doctors," Bensen says, "and a few times earlier today, at the office, it was almost as if I shifted to a different place in myself, a different level. I don't know how to describe it better than that. There's the usual me-against-them feeling, what I think of as my powering-through mode, more confrontational. But then there's this other thing, that comes from deeper down . . . and has a different kind of power."

He recalls the surprise, and then the pleasure, on the faces of his assistant, Marie, and that young man with the survey results, when he was open and expressed genuine interest in them.

The Seed of Relationship: Always Connect

"I'm thinking that maybe being driven and driving other people isn't the only way to get things done, or even the best way. It would definitely be less stressful—and possibly more effective—to relate to people on that human level."

"You won't hear any arguments from me about that!" Emily says, opening the driver's-side door and sitting down. But Bensen is still working out these new ideas, and is not ready to let her go.

"It's one kind of satisfaction to perform effectively and achieve a lot," he says, "to move the world from your power seat. But I'm really starting to get that there's another kind of satisfaction, that comes from making these connections. And it may be deeper and more gratifying."

"Well, there's no reason not to do both, is there?" Emily says. "You seem to be creating a dichotomy, as if the two are contradictory. Do you think it's impossible to be an effective leader and a caring person, too?"

"I guess not, logically. But you know, I have this deeply engrained sense that they are incompatible."

"Well, you're the CEO, not me. But I think you could lead just as effectively if you motivated people by offering them respect and a sense of shared purpose, rather than instilling fear or relying on their desire for some kind of reward. But we can continue this at home."

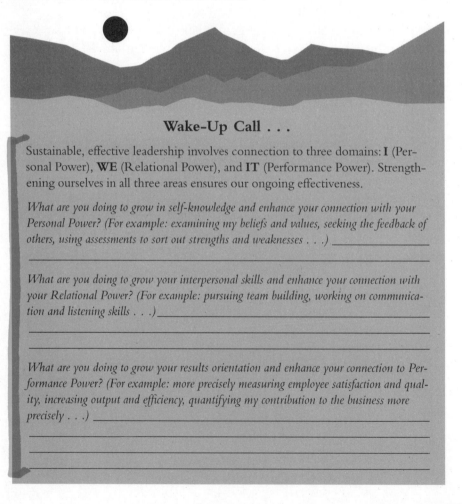

Wake-Up Call . . .

Sustainable, effective leadership involves connection to three domains: **I** (Personal Power), **WE** (Relational Power), and **IT** (Performance Power). Strengthening ourselves in all three areas ensures our ongoing effectiveness.

What are you doing to grow in self-knowledge and enhance your connection with your Personal Power? (For example: examining my beliefs and values, seeking the feedback of others, using assessments to sort out strengths and weaknesses . . .) _____

_____

What are you doing to grow your interpersonal skills and enhance your connection with your Relational Power? (For example: pursuing team building, working on communication and listening skills . . .) _____

_____

_____

What are you doing to grow your results orientation and enhance your connection to Performance Power? (For example: more precisely measuring employee satisfaction and quality, increasing output and efficiency, quantifying my contribution to the business more precisely . . .) _____

_____

_____

_____

"Okay," Bensen says. "It would be nice to have a little time with you not in the hospital or a parking lot."

He watches her drive off, and walks toward his own car. A few minutes later, he turns on the radio to catch the headlines and sports scores. An advertisement is in progress for a wireless phone service, which signs off with the words, "Wherever you go, you're always connected with Skynet Wireless."

The words strike home. "Always connected," he echoes, turning down the volume. "Wouldn't that be great! What if I could always be connected to who I am, and to what I believe in? What if I could always feel connected to the people important to me? What if our managers, employees, and customers all felt they had that sense of connection? That's it—my new commitment: Always Connected."

14 Awakening to Essence

No matter how valiantly Bensen struggles, the current keeps dragging him farther out to sea. He had gone out alone in his old ocean kayak, paddling along the coast as he has done many times before. Strong, athletic, and at home in the water, he felt comfortably in control, but now, despite his best efforts, the shore keeps receding and the growing expanse of water between himself and the land fills him with fear. A strong offshore wind blows stinging saltwater in his face and eyes. Finally, his arms and shoulders aching and his lungs burning from the effort, he stops straining, holds the paddle close to his chest, and allows himself to drift. Almost magically, the currents abruptly change, the wind stops, and without any effort he finds himself floating on gently rising and falling waves back toward shore.

Awakening from this dream in the predawn hours, Bensen cannot find his way back to sleep. The dream seems to parallel his internal deliberations; he feels that it symbolizes something, is telling him something that he needs to learn, but he is not sure what it is. He wants to talk about it, but Emily, always willing to listen and always insightful, is exhausted and needs to sleep. As carefully and quietly as he can, he slips out of bed and down the stairs.

He knows these early morning hours well, but ordinarily he's in the workout room in the west wing of the house, lifting weights, riding the stationary bike, planning his day—with CNN and the financial networks playing in the background—all his energy and attention focused outward, on growing the business. Now, since Katie's accident, it's as if that powerful current has turned around and gone inward. He doesn't feel like exercising, isn't motivated to get out and move the world. Instead, he's begun looking inside, examining his life and wrestling with the big questions—about death, and meaning, and the ultimate purpose of our being here—things he hasn't thought much about since Philosophy 101.

Pacing restlessly in the living room with the curtains open to the still-dark garden, he thinks about Kenji, aware that at least some of his newfound inwardness and self-reflection are due to his conversations with the gardener. "It's remarkable. Everyone knows I'm not the kind of man who's influenced much by other people, certainly not by my gardener! He can't possibly understand the complexity of the world I move in every day, yet when he talks to me about taking care to plant the right seeds, or questions me about what's truly important to me, I feel that he's helping me gain vital insight into my life and my effectiveness as a leader." With a trace of sadness, Bensen realizes that although he knows hundreds of people, and there are many he can count on for advice about business matters, he hasn't had a close friend in a long time, someone he can talk to about important things. "Well," he thinks, "that's because all that's been important to me for twenty years is my work."

Now other things are becoming important, so much so that when Kenji arrives not long after sunrise he finds his employer sitting on the bench in the garden with two cups and a thermos of hot coffee, eager to talk. "Kenji," Bensen says, when they are settled together on the bench, "I feel like I'm at war with myself!"

"And who are the opposing parties?" Kenji asks.

"Well, there's the familiar Bensen Quinn, the aggressive, high-achieving, control-everything-and-everybody leader. And then there's someone I'm just getting acquainted with, a man who seems to be more patient and caring about people, and who doesn't feel comfortable with that old familiar style."

"And does the old, familiar executive feel any more friendly toward the new version?"

"Not really; that's why it's such a conflict."

"Just the other day, you were saying how well your tough side has worked for you."

"It's true. Yet I must say that I'm drawn toward the emerging model. The problem is, if I take this new approach I'm not sure I can still be a leader and accomplish what I need to accomplish. I don't know if it will work, if I can be effective. I'm afraid I might lose my edge."

As if he hasn't heard Bensen's remarks, Kenji stands up, walks a few paces, and kneels down next to several flowering plants with large, brilliantly colored red and yellow flowers. "Look at these magnificent hibiscus blossoms!" he says, taking obvious pleasure in the sight. "I have only a limited role in the life of this plant. I can place it in the earth. I can water and fertilize it, and make sure it gets sunlight—but I can't make it grow. I can create positive conditions for the plant, but then I have to step back and let nature take care of the rest. The longer I work as a gardener, the more I find that success comes from creating the right conditions and then letting go."

"I know what you mean," Bensen says enthusiastically. "Yesterday, in a meeting with the doctors who are treating my daughter, I was upset and insisting that they do more for her. Suddenly I saw how I was behaving, and it became clear to me that I wouldn't accomplish anything by being pushy. They are specialists, top professionals. Why would they be inspired to work harder for a guy who didn't trust them, who was accusing them of not doing their jobs?"

"So what did you do?" Kenji asks.

"I let go of my compulsion to be in control. I even apologized, and expressed my fear about Katie and my sense of frustration. The moment I told the truth about how I felt, they rushed to my support! When I was pushing, they resisted me and defended themselves. When I released, they came forward."

"That's precisely how it is in my work," Kenji says, rejoining Bensen on the bench. "I can't force nature. After I plant the seed and foster the best conditions, then the more I step back and allow Essence to take care of the garden, the more beautiful it gets."

"Essence?" repeats Bensen. "You've used that word before."

"The heart of things," Kenji responds. "The life force within all things."

"You mean God?"

"Some people may wish to call it that. To me, it's the great intelligence of the universe. It's within everything, leading everything. Look at the galaxies, those giant collections of stars—think of it, Bensen, billions and billions of stars, moving in order through unfathomable space! What is governing it all? You plant a seed, and it becomes a tree. What makes it do that? A child is born, and grows up to be an adult. How astonishing! If we are attuned to that life force, aligned to it, nourished by it, we become great, as *it* is great."

"That's beautiful, Kenji, very poetic, but I'm not sure I understand."

"Essence is always flowing through us, and through all things, creating beauty, balance, and harmony. It is natural law, the hidden, mysterious intelligence that guides and supports the growth of all. You can't see it, touch it, or grasp it with any of the five senses, but it's there. It's the source, the most fundamental level of life. It is everywhere, in everything; it *is* everything. Everything is it."

"Then it must be part of *us,* too," Bensen notes.

Kenji nods. "That's why we can attune to it and follow it. It is part of our nature. Unfortunately, most of us are more attached to our individuality, our ego, than to that deeper, more universal essence of our being."

"Ego?" asks Bensen. "What do you mean by that?"

"Ego is what stands up and says, 'It's about *me!* I want things my way!'"

Bensen laughs. "I certainly know about that."

"We all do," says Kenji, "but that narrow sense of self is just what makes us feel separate and disconnected. When we identify with ego, when we believe that our individuality, our personality, is all that we are, then we feel that all aspects of our life—our success, even our survival—are entirely up to us."

"But aren't we ultimately alone?" Bensen asks.

"No, Bensen. A branch may feel that it is separate from the tree, but it isn't; that sense of separation is a mistake, an illusion. If the branch decided to act independently and could somehow cut itself off from the flow of nourishment coming from the tree—why, it would die. To survive and grow, it must stay connected.

"Ego," Kenji continues, "like the branch connecting to the current of sap from the tree, can open to the flow of Essence, and be guided by it. You and I, and this garden, the mountains and oceans, the galaxies, all things and all beings are all part of the one great universal Essence that nourishes and upholds all beings, like a mother. If we understand this truth, and act with our awareness rooted in Essence, we flourish. Other times, when we go against the flow of natural law, we may suffer for it."

"So," Bensen offers, "ego is the problem. How do I get it out of the way?"

Kenji laughs. "Spoken like a true man of action, Bensen! The thing is, ego, in one form or another, you will always have. Ego is who we take ourselves to be, our sense of identity or what we call 'I.' It is only a problem when we are not in touch with the depths of our being, our Essence. Not knowing about that inner richness, not experiencing it, we think we are only our body, our profession, our thoughts and ideas, our fears and desires. 'I am Kenji. I am a gardener, a father. I like rice.' Well, I *am* Kenji and all the rest—but that is not *all* that I am."

"So the problem is *not* the ego?"

"No, the problem is our belief that we are nothing more than our bodies and our limited, bounded personalities. So long as this belief colors our experience, we will continue to live on the surface of life, in the shallowest levels of awareness, while our true greatness lies within, untapped, unlived."

"What you're saying about the surface and the depth makes me think of the ocean," Bensen says, "and a dream I had last night."

"It *is* like the ocean," Kenji replies. "Waves on the surface, and the silent depths within. A wave rises up, and in a moment settles down and is gone, but the sea goes on and on. The wave, in its ignorance, may say, 'Look at me! How beautiful and powerful I am!' forgetting that it is an expression of the sea. The wave *is* the ocean, and that's what makes it great!"

"Yes," says Bensen, "I see that."

"Think of how tired the wave would get," Kenji continues, "if it tried to manage its own destiny—lifting itself up, moving itself forward, day after day, hour after hour, struggling to preserve itself, to stay in control. If it remembers, 'Oh, I am the ocean, after all!' it can relax and let the vast sea lead its affairs."

Bensen sits quietly for a minute. Then he says, "That may be the most profound concept I've ever heard. Thank you."

Kenji smiles. "You're quite welcome, Bensen. And I believe your assessment is correct. What knowledge could be more profound, or more transformative, than to understand our true nature? But you know, it's not just a concept. It is the reality."

"In the dream I had last night," Bensen says, "I was in a boat, trying to go in one direction, and not getting anywhere. Then I got tired of struggling. I relaxed, and the current carried me."

"Yes," Kenji says, nodding his head.

"I think the dream was saying what you're saying now: that not living from my essence, this deeper level of myself, is like trying to swim or paddle upstream, against the flow. Right? So that, even if I do reach my goal, I'll get tired and stressed."

"Exactly," Kenji says. "I've learned that if I only follow my ego—if I define or identify myself as a wave—I'm limited by my own stock of knowledge, my own perspective, my determination to be in control of things, and I can make a terrible mess! I may try to set too many plants in a small area, and they'll crowd each other or fight for water. Or maybe I'll put a plant someplace because I think it will look good there—but it won't get enough sunlight. Or it may block the light a smaller plant requires. I can't change the rules, the laws of nature.

"A gardener who follows Essence," he concludes, "who aligns himself and flows with natural law, will have a beautiful garden."

After a long silence, Bensen says, as if making an announcement: "*Rules for the Garden of Life.* Maybe you should write a book, Kenji!"

Kenji laughs, but then says with seriousness, "The point of all this, Bensen, is this: If you want to be most effective as a leader, be like a good gardener. As the gardener plays a small part, but leaves the larger role to all-wise and all-nurturing Mother Nature, to the sun, the rain, the soil, the cycle of seasons, so you must learn to rely on something that's bigger than you, a place inside that is wiser than you are yourself."

"How do I do that?" Bensen asks.

Kenji points to the hibiscus. "If you want these flowers to thrive, you have to nourish the sap. The sap is the essence. It's hidden. It's inside. But if you probe into the petal, into the leaf, into the stem, you'll find it everywhere. In fact, the sap has become the flower. Every part of it, if you think about it, is nothing but sap, expressing itself as the petal or the leaf."

"And what you're saying is that there's something inside us analogous to the sap—a field of intelligence or wisdom—that can guide us and help us make the right decisions?"

Kenji nods. "Yes. Ego tends to have a more localized vision. It seeks to control, to adapt, to cope. On the other hand, Essence transforms. If we attune ourselves with our essence, if we allow our connection to a deeper, more authentic reality to be the master and to lead us, while ego acts as the servant, we will achieve better results with less struggle. Great beauty will come into our lives. And tremendous energy. And joy."

Bensen sits quietly, taking it in. Then he asks, "You said this intelligence or whatever we call it, the Essence, is like the sap in the flower. It seems to be hidden away, but it's the source of everything, in a sense it *is* everything. Okay. If I am that intelligence, that big creative power already, why do I have to get more in touch with it? And if I do have to, how do I do it? How do I learn to operate from that place of essence? How do I get more in tune with it? How do I connect with that part of myself? How do I recognize it?"

Bensen's flurry of inquiries amuses Kenji. "You ask the perfect questions, but too many of them! First, it's more about opening up to it, or allowing it, rather than about finding it, since, as you say, it's already there. And second, it's not so much about doing, as about not-doing."

"I'm not used to that," says Bensen. "Actually, I hardly know what you mean."

"It's a matter of learning how to *do* less, and *be* more. Do you have half an hour now to sit quietly?"

"I could take it."

"Good. Are you comfortable the way you're sitting?" Kenji asks, removing his shoes and folding his legs in front of him on the bench. Bensen shifts around a little, and then nods.

"All right," Kenji says, "now, close your eyes," and after a few moments, he quietly imparts some simple instructions. As Bensen follows Kenji's directions, his attention begins to turn inward. Almost immediately he runs into a storm of inner turbulence; he feels agitated and his mind is restless, filled with worries about his daughter, plans for the day, decisions to be made at work. "My mind is buzzing with thoughts," he says to Kenji, who replies, "Never mind, that's completely normal at the beginning. Let's continue sitting."

Soon Bensen does begin to settle down. He becomes aware of his body's weight on the hard bench, the muscles deeply relaxed, the in-and-out flow of his breath as it moves through his nostrils, his abdomen gently swelling and emptying with each breath, his chest rising and falling.

Again thoughts intrude. He feels time passing, the day progressing; he starts making a mental list of things he has to do, visualizes the people at the office waiting for him, and feels his body tense up with the pressure of responsibility. "What in the world am I doing," he asks himself, "sitting in my garden with my eyes closed, taking instructions from my gardener? This is crazy! I've got to get to work."

With that, his awareness shifts outward, to the environment, and he senses the garden, hears the wind rustling the leaves, the song of birds. He thinks he feels Kenji's calm, soothing presence nearby.

Then the garden is left behind. Like choppy ocean waves settling, settling, becoming still, his restless mind quiets down and opens into a calm expanse in which he feels he just *is,* with his awareness submerged in silence and inward peace. For a moment, the mental imagery and flow of thoughts cease, and all is still.

Emerging from that experience of expanded awareness he thinks, "That's what Kenji means by *being.*" When he opens his eyes he feels the peace lingering. "What was that?" he asks. "What happened?"

"You just experienced who you are," Kenji says. "That's your center, your place to stand as a basis of action. It's your essence." Bensen feels the truth of the remark.

"Every day, practice this," Kenji tells him. "Connect with that broad, quiet awareness within you, and as much as you can, stay open to it. Remember it. When you forget, return to it again. It is always there."

Sitting in the glow of his meditation experience, Bensen senses that if he could stay attuned to that space within him, he would be unshakable, calm, focused—as he perceives Kenji to be. In a flash of insight he comprehends what Kenji is all about, why he is who he is, and why his mere presence has affected him so profoundly: He lives from this expansive, tranquil place. No wonder his eyes are so steady and he seems to radiate such strength.

"You know, Kenji," he says, giving voice to his feelings, "I believe that if I could stay connected to this awareness that I have now, I could be happy and at peace no matter what came along in my life. I could deal with anything, lead myself and others through anything."

Kenji nods approvingly. "You are a good student, Bensen," he says softly.

It is the first time Bensen realizes—and he realizes it deeply and poignantly—that he is indeed Kenji's student, and that this

> *The Seed of Essence:*
> *Engage Essence as the Master,*
> *Employ Ego as the Servant*

little man in the faded overalls, with the wrinkled face and short-cropped white hair, his hands calloused from digging in the earth, is his teacher: perhaps the most important teacher he's ever had.

At that moment Bensen's glance travels past Kenji to the other side of the stream, to the small shrinelike area Kenji had been working on. There, amidst the flowers and tall grasses, Kenji has artfully created a waterfall, about three feet wide, tumbling down several levels and then dropping into a small pool.

"How lovely!" Bensen exclaims. "It looks so peaceful."

Kenji, following his glance, replies, "I put it there to remind you of what you have just experienced. Bensen, you're a man of action, a man of doing. To live the totality of who you are, you must also become a man of being. So, in the midst of all your action and achievement, always remember to take a few minutes each day to connect to your essence, the source of your creativity."

"Amazing!" Bensen responds, suddenly animated. "Just yesterday I made a vow to myself to always connect: to be more connected to other people, and to my own guiding principles. Those words have a richer meaning now, an added dimension."

"Yes. Always connect: first to Essence, to yourself, the deepest level of your own being. The more you connect to it within yourself, the better you will be able to connect to others. The more you are in harmony with your deepest self, the better you will be able to follow your principles and to create value in your community and in the world, to help others have a better life."

"Oh, I don't know that I'm cut out to be some kind of do-gooder. That's far from my area of expertise."

"There are many ways to be helpful, Bensen. You will find yours."

"I appreciate your confidence, Kenji. The truth is, there have been times when I've been acutely conscious of people's struggles and their suffering, and I have tried to help. Somehow, I seem to have forgotten about all that."

"You have just awakened to a hidden aspect of your being, Bensen, one that you didn't even know about. It will not be hard to reawaken to something you *did* know."

———

Bensen looks at his watch, stretches out his legs and appears ready to get up, but then he leans back again and looks thoughtful.

"Is there something else, Bensen?" Kenji inquires.

"What about prayer, Kenji?"

"What about it?"

"I keep having the impulse to pray for Katie . . . for her recovery. I used to pray when I was a kid and went to church, but I haven't done it for so long I'm not even sure what to do. I don't think I was ever very good at it." A moment later he turns to Kenji and asks, "Do you think this would help—what you just taught me?"

"Yes, I can't think of a better preparation."

"So, if I feel I want to pray . . . ?"

"Whatever tradition you have," Kenji says, "whatever religion, follow that. But first, connect to Essence. Center yourself, quiet your mind, and then pray; your prayer will be more effective. Just as everything you do will be more effective, whether it's an outer activity or an inner one, like prayer."

———

Before leaving for work, Bensen goes into the house to say goodbye to Emily, to connect with her and see if there is any news about Katie. She is sitting at the kitchen table with her breakfast, and the moment he walks in she exclaims, "What happened to you?"

"What do you mean?"

"You look so peaceful, your face is so relaxed."

When Bensen doesn't reply, she adds, "You've been talking with Kenji, haven't you?"

He laughs. "Yes, I have."

"He's a very wise and caring man."

"You've spoken with him?"

"In eight years? With my office in the house, and being home with Katie, and being the one who pays him and discusses what work he'll be doing? . . . No, probably not more than a few hundred times."

"No, I mean . . . you've really talked with him."

"Yes, Ben. Quite a lot. But not the way I've seen you two talking. There's something special going on between you two."

Bensen nods. "Very special," he says. "I truly don't know what to make of it. He's an extraordinary man."

"He certainly is," she says. She stands, walks over to her husband and puts her arms around his neck. "And you know what? So is Bensen Quinn."

Wake-Up Call . . .

Taking the time to pause and reconnect with the deepest level of ourselves seems counterproductive to many achievement-oriented people. Most leaders I coach say, "I don't need a pause; I need to *do* more." However, to *do* more, we first must *be* more. Essence enriches our being as a preparation for more dynamic, productive performance. It's like when an archer pulls the bow back and then pauses to create a more forceful, accurate shot.

When in your life have you had a real pause, an authentic taste of Essence?

_____
_____
_____

What practices do you have (or want to learn) to help you more regularly connect to your state of Essence? _____

_____

How would your life change if you had a more peaceful, centered state of mind amidst all of life's challenges? _____

_____
_____

The Blossoming Bud 15

"Ben, I need to talk to you."

Anne Holmes, one of the few people with carte blanche to walk into Bensen's office unannounced, is standing just inside the doorway. He finishes the memo he's been reading, writes a few words of reply at the bottom, lays it on the "finished" stack on the side of his desk, looks up and motions to the big couch across from him. Anne steps back to close the door, saying, "It's kind of private."

"Must be important! What's up?"

She settles herself on the couch, takes a deep breath. "I've had a job offer." She pauses. "I wasn't looking for it, or anything." Another pause. "It's from OneWorld."

Bensen immediately recognizes the name: a hot firm, only a few years old and growing rapidly.

"It's a once-in-a-lifetime offer, Bensen, and I want to take it."

Bensen is stunned. Anne is one of the few people at HighQuest he has counted among his friends. Soon after her arrival at the company he saw her potential as a high-level executive, even a successor, and he's been coaching her and closely observing her development as a leader. His reaction is knee-jerk and abrupt: "How much are they offering?"

"Ben, it's not about money," she shoots back. "It's about meaning. They're committed to truly making a difference."

"What? I didn't know they were a nonprofit," he quips.

"I came here to *talk* to you about it," Anne says.

"Sorry. I'm kind of upset. I wasn't expecting this."

"I'm sorry too. I know all kinds of things have been coming at you in the last few days. I didn't want to add to it."

"No, it's . . . it's okay. Please go on. What do you mean, it's about meaning?"

"Well, several things. First of all, it's become important to me for my job to be more than a way to achieve financial security. I want to be doing work that inspires me and serves others in a meaningful way. Long before they called, I'd been thinking about it, asking myself, 'Why are we here? To make money? What's *that* all about? What meaning does it have?' I've got nothing against money, believe me, but I've learned that for me it's not enough."

"Growing a company and advancing your career doesn't have meaning?" he interrupts. "Sorry," he says, observing her expression. "Go on."

"Okay," she says, leaning forward. "I've also become aware of a kind of split between my private life and my job, where my personal life is for meaning—my close relationships, my spiritual development, things I do for my health or growth, the meager amount of volunteer work I have time for—while my job has become almost entirely economic. I'm tired of putting my life into compartments; I want it all to weave together. I want my work to be something I can put my heart into, that is creating real value in the world." She looks him in the eyes. "More than just making sweatshirts and mountain-climbing gear. Something that really adds value—that makes people's lives better."

In a quiet voice, Bensen answers her. "Believe it or not, I understand."

"I thought you might, even though you fight me every time I try to bring ideas like this up. But Bob clued me in about how different you seemed Tuesday morning, when you asked them to think about why we're all here. So I hoped I could talk to you about this directly."

"I'm definitely different," Bensen agrees, "and I'm listening. What else?"

"Okay. The other principal issue for me is that I strongly believe the business world is changing. There's the old paradigm of how things have been done, the usual story about short-term results and the quarterly report, the shareholder and the stock price, cutting costs and squeezing out near-term profits—the old, familiar model we all grew up with."

"What about it?"

"I don't think it's sustainable. It's worked for a while, it's produced incredible wealth for a few people, but in the big picture, it's *not* working. I'm looking for a place where I can create profit *and* improve the lives of people. I think about this all the time, and I really care about it. Major changes have to be made, and I want to be on the cutting edge."

"Especially if you can get paid a lot."

"Ben, that's not fair."

"Maybe not. Maybe I'm stuck in your old paradigm. But it seems to me that we're contributing a lot here, we're doing something that *is* meaningful. Not only do we put together products that a lot of consumers seem to want, but we also employ thousands of people. Have you figured out lately how many families we support, around the world? Those people can buy food and clothing for their kids, and send them to school. They pay taxes, and we as a corporation pay taxes. That finances public education and hospitals and paves the streets and connects up the water supply. What's so bad about all that?"

"Nothing's wrong with it, it's all true," Anne says. "But it's only part of the picture, the pretty part. What bothers me is that business is still operating in some sort of fantasy land, where actions have no consequences for the greater whole. It's not just the focus on profit margins and earnings growth. Most of the companies I've run into don't seem to care about their employees; they'll lay off thousands whenever the stock price needs a boost. They haven't cared about their customers; they try to sell the cheapest possible stuff at the highest price the market will bear. They haven't cared about the environment and the earth; they'll use up resources and dump toxic or nondegradable waste as if future generations truly do not matter at all.

"And yet, we're all interconnected and related on this planet. So this way of doing business is not sustainable in the long term. It can't go on indefinitely. I think people who see and understand this have to take a stand for a better way. And I feel OneWorld is doing that. They're determined not to fall into the old model that only looks at near-term profit."

"They don't want to make money?"

"Of course they do. But they want to do it in a way that makes at least their corner of the world a little better. They're committed to their employees. They have a gym, onsite childcare, paid parental leave, and a real vision of stewardship that encompasses employees, customers, the community, and the environment as well as shareholders."

In the course of their work together, Anne had more than once taken Bensen aside and urged him toward a more progressive view, and he had always resisted. Today, despite his occasional barbs, it's as if he hears what she's saying for the first time. She perceives his focused attention and thoughtful consideration of her words, and looks closely at him.

"What?" Bensen asks.

"What is it with you today, Quinn? You're listening to me."

"I always listen," he protests.

"But today you're listening with your heart, not just your head." After a moment she adds, "It's Katie. What happened has really shaken you up." Caught off guard, Bensen has no time to put up any defenses. Strong feelings surface and he finds himself unable to speak.

"Sorry," Anne says. Then, trying to lighten his mood, she adds, "It's a good thing the door is closed. We wouldn't want anyone seeing signs of emotion or vulnerability in *this* office, would we?"

Regaining his composure, Bensen parries, "I'm not choked up over *you*, you know!"

"So you're ready to let me go, then? Maybe happy to get rid of me?"

"No, I'm not ready to let you go. In fact, I can't believe you're thinking about leaving, after all we've worked on together. You do know, don't you, the future I've envisioned for you here?"

"I do, Bensen; that's why I'm here talking to you about it, rather than sitting at my computer composing a resignation letter. I appreciate all that you've done for me. If I'm leaving, I want to do it this way—I want you to understand."

"So, it's still open? I heard an 'if' in there. You haven't decided absolutely?"

"I said I was interested. My heart was saying yes, but you taught me to always say 'Let me think about it' before committing, so I said I'd think about it."

"Would you tell them you need a couple of weeks to consider it?"

"That's a long time."

"Try. If they pressure you, and you really want it, then of course it's your call. But if you can hold off for a couple weeks—I feel that things are starting to move in a new direction around here. I can't say more than that right now. Between you and me, I'm not sure I know yet. But what you said today makes sense."

"I'll try to hold off a while."

"Good. And in the next few days, what do you say we discuss a new vision of what this place could be. Formulate a draft for me, would you?"

"You really want to hear it?"

"The whole thing. Lay it on me. Take your best shot and then let's discuss it."

———

The day winds down, and Bensen returns home with troubled thoughts. When he notices that Emily's car is not in the garage, instead of going inside the house and facing the emptiness that has taken up residence there in Katie's absence, he walks to the garden and plops wearily onto the bench. It has been a rough day, packed with nonstop phone calls, meetings, fires to be put out immediately, and longer-term problems to solve, followed by a working drive home, returning phone messages and conferring with management in various time zones.

As soon as he starts to relax, the meeting with Anne begins to replay, concluding with his attempt to delay her departure with vague promises of change and reform. He had been sincere, but really, what would he do to change things at the company? What does he *want* to do? It isn't at all clear.

Since the night of Katie's accident he has been in a whirlwind of change—personal change, very different from the ever-shifting sands of the business world, and much more bewildering. Diminished enthusiasm for his work; self-doubt about what seems to be an overly brusque way of relating with people; Kenji's thought-provoking questions about the kind of legacy he would leave behind; Anne's unanticipated announcement—when he adds all that to the anxiety and pain he feels about Katie, it is overwhelming.

Looking around in the deepening twilight, his glance falls on Kenji's waterfall, and he recalls the experience of lightness and freedom when he meditated with Kenji. Even though it was only this morning, it feels not only long ago, but very far away, in another realm, unconnected to the pressures and problems piled one on top of another. It had seemed so effortless and natural to slip into that peaceful center, but he hadn't thought of it again all day. He closes his eyes, hoping to recapture some of that bright inner awareness.

Suddenly he hears footsteps approaching on the path, and finds himself with head slumped forward, chin resting on his chest, startled out of a heavy sleep. Kenji is standing a few feet away, a kindly expression on his face. "Have you been here *all day?*" Bensen asks, incredulous, with a glance at his watch. "It was more than twelve hours ago that I talked to you!"

Kenji seems amused by the question. "No, I'm much too old for such a long workday. I'm on my way home from a meeting." Only then does Bensen notice that Kenji is not wearing his customary work clothes: he's attired in light woolen dress slacks and a fine cotton shirt. "I was passing through the neighborhood and I thought I might catch you. I wondered how the day went for you."

At those words, Bensen lets out a groan and leans back against the bench. "You don't want to know. Why ruin two people's day?"

Again Kenji chuckles. "I thought it might be a happy story, after our time together this morning."

"I'm afraid not. Trouble started as soon as I got to the office. Anne, a woman I've been grooming for a high-level position, informed me that she's quitting—well, *thinking* of quitting and moving to another firm."

"You must have been disappointed."

"I was shocked! But most shocking was when she told me what catalyzed her decision. It wasn't the new responsibilities or the money they were offering—which I know has to be a lot—it was their vision, their sense of purpose. They told her, 'We're changing the world. We want you to join us.' They painted a vision that was compelling; it inspired her."

"How did you respond to that?" Kenji asks.

"I started tackling the problem in my typical way. I asked myself, 'How can we compete with these cutting-edge companies for talented people? How much more money do I need to I offer her?' But when I brought up money she said, 'That's not the point, Bensen. It's not about money. It's about meaning. It's about making a difference.' And she meant it. I know her."

Bensen pauses a moment, remembering Anne's earnestness. Then he looks up. "I'm sorry!" he says, sliding over on the bench to make room. "Please sit down, if you'd like to."

Kenji does sit down, and Bensen then continues, "Initially, I gave her a hard time. Then, when I started to truly listen to what she was saying—when I stopped feeling threatened, competitive, and upset about losing a quality employee and a friend—I realized that I've been thinking along similar lines lately."

"Yes, you've been expressing such thoughts to me," Kenji puts in.

"For some reason, listening to her express these ideas helped me understand them more fully. It also gave me a sense of perspective; I saw that what we value as a culture, the way we live—it's just *now*. It's our current model, our paradigm, as Anne put it. Things weren't always this way, and they won't be this way in the future. Most of us get caught up in the moment and we think, 'This is how life is.' But not necessarily. There have been other ways to live. There *are* other ways to live."

"Yes," says Kenji, "And other values, different from what we think is important, have been held in high esteem. Values like honor . . . duty . . . service. Many cultures are still guided by them."

"Exactly. We're all compulsively wrapped up in the business world—at least I have been—and in a particular *model* of business, that evaluates success only in financial terms. But there's nothing written in stone about this model. It can change. In fact, it needs to change, as it has changed from something else to be like this. Am I making any sense?"

"Very much. You're telling me that you are changing, inside, so your world is changing too."

"Oh! Is *that* what's happening? Things are moving so fast I'm confused by it all. I'm not accustomed to feeling this way, I assure you!"

"This confusion is good, Bensen. It may be uncomfortable, but it's a sign of growth."

"But what do I need it for?" Bensen demands, suddenly irritated. "My life has been very good, successful beyond any dreams of success I had when I was young. It seems that ever since I've been talking to you . . ."

"You need it," Kenji interrupts, "because what was good for you before, what worked in your life, isn't sufficient any longer. Ways you have defined success, ways you have been leading, goals you have reached for, they're not enough for you now, not appropriate for where you stand in your life, and you're looking for what *will* work."

"You're right," Bensen admits, slumping further into the bench. "While you were speaking just now, the 'corporate vision' meeting I told you about awhile ago popped into my mind. I can still see the whiteboard, with the objectives we articulated, like increasing profits and expanding sales. Those goals sound flat and hollow to me now. Don't get me wrong, I know they're important, I know we need to accomplish them, but they're just not enough. They reflect where I have been, and where my team still is. But what *I* consider important, what *I* value—all of that is starting to change for me . . . and I think that a better way to accomplish those goals needs to emerge."

"Yes, Bensen. As the leader of the company, you'll have to guide *it* to change, too. That's what integrity is about—lining up outer behavior with inner values. But you'll see: Much of your growth will start showing up in your actions, and almost without thinking about it, you'll make adjustments in company policy. It won't be as difficult as you might think."

"Yeah, right!" Bensen inwardly responds. "That's easy enough for *you* to say. What do you know about how a business like this operates?" He holds his tongue, but he knows well that it won't be a simple task to initiate far-reaching, systemic change in a huge, multilayered international corporation, even if he is the CEO. "It would certainly be easier if I knew *what* changes we're talking about here," he thinks. "That's the crucial question, and it still needs to be answered."

He senses that while his mind is racing along—trying to get a handle on his new direction, momentarily imagining himself in front of his conservative

Board of Directors to offer a new vision for the company, making judgments about Kenji and then feeling guilty about it, and confronting a hundred other fleeting images and ideas—Kenji has become inwardly still and is just *there,* being with the moment. He backs away from the chatter and allows his mind, too, to settle. Both men sit quietly, observing the small signs of imminent nightfall, a coolness in the air, birds letting out a small chirp or two as they settle in for the night, the waxing moon increasingly bright in the sky above them.

"Look at those lovely rosebuds, Bensen," Kenji says, pointing to the bushes lining the walkway near their seat. Even in the twilight Bensen can discern the roses' lush colors and their outlines in all stages of unfoldment, from bud to full bloom. "If you had never observed roses before," the gardener continues, "you'd never know a bud will continue to develop, opening . . . opening . . . until it is a beautiful, fragrant flower. Nature has given it a profound wisdom: No matter how beautiful or wonderful it may be, it is always ready to grow to the next level.

"The bud is true to itself—but not to the rose it will become. And as it blossoms, it continues to be authentic, genuinely and fully itself, at every stage of growth.

"A seed, too, is true to its seed life," Kenji adds, nodding toward a small stand of young fruit trees a few yards beyond the roses. "It can't, at first, be the tree that it will become, its full potential. When it's a year old, a slender trunk you could bend with one hand, it can express only a limited amount of strength and fruitfulness. But when it is fully grown, it gives shade and fruit."

"So," Bensen says, speaking slowly, "it's time for me to start showing up with my new understanding of things."

"Yes. But don't be hard on yourself, my friend," Kenji replies. "You have been true to your vision of your life and work, to what you understood life to be about. Now your vision is changing. You are seeing that profit and the bottom line are important, but there's more; there's something else you're looking for, and now is the time to be true to that as well."

"I believe I would be true to it," Bensen says, "if I could pin down what it is I'm looking for."

"If all you know is that you're dissatisfied," Kenji replies, "and confused, and searching for the answer, then be true to *that.* There was a poet named Rilke who wrote to a younger, fellow poet, 'Be patient toward all that is unresolved in your heart, and try to love the questions themselves. They are like locked rooms, or books written in a foreign tongue.' He told him that if he lived with the questions, eventually the answers would come, the locked doors would open."

"First you quote Emerson to me, and now Rilke?" Bensen exclaims, shaking his head in wonder.

"I like to read," Kenji says, chuckling; "What can I do?" He bursts into laughter, and Bensen quickly joins in. Then he says, "The truth is, Bensen, that you have done exceptionally well. But you are about to go beyond what is and what has been, to transform. Your expectations of yourself, and what you need to do, are going to change. It is the next stage of growth."

"I guess all change is kind of scary," Bensen acknowledges. "But then you go through it, and you come out the other side in a better place. I should be used to that by now."

"No transformation is possible without a breaking down of the old, so that the new can emerge," Kenji replies. "You know the story of the caterpillar and the butterfly. Imagine, if the caterpillar could think about it, what it might feel as its body begins to disintegrate so a new one can be structured! Imagine how terrified a rosebud might feel, as it felt its familiar, compact boundaries loosening. 'I'm falling apart!' it might scream—but then it becomes a rose!"

"So you think I'm blossoming?" Bensen asks, with an edge of sarcasm.

"Don't you feel that the old way is no longer acceptable?"

"I do."

"So work through it, take a leap, go for it," Kenji says with joyful enthusiasm, savoring the expressions as they tumble out of his mouth. "There comes a time when staying locked within the boundaries of the bud becomes more painful than the courage it takes to let yourself bloom."

After a long, reflective silence Bensen asks, "Do you remember, Kenji, when you were explaining to me that life is a totality that includes both good and bad, and that the better part of wisdom is to embrace the wholeness, the thorn as well as the flower? That growth and goodness sometimes come from obstacles and problems?"

"Yes, of course."

"And I said, 'What about my daughter, what good could possibly come from that?' And I got pretty defensive about it?"

"I remember."

"Well, as difficult as it is to say this, something good *is* coming from it, I think—this reevaluating of my life, a redirection, a fresh dedication to living according to what I believe in, what I value. I couldn't see it, then."

"Of course not. You were feeling overwhelmed."

"But you saw it."

"Yes, Bensen, I see many things."

Again the two men fall silent. Then Kenji adds, "You know, to do that—to be all that we are capable of being—we can't stay the same. We have to grow. And that requires nothing more of us than simply being open to growth. Life is fluid, not static. It is always changing, always transforming. As we move forward, the landscape alters; the horizon gives way to other horizons, ever new. There's no stopping the eternal flow of life.

"Trust the flow, Bensen; it cares for all beings. Everywhere things are unfolding, like the rosebud and the apple seed, growing and evolving in harmony with natural law. Move with it, grow with it. Resistance to flow creates suffering; growing with it creates possibility. Whatever is flexible and flowing will be transformed. And don't worry, Bensen. Because of who you are—your strength of character, your ambition, your commitment to integrity—you will be even more successful, and more fulfilled, in this new life that is unfolding."

Wake-Up Call . . .

A while ago, a senior executive in a major company involved in food and personal care products sat down with me for a coaching session. His ordinarily upbeat demeanor was unusually deflated. "Kevin," he said, "there's got to be more to life than this. Developing new deodorant formulas just doesn't fill my heart with inspiration any more!" After a great laugh, we got down to the business of uncovering what *would* inspire him. He soon realized that his problem wasn't about products; it was about his sense of meaning and purpose in life, which he was able to define as *unleashing creativity*. As long as he could be consistent with that core purpose, he was enthusiastic about his life and his work, and everyone around him was enlivened, too.

What is meaningful to you but not being expressed or lived in your work?

_____

_____

_____

What is meaningful to you but not being expressed or lived in your organization? _____

_____

How can you come forward to bring this meaning into your work and your organization?

_____

_____

To align with what is meaningful, do you need to make a change? In yourself? In where you work? In how you live? _____

_____

_____

"Ben, you haven't mentioned anything about Jim," Emily comments early the next morning. "That sounded pretty serious. What are you going to do? Have you talked to him?"

Bensen, standing at the bathroom mirror shaving, turns to face her, razor in hand. "Yes, I've talked to him. Several times now. And no, I don't know what I'm going to do. It's a difficult decision for me. It seems simple, but it's full of ambiguity."

"What happened?"

"The situation itself is pretty straightforward. In many countries, it's customary to give something to somebody in order to make a sale or land a contract. On a small scale, you hand the store owner a pair of tickets to a show. On Jim's level, if you're selling sixty thousand garments to a retail chain and you're looking to develop a long-term relationship, you charter a yacht and send the CEO on a vacation, or you arrange for the chief buyer to have a new car. It's standard business practice. To many people, of course, that counts as bribery; we know we're not supposed to do it.

"Now, with globalization, there's a lot of attention to this issue. On one hand, there's an effort to create and enforce international antibribery regulations. On the other hand, on a practical level, most of our companies are getting over their scruples and going with the prevailing standards."

"And that's what he did?"

"It's *exactly* what he did. As I said, you could make a good case that everybody does it. The problem is, first of all, we have an explicit company policy against it. And second, when the media get hold of a clear-cut case of corporate misdoing, they tend to make a lot of noise about it."

"And this is clear-cut?"

"The media will see it that way, even though according to him no money changed hands. I believe him, because he's Jim, and because he seems to be open about it, not evasive. But he definitely broke company policy. And he definitely handed out gifts to gain contracts and increase business."

"He must be going through hell."

"He's been great about it. He *is* going through hell. But he doesn't deny anything."

"So what are you going to do?"

"My options are pretty slim. If the gift-giving had been a little less open, we could just deny it, but in this case that's not a viable option. We could issue a reprimand and say something like, 'We thought it would be okay to do business like that since it's standard practice, now we realize it wasn't right.' But that's pretty lame. From a purely profit-and-loss perspective, Jim has brought in some of our most lucrative contracts; he's been a major factor in opening new markets for us in Latin America. He's a valuable asset, and I should do whatever I need to hold onto him. From a PR perspective, I should fire him and take a self-righteous public stand about HighQuest's code of ethics."

"What about from a moral perspective?" she asks. "And legal?"

"Well, from the legal angle, if there's no evidence that money changed hands, it may be defensible. The lawyers are looking into it."

"And ethically?" Emily presses.

"Well, that's not black and white either. There's that old saying, 'When in Rome, do as the Romans do.' No one can deny that customs and values differ. Who's to say what's right and what's wrong?"

"You are, Bensen. You're the CEO."

Bensen cringes at that remark and says nothing.

"And as his friend?" Emily asks.

"As his friend—well, he knows this will be bad for the company. He knows it puts me in an awkward and difficult position. And he knows what it could mean for his career. I'm concerned about that. And about being the one to drop the ax, if indeed the ax must fall."

"Do you think he was aware that he was doing the wrong thing?"

"He was doing the *right* thing, in terms of the ethics of getting business results. But I'm getting to the point where I don't think there should be a special subset of ethics: if something is wrong, it's wrong. I think Jim's feeling that way now, too."

She looks at him for a long moment, then says, "Sounds like you know what you need to do."

———

On the way to the car, he stops briefly to say good morning to Kenji. "Is there bad news about your daughter?" the gardener asks.

"No, why?"

"You seem more weighed down than I've seen you lately."

"Sometimes I wish you weren't so observant!" Bensen retorts. "No, there's no news at all, nothing new, which is bad enough. But there is something troubling me."

"Do you want to talk about it?"

Prompted by Kenji, Bensen tells the story again. "With anyone else, I'd just fire him," Bensen says. "But Jim and I played football together in college! We've known each other for thirty years. I know I shouldn't let things like that interfere when it comes to business but this is different."

"Do you think what he did was wrong?"

"That's precisely the problem. I'm not sure. It's confusing to me. I live and breathe in a corporate culture where that kind of behavior is a daily reality. So I accept it. I've never—I'm embarrassed to say—given it a second thought. Now that I have to think about it, I'm discovering that deep down, I do think it's wrong. I'm not sure I could tell you exactly why, it just feels that way."

"But hurting your friend also feels wrong."

"Precisely."

"Well then, you have a dilemma. Have you thought about asking your top staff what they think?"

Bensen, completely taken aback at the prospect of asking for advice on such a delicate issue, stares back in disbelief. "I very rarely do that."

Kenji says, "In my country we have a saying, 'None of us is as smart as all of us.' Sometimes it helps to draw on the wisdom of the group."

———

As it happens, there's a staff meeting that morning. At the back of his mind during the early discussions, Bensen anxiously considers bringing the question before the group. He doesn't want to appear weak or indecisive, qualities he considers antithetical to the leadership image he has always cultivated. Kenji's words about consulting the wisdom of the group appeal to him, yet he hesitates, not just to protect his image, but for a good reason: As a leader, he knows that sometimes the group can be dead wrong. They might not see or understand something crucial, and—more often than he'd like—his job is to move them in the direction he perceives to be best.

But this is not one of those situations. Far from certain about what is best, he's conflicted and unsure. Moreover, he realizes with a feeling of pleasure and satisfaction, he trusts his team, these core people he has carefully gathered around him. When they finish their reports and turn to him for direction for the rest of the meeting, he looks around the room and says, "I'm going to do something now that's hard for me." Seeing shock on their faces, he chuckles, "No, no, I'm not firing anybody. I'm going to do something that may seem even more radical: I'm going to ask for your help. I have a decision to make and I'm having a helluva time with it. It's about Jim Morris."

Bensen lays out his predicament, acknowledging the fact that Jim is a close friend. "What it seems to boil down to is, should I fire Jim and make a statement about HighQuest not tolerating unethical behavior, or should we try to cover it up to protect him? I've got to say that the latter will not be easy to pull off. I'd like your feedback. What do you think is the right way to go here? Do you see any options I'm missing?"

The VPs aren't sure how to respond, and for the better part of a minute no one speaks while the wheels turn in their heads. Is this a test of their loyalty to the company? Why would the CEO and Chairman of the Board even consider a personal friendship before the interests of the corporation? And why would he ask *them* about it, even if the consideration entered his mind? They know Bensen Quinn to be a decisive, in-control executive, not prone to long deliberations or to seeking assistance on tough decisions. Even though he seems sincere, they're not sure he really wants to listen.

Accurately reading their silence, he says, "Don't be afraid to speak your minds. I need all of you for this. I wouldn't have brought it up if I knew what to do. I just don't have the answer."

One by one, they offer their views. The turning point comes when Lou Leonard, VP of marketing, reminds everyone of the forthcoming *New York Times* series about conditions in offshore factories. "Listen," he says, "we're going to look bad enough when the *Times* articles hit. I say we do some damage control now and show up with some ethical values. We've got a good public image, and I believe we can keep it if we express outrage and regret that someone in our company has behaved in this despicable manner, et cetera et cetera."

"Now, wait a minute here," Bensen says. "Do we want to look good, or do we want to do the right thing?"

"Who knows what's right, Bensen?" Lou counters. "It's a complicated issue. But we know we've got to come out of it looking squeaky clean. That's critical."

"I'm not going to sacrifice Jim for the HighQuest image," Bensen responds heatedly. "If what he's done is wrong, that's different."

"Bensen," another executive says quietly, "you asked for our opinions, and we're offering them. Whether to maintain our image—which I'm sure you'll agree is important—or because it's the right thing to do, it looks like you need to let him go."

"We know he's your friend," Lou adds, "and we understand that what he's done is not so bad. I think I can speak for all of us in honoring your decision to hire him in the first place; he's been a tremendous boon to the company, and he'll be hard to replace. But we've got to do it."

Bensen looks around the table. "You're all feeling that way?" he asks. All the heads nod affirmatively. "Well, I'm leaning in that direction, too. Firing him would protect our reputation, and I certainly don't want to belittle the importance of that. But on the other hand, if it doesn't draw media attention in this country, I'd be somewhat inclined to let it go, and learn a lesson from it. Tighten up our policy."

Looking around the table, however, he sees that the execs are not happy with those words. "Okay," he says, "I hear you. I *am* getting to the point where I want to do the right thing for the right reason. Like many businesses—most, if I'm not mistaken—we've overlooked this type of behavior repeatedly. But I do believe it's wrong. I think we need to commit to a higher standard."

"So what are you saying, Bensen?" asks Lou.

"I'm saying that in my gut, I see it as bribery and I don't like it. I don't think I can live with that any more. Thank you. You've all been really helpful."

"Do you want one of us to take care of it?" asks Lou.

Bensen gives a snort of laughter. "That would be convenient, wouldn't it! No, he's having a hard enough time as it is. We've been friends too long for me to be such a wimp. I'll handle it."

"There's still one important item of business remaining," says Bob Barnett, the company's Chief Operating Officer. "Lou mentioned the *Times* article. How are we going to deal with it?"

Pressed for a decision, Bensen stalls. "I need a little more time to ponder that," he says. "Let's talk about it together Wednesday morning, early. I'll have Marie work with you on coordinating our schedules. If you have a strong opinion, e-mail it to me."

———

Alone in his office after the meeting, Bensen feels relieved that the decision about Jim has been made. He senses that the wisdom of the group truly did speak and that his team is stronger because of his willingness to listen and to value their opinions. He also feels centered and at ease with himself, which jibes with what Emily and Kenji have been helping him understand about authenticity. "I must have revealed more of myself in that short meeting than in the last ten years," he thinks, both amazed and amused at himself. "And it wasn't so bad! They responded like the doctors—when I told my truth and asked for help, they offered it. That is, after they stopped calculating whether it was safe or not!"

Yet he also feels a deep uneasiness about the factory situation and the possible fallout from the *Times* articles. *Sweatshops,* the word Katie threw in his face, the word he had so vehemently resisted and denied, keeps playing in his head like a catchy advertising jingle that won't quit.

"What is going on with me? I've always assumed that we were doing just fine at our factories. Why am I questioning it now? I'm just trying to run a good, profitable business. I'm employing thousands of people, I'm trying to take care of my family, and they're all on my case about sweatshops. I'm sure it can't be that bad. It's the damn media! They're such a pain in the ass! Why don't they get off our backs?"

In an attempt to appease his conscience, he mentally plays back both his negotiations with owners of the various contract facilities that produce their goods and his discussions with the managers of HighQuest's own plants. "I always clearly stated that one of HighQuest's conditions for doing business was that workers be paid no less than the prevailing wage in the area, and be provided with acceptable working conditions," he recalls. "Everyone smiled and nodded and gave us all sorts of assurances about fair wages and workplace safety."

But he also remembers this: In one of the first negotiations, when he began pressing for specific numbers and contractual guarantees for worker health, safety, and wages that could be held accountable, Bob, who was sitting next to him at the table, had turned to him and muttered, "Don't push too hard on this good-guy stuff, Bensen. If they do even fifty percent of what they're promising, it'll be equivalent to what any other company is offering. If they do more, we won't be competitive." Before he could open his mouth to object, Bob tapped the stack of papers in front of him, filled with cost analyses. "It says so right here, trust me."

And that was the end of it. All the rest of the talks were about maximizing productivity. "The truth is," he admits now, "I never followed up to find out how well those promises were honored, or even to ascertain what a *living wage* would be, that would allow people to support their families."

Then the thought arises, "Maybe it's time to do that now—to send someone to investigate. If I find out that things are worse than I've wanted to believe, it's possible that we could offer a little more to the workers without hurting ourselves. On the other hand, maybe conditions are actually *better* than I imagine, and I can stop obsessing over this! I know things aren't perfect in those factories, but we *are* providing work for those people. Where would they be without us?" Encouraged by that thought, he concludes, "We're doing the best we can!" and tries to drop it.

But his mind won't quit, and as he begins to spin through another cycle of doubt, he decides, "I'd better send a team to one or two of our plants. Then I'll know for sure."

Mentally running through his top candidates for the team, he quickly realizes, "Whoever I send is going to give me what they think I want to hear, no matter how I prep them ahead of time. Even if conditions are terrible, they'll build a case for leaving things just as they are, because our operations are cost effective right now and they know that's what the CEO cares about. I'll never find out the truth."

Unable to let it go, he tells his assistant, "No calls for ten minutes," leans back in his chair, closes his eyes, and settles into himself. A few minutes later, his mind calm and his feelings less agitated, he makes a spontaneous decision. Turning to his computer, he calls up a list of production facilities in Latin America, selects one nearest to an airport, and buzzes his assistant.

"Marie, get me on the next available flight to San Diego. I'll need a hotel room for tonight, and a car—not the top of the line, but a good one. And returning tomorrow, late afternoon or early evening."

"What about the corporate jet?" Marie asks. "It's . . . hold on a second . . . it's available, I just checked."

"No, I don't want the jet, and I don't want any entourage. Just get me detailed directions from the San Diego airport to our *Las Flores* facility outside Tijuana. If you could download a map, that would be helpful. And Marie—no one is to know about it until I'm back. I'm counting on you."

Next, he dials Jim's private number in Mexico City, but gets no answer. "Jim," he says to the voice mail, "it's Bensen. I'm coming to Tijuana tomorrow morning. I want you to meet me at the *Las Flores* factory around midday. We need to talk. It'll be a tough meeting, but you and I both know we have to do it.

"Also, I want you to arrange an in-depth tour of the facility for me. Call your plant manager at *Las Flores* and tell him a consultant . . . a Mr. Davis . . . Ted Davis . . . is on his way from corporate headquarters to look for ways to streamline production and reduce costs, and is to be shown all aspects of factory operations, starting first thing in the morning."

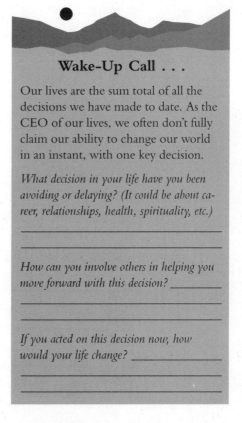

Wake-Up Call . . .

Our lives are the sum total of all the decisions we have made to date. As the CEO of our lives, we often don't fully claim our ability to change our world in an instant, with one key decision.

What decision in your life have you been avoiding or delaying? (It could be about career, relationships, health, spirituality, etc.)
_____
_____

How can you involve others in helping you move forward with this decision? _____
_____
_____

If you acted on this decision now, how would your life change? _____
_____
_____

With the decision made to talk directly to Jim, and to inspect factory conditions himself, his heart feels easier. "I've got to find out the truth about what really goes on there," he says to himself. "Then I'll know what to do."

17 Heart to Heart

With a couple of hours before his flight departs, Bensen heads for the hospital to see his daughter.

Like all the other times he's visited Katie's room, he doesn't know what to do with himself. He can't take any action, and that lack of power and control adds to his discomfort and agitation. He paces back and forth in the small space, looking from Katie's unchanging, inexpressive face to the array of monitors and the translucent tubing that represent her life support system. Eventually, he settles down enough to sit quietly at her bedside.

Desperate to help her, he remembers the doctors saying, "Talk to her," even while admitting that they didn't know if she could possibly hear. Emily, too, has been urging him to speak to her. "Some people claim to have clear recollections of near-death experiences, or to recall precise details of what happened when they were on the operating table under anesthesia," she has told him. "Maybe people in comas are also conscious on some level." Not entirely believing in this kind of thing, but willing to try anything, Bensen takes Katie's hand and begins to speak quietly to her.

"Okay, Katherine Quinn, this is your dad here. I love you very much . . . and I want to tell you, I'm sorry about many things. We got off to a wonderful start when you were little, but I haven't been a great father for you lately, I know. You were right to say, 'Your business is more important than I am.' It's *not,* Katie—not deep down, in my heart—but I've been acting as if it is. I promise you, those days are over now.

"I can understand why you've been angry with me. It's been years since we did things together the way we did when you were little, like when we went swimming together, or played soccer, or that time we drove up into the mountains, just the two of us, and spent the weekend skiing, laughing, and eating fondue, and you fell asleep by the fire in the ski lodge."

Rendered silent by the deep feelings rising up with these memories,

Bensen stops talking and lets his mind drift back through special moments with his daughter. Suddenly he laughs out loud, recalling a time in the backyard of one of their earlier homes, when she was still a young girl. He was teaching her how to play baseball with a plastic bat and a whiffle ball. Each time he gently tossed the ball to her, she swung wildly, spinning around, falling to the ground, and bursting into surprised, uproarious laughter. The whole process was so delightful to her that she couldn't get enough of it.

Then without warning the scene shifts back many years. He was playing stickball in the old neighborhood, on the street with all the wonderful smells drifting out from the Napoli Pizzeria, Irving's Deli, and Chow's Chinese Restaurant. He can see the bank on the corner next to the subway entrance, and the Cottage Book and Gift Shop with its display of toys and flowery greeting cards. And he can feel the smack of the stick as he connected with the pink rubber ball and sent it flying down the street, where it landed atop a parked car and bounced over, a ground rule double.

Then the terrible thing happened, that he hadn't thought of in decades. Far down the street he saw his father stumbling toward them. He cringed in fear of what might happen—and it did. His father was drunk and belligerent, and when he reached the group he grabbed the stick from one of the boys and grunted, "Lemme show you how it's done. I used to be a professional ball player, you know."

"Everyone knows, Dad," Bensen said weakly, but Jimmy Quinn was not to be deterred.

"Come on, throw it in," he growled.

One of the boys pitched to him. He didn't like the pitch, and let it pass. But at the next toss, he took a big, clumsy swing, missed, spun around, and fell down, hitting the ground hard. No one said anything. For a long time he lay on the ground, in the street, and the boys became frightened. Then slowly he pulled himself up and walked away, muttering to himself. Bensen, frequently embarrassed by his father's behavior, was mortified.

Now, coming out of his dreamlike reminiscence, he wonders, "Have I been an embarrassment to Katie, in terms of what I've been swinging for—the home runs of corporate life? Does she look at what I do, the way I live, and feel embarrassed rather than proud? Am I just a more sophisticated version of my father?" But he quickly pulls back from that thought and continues to speak to her.

"Honey, I'm going away for a day or two, and I won't be able to stop by to

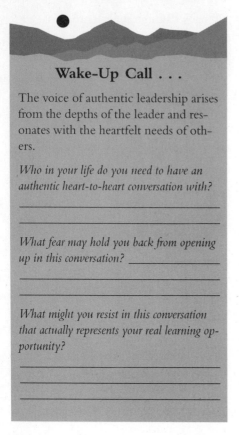

Wake-Up Call . . .

The voice of authentic leadership arises from the depths of the leader and resonates with the heartfelt needs of others.

Who in your life do you need to have an authentic heart-to-heart conversation with?

_____

_____

What fear may hold you back from opening up in this conversation? _____

_____

_____

What might you resist in this conversation that actually represents your real learning opportunity?

_____

_____

_____

see you. Something important has come up, and you actually have a lot to do with it. Remember when you told me about those factories in Asia and Latin America that are like sweatshops? You were so up in arms about it, so outraged that American companies, with all our money, were paying people twenty-five or thirty-five cents an hour. I thought our company was doing a pretty good job with our workers overseas. Now I'm not so sure. A reporter investigated some of them, and he says conditions are pretty much what you told me. If it's really true, Katie, I want to do something about it. So I'm going to one of our factories to find out.

"I've always thought of myself as basically a good guy," he continues. "But I'm the head honcho of a company that may be doing some things that are not so laudable, and if that's true, I'm not going to be proud of it. It looks like you may have been right, and I was wrong. I'll let you know when I get back."

Bensen is amazed to hear himself talking in this way, revealing feelings he might not expose if he knew she could hear him. Somehow, it is liberating. He sees now that instead of listening to what Katie was telling him, he had assumed an arrogant, authoritarian stance and wouldn't let up, either in the face of evidence about the company, or out of respect for her. With the newfound vision of his awakened heart, he can see the beautiful spirit that impelled her actions.

"And," he reflects as he feels electricity course through his body, "*my* beautiful spirit. I may have been too focused on my academic programs and my career goals to dedicate as much time as I wanted to the cause of civil rights, or to raise my voice effectively in protest over the Vietnam war. I guess those weren't my battles to fight. But now, at this point in my life, to take a stand for what I *believe,* not only for what is good for my cash flow: *That* would give my life meaning and purpose."

The moment he has these thoughts, he's eager to talk to Kenji. He can sense his teacher's response. "That's good, Bensen," the gardener would say. "But *what* are you going to fight for? What is it that you believe in?" And once he answered that—once he knew the answer—the next question would be, "Okay, now that you've become aware of what you believe in, what precisely do you intend to do about it?" All he knows at this point is that the answer, or at least a crucial step on the road to the answer, lies in a factory just over the Mexican border.

"Now here's the deal," he says, once again addressing Katie. "While I'm gone I want you to consider coming out from wherever you are. I may not deserve for you to do this for me, but please consider doing it for yourself. And for your mom,who loves you very, very much. You're such a bright light, Honey, you're so smart and so funny and so capable; you have so much to live for, so much to contribute."

Words stop coming, and Bensen sits a few minutes longer in silence. The photo of Kenji's tiny granddaughter floats into his mind, and he hears the gardener's voice: "Are you playing the music you want people to remember you by?"

Still holding Katie's hand, he makes a sacred vow. "Whether you come out of this or not, I am going to do whatever it takes to create a legacy you would be proud of—and that I will be proud of, too. I don't know what that will look like, right now, but *I will do it.*"

18 Piercing the Veil

Bensen can't believe his eyes. The last couple of miles, bouncing his rental car toward the *Las Flores* factory along dusty, unpaved streets crowded with dilapidated shacks, had been bad enough. Now, when he sees the high cement-block walls topped with barbed wire surrounding the *maquila* and is stopped at the gate by a pair of guards armed with semiautomatic weapons, he is genuinely shocked.

"Is this the way it is at all the production facilities?" he wonders. He had assumed that the descriptions Bob had managed to obtain from the upcoming *Times* article were exaggerated, a little poetic license taken by the author, to create an effect. Now he feels the descriptions may not have been graphic enough. He's also a little frightened: When he's not in a company jet or limo, he's accustomed to traveling first class, with an escort, often a bodyguard. Had he been crazy to come to the factory alone?

The guards block his entry, demanding identification. He tries to communicate to them that he's expected, that he comes from corporate headquarters, but they don't appear to understand, and are growing belligerent, gesturing that he should turn his car around and leave, when two men in shirtsleeves emerge from the building and stride energetically to the guard station. A few words to the guards suffice, and they back off.

The two men turn to him in greeting, and he ventures out of the car. The younger one, a dark-haired Mexican in his middle or late thirties, looks at him closely, then says enthusiastically, "Mr. Davis?"

"Yes," Bensen replies and puts out a hand.

"I'm Juan Ramon Hernandez," the man says, grasping Bensen's hand and pumping it. "I'm glad to meet you, very glad. I apologize for the guards. Routine precautions. They must not have received our instructions about your arrival.

"Señor Lopez," he continues, "our plant manager, has asked me to take you around today. I'm assistant manager, and my English is a lot better."

At those words, the other man nods vigorously and says, "Please to forgive me, señor, for not conducting you myself, but my English is still learning. Señor Hernandez knows everything. He will show you what you need to see."

"Thank you," Bensen says. "I'm eager to get started. This afternoon, after we've looked around, can you provide me with a detailed cost analysis for the plant? I'd like to look at it with you, and I'd like to be able to take it with me."

"Yes, yes, of course," says Lopez after a quick consultation with the assistant manager. With that, after persuading Bensen to remove his suit jacket and leave it in the car, the two men escort him from the guard station into the building, and Lopez departs.

Inside, Bensen continues to be appalled. Before he has time to assess working conditions, or even to take in the factory layout, he's immediately struck by the spectacle of row upon row of young girls bent over machines, cutting, stitching, transferring patterns and logos. "My God," he says aloud, "they look like children."

"Some of them are," replies Juan Ramon. "Many of the girls here are fourteen and fifteen. They have very nimble fingers."

"I see."

"Of course, not all are so young."

"I don't think I see anyone over twenty-five."

"No, you probably won't. Or perhaps a few."

"And men? I don't see any. . . ."

"You'll see a few, doing the heavier work, driving the forklifts and other equipment. And of course, supervising. All our supervisors are men."

Bensen scans the factory floor. The huge plant—he can barely see the far end—is divided into sectors for specific tasks and stages of production, from the cutting and joining of small pieces to the final stitching together of entire garments. In each area anywhere from a dozen to a few hundred women and girls sit on backless chairs and stools, looking serious and tense, apparently working as fast as they can to meet their quotas. Their quick, jerky movements as they snip loose threads, trim ragged edges, and pull the garments through the sewing machines give them the look of frightened birds. In each area, a male supervisor hovers over and around the seated girls, shouting and gesturing, grabbing finished pieces and tossing them into quickly filling bins awaiting the next phase of production.

As he orients himself to the factory, more impressions pour in: poor lighting, air filled with dust, smells of chemicals from dyes and from the recently manufactured synthetic materials. His ears are assaulted by a loud and incessant racket, the clatter and whir of sewing machines, and male voices shouting orders in Spanish as a steady stream of new fabric is moved onto the floor and goods are sewn, trimmed, loaded on handcarts and small electric trucks, and moved from one part of the huge plant to another. "Isn't there any air conditioning?" he inquires, "To filter some of the dust and chemicals out of the air?"

Juan Ramon seems amused by the question. "I'm afraid not, sir. There weren't even fans until a year or so ago. Some workers' rights group began getting favorable press in North America, and I suppose headquarters felt compelled to respond. Perhaps you heard about it," he says, turning to Bensen, then quickly looking away.

"No, I wasn't aware of it," Bensen says, wondering why—if the company had indeed received unfavorable press—he had not been informed.

"They instructed us to install fans and build a new restroom or two for the girls," Juan Ramon continues. "Really, all that the fans accomplish is to force the hot air down at the workers and blow the dust around."

"Well, we'd better get moving," Bensen says, assuming his usual commanding style. "Take me through the steps—let's say, of how one of the High-Quest sweatshirts would be made. I want to see everything."

"Of course," Juan Ramon replies. "How else can you tell what's going on here, and what you need to improve?"

Bensen shoots him a quick, inquisitive look, but Hernandez is expressionless as he leads the way, shepherding Bensen from station to station in the production process. When they pass supervisors and foremen, all of whom greet Hernandez with obvious warmth and respect, Bensen notices that his guide's voice grows louder, and he speaks in an authoritative tone of "cost-cutting measures" and "increased productivity from longer shifts with these skilled workers," assuring Bensen he will find "very little room for improvement in production efficiency." When they are more or less alone, protected by the constant din from being overheard, Juan Ramon speaks more quietly. "These girls regularly work twelve or fourteen hours a day, Mr. Davis. Every day. That's not including overtime."

"Overtime?" Bensen asks, incredulous. "Beyond fourteen hours? These young girls?"

"The company gives them the opportunity."

"*Opportunity*?"

"Yes—to keep their jobs, actually, if you know what I mean."

"So, how many hours a week do they work?" asks Bensen.

"Between eighty and ninety is quite common."

"They must be exhausted."

"They're young," Juan Ramon says. "They have a lot of energy."

"Yes," says Bensen, "but they're human."

Almost in a whisper, his voice filled with emotion, Juan Ramon echoes Bensen's words. "Yes, sir, they are human." Looking intently at Bensen, he says, gently but firmly, "That's why I'm telling you this."

The two men advance steadily through the factory, stopping occasionally to observe and discuss. To Bensen's surprise the women, their black hair bound up in colorful bandannas, their faces focused on their work, scarcely seem to notice him. Occasionally one lifts her head and meets his gaze for a moment before hastily returning to work. Is that fear he senses in the hurried way they drop their gaze? Bensen is struck by the dark circles under their eyes and the guilelessness that he senses still lies unbroken beneath the troubled surface of their lives.

One girl in particular captures his attention. No more than fourteen or fifteen, she's wearing a billowy white blouse, beautifully hand-embroidered with multicolored tropical birds and flowers, though somewhat worn and discolored with long wear; her thick black hair is pulled back and tied in a yellow ribbon that offsets her light brown skin. When she looks up at Bensen, her gaze lingers a moment, long enough for him to take in the wide forehead, prominent cheekbones, and dark brown eyes. He smiles at her, and she immediately and fearlessly grins back. Although she doesn't resemble his daughter at all, something about her touches his heart and leads his thoughts back home. Distracted, he almost doesn't hear Juan Ramon, who is saying, "I know I'm here to show you around, not to give you my opinions. . . ."

"No no," Bensen interrupts. "You're knowledgeable about operations here, and I'd value anything you want to point out."

"I can't help thinking," Hernandez continues, moving closer to Bensen and lowering his voice, "how much better it would be if these girls had more rest and a less grueling schedule. Good for the company, I mean. They would make fewer mistakes, and could work faster if they weren't so tired."

Before Bensen can reply, Juan Ramon continues, "And of course, it would be better for them, for these women. Right now, they work out of fear. The supervisors are shouting at them all the time, 'hurry up, hurry up.'"

"What I'm wondering," says Bensen. "is why so many girls are here, in the factory, and not in school."

"When would they go? Their families need the money. They start work-ing when they're children, and they work until they become pregnant. Then they get fired."

"But that's illegal, isn't it?" asks Bensen. In reply, Juan Ramon just looks at him.

Agitated, Bensen takes his cell phone from his pocket and says, "I need a few minutes to make an important phone call."

"Certainly, sir. I'll wait right over there, near those girls who are stitching the sleeves. Or would you prefer to use an office?"

"No, this is fine," Bensen says and presses in Jim Morris's number.

"Jim, Bensen," he begins. "I'm in the factory. Jim, why the hell didn't you tell me what goes on here?"

Morris laughs. "Bensen, I tried, over and over."

"What do you mean, you tried?"

"Every time I brought it up, you shut me down. Don't you remember all those times you told me, 'We can't afford to make any changes down there'?"

Bensen vaguely remembers, but starts to protest. "But we're friends. You don't have to buy it when I say I don't want to talk about something. You can bring it up again."

Jim laughs. "Yeah, we're friends. But you're also the CEO. And you have a way . . ."

"And is this what you were talking about this morning, when you said you thought I'd understand things differently after I saw the factory?"

"Well, I don't know exactly what you've seen so far. . . ."

"I've seen more than enough to know we need to make some changes here." He pauses, and Jim says nothing. "Okay," Bensen continues. "I'm look-ing forward to our meeting. It'll be good to see you. But I'm still very upset at having to deal with this bribery business. . . ."

Jim cuts him off. "That's strong language, Bensen."

"Well . . . okay, fine, we'll talk later." He shuts down the phone, and walks over to Juan Ramon.

"Can you tell me roughly what the average wages are at different levels?" Bensen inquires, jumping back into his investigation. "We can look at the pre-cise numbers in the afternoon."

"How much they're supposed to get, or how much they actually get?"

"What do you mean?" Bensen asks, surprised at the reply.

"First of all," Juan Ramon explains, "money is deducted from their wages for room and board. You know, don't you, that most of them live in dormito-ries right here?"

"In this building?"

"Yes, and in another behind this one."

"Could we look at that?"

"Perhaps. That will be a little more difficult to arrange."

"Arrange it. But you said 'first of all.' What else?"

"What's on the books doesn't necessarily reflect what the girls are paid."

"You're suggesting that the records are falsified? Are you sure?"

Looking around carefully before speaking, Juan Ramon replies, almost in a whisper, "It happens every day. In fact, there are two sets of books. One is for possible visitors from corporate headquarters—like you, sir, if I may say so. Or for the highly improbable appearance of an inspection team. The other one, the true one, is for the people who run the factory."

"And you know this for certain?" Bensen asks again.

Juan Ramon replies with a brief, sardonic laugh. "I am the assistant man-ager, after all."

"So what you're saying," Bensen presses, "is that the people at corporate headquarters might believe they are paying a decent wage, because those are the numbers submitted to us—to them—but in truth, the workers never see all the money they're supposed to get?"

"Precisely, yes."

"And this could apply to other issues too, like safety regulations, air quality, noise level, availability of medical care. . . ." His guide nods in assent, and Ben-sen continues, "Juan Ramon, after we finish our tour, can we go somewhere to talk?"

———

But there is nowhere to talk comfortably without the possibility of being over-heard, and no restaurants or cafes are located nearby. So Bensen and Juan Ra-mon leave the building, walk past the armed guards at the checkpoint, and go to purchase lunch from the row of food vendors set up across the street from the *maquila*. Bensen is concerned about the cleanliness, but fascinated by the slap-slap of women molding cornmeal into tortillas, the pots of boiling corn on the cob, the pushcarts filled with fruit. They make their choices and carry their steaming tamales, beans, rice, and tortillas to Bensen's car. "Is there any kind of park," Bensen asks, "where we could find some shade?"

"No park, I'm afraid. Most of these *maquiladoras* were built *donde no hay nada,* in the middle of nowhere, as you would say. But let's drive away from here. Finding some trees may not be impossible."

A few minutes later, sitting in the car with the motor running to keep the air conditioner on, Bensen tells Juan Ramon, "I am very disturbed by what I am discovering here. I know that the company has pressed hard to keep production costs low. That's a vital concern . . ."

"As it must be for all businesses," Juan Ramon interrupts, nodding in assent.

"But I also believe," Bensen continues, "that they negotiated in good faith for what they considered livable wages and decent working conditions. Granted, they didn't demand conditions equal to factories in the U.S. The standard of living is different here, expectations are different. And HighQuest *is* in business to make a profit."

"Of course."

"They thought they had a fair arrangement worked out. There are regular reports. What you're telling me is that those reports are probably bogus. This is extremely upsetting to me."

In the next hour, Juan Ramon tells Bensen what he has learned about the international textile factory system, and the Las Flores *maquila* in particular. Most of it Bensen already knows, but some is new, and he listens patiently, letting Juan Ramon unfold the story as he understands it.

"Although this particular factory is owned by HighQuest," Juan Ramon explains, "most production takes place in contract facilities, where products are manufactured for as many as thirty companies. The factories—not the multinational corporations who are their customers—hire the workers, set the wages, and determine factory conditions. The corporations just pay the bill. This arrangement makes it easy for them to turn their eyes away and deny responsibility for whatever may go on. And of course, the lower the bill, the happier they are.

"Okay, HighQuest owns this factory," Juan Ramon continues. "But in fact, the situation is only slightly different. All the hiring is still done locally. We set the wages, as long as they fall within government regulations. . . ."

"The government regulates wages?" Bensen asks.

"Yes, and they are careful to keep them low. They want to attract big corporations from around the world to open factories here, and the less it costs to do business, the more likely that they will come. Lately, I must say, they have allowed wages to rise somewhat."

"Which is why more production is shifting to Asia," Bensen mutters.

"Yes sir. But we determine everything else, factory conditions, the length of work shifts. . . . The company gives us guidelines, but only once since the plant opened has anyone from corporate headquarters looked in on us, until today."

At this point in his narration, Juan Ramon pauses and looks at Bensen. "I'm sure you're wondering, señor—and you may be quite concerned—that a manager at one of your plants is talking like some kind of union organizer. I assure you, I am loyal to the company. I want it to be successful, for in its success is my own, and the fulfillment of my aspirations for my family. Working here is a huge opportunity for me, one that may never have occurred if HighQuest had not moved to Mexico, and I never forget that.

"But I must tell you," he continues, his voice trembling slightly with emotion, "I have been increasingly upset by what I have seen here. I don't believe workers have to be intimidated in order to be productive. I don't think it's right for these young girls to work twelve hours day after day. I think a lot of the ways the workers are treated are unfair, and unnecessary. And I have, as management, been involved in practices I don't like."

Again Juan Ramon becomes silent, and his eyes search Bensen's face for a clue as to how this powerful gringo from corporate headquarters is responding. "I hope you can appreciate, señor," he says at last, "how great a risk I am taking, telling you all this. I know this could be my last day on the job. But I am hoping—and I believe—that I can trust you, that it is not foolish of me to talk to you this way."

"Have you never spoken of this with anyone?" Bensen asks.

"Yes," Juan Ramon replies. "First, I went to Señor Lopez with my concerns, and presented him a practical plan to improve conditions here for the workers. But he just laughed at me, and refused even to take the papers I had prepared, even though he knows I understand how the plant works better than he does. I tried to explain that if the girls were not always so tired, if they were better nourished, if they could take short breaks to refresh themselves, they could meet and perhaps even exceed their production quotas. I argued that wages could be considerably higher without approaching the government's upper limit or threatening our profitability. But he was not interested."

"You said, *first* you went to Señor Lopez," Bensen gently presses.

"Yes. I also spoke to Señor Morris, the Latin American director. I understand you will be meeting him later today."

"Yes, this afternoon. What did he say when you spoke to him?"

"He was much more sympathetic than Señor Lopez. He told me he would do what he could, and I believe he was sincere. But apparently corporate headquarters was not interested. So the resources needed to accomplish these improvements were never available."

"So you are trying again, with me?" Bensen asks.

Juan Ramon smiles wistfully, both sadness and hope written on his face. "Yes, señor, I am." Again he looks searchingly at Bensen, remains silent a long moment, then says, "I am speaking to you about this because earlier, when I was telling you about how long and how hard the girls work—and I tried to speak like a manager proud of how I am driving my workforce—you said, 'But they are human.' I knew then that you are a man of heart, a real man."

Bensen laughs a bit uneasily. "Funny that you should say that, Juan Ramon. It wasn't too long ago that I would not have been characterized that way." Then, quickly regrouping, he adds, "I must say that I've been surprised—shocked, really—by some of what you've told me. I didn't expect to hear these things, and I don't like hearing them. But I appreciate your candor. What you say is consistent with what I am observing. You have nothing to fear from me, I promise you. Please continue."

"Thank you, señor," Juan Ramon says, visibly relaxing. "All right. I already told you about the accounting and record keeping here. Another thing: Money is always paid to government officials, to 'encourage' them not to enforce labor regulations, if you understand how I'm speaking. For example, this factory has petitioned the government for permission to pay what is called apprentice wages to the workers in their first three months, even though new girls, after a week of training, do the identical work as most of the others. We've also been excused from paying the minimum wage to all our workers, because we've claimed financial hardship for installing those fans and toilet facilities and repairing some leaks in the roof."

"And those exemptions are paid for in bribes, is that what you're saying?" Bensen asks, becoming increasingly agitated by this discussion.

"Yes, of course. That's how it is done. I'm speaking frankly with you, sir. I hope you don't take it wrong."

"So a few people are doing well—the factory owners, government officials. And of course, the corporate officers. While the workers . . ."

"According to my calculations, factory workers here make an average of eighty-seven cents an hour. Yet international observers have established that a person cannot live—cannot eat and have clothing and a place to live—for less than $1.44 an hour. And that's a bare minimum, and only for one person. To support a family, obviously, requires substantially more." After a pause he adds, "So you see, sir, why the girls work overtime."

Bensen is quiet for a long moment. Then he asks, "So, how *do* the people live? What kind of life can they have, on so little money?"

"Do you want to see?"

"I think I need to. I've seen enough of the production capabilities and conditions. I'm concerned, now, about other things."

"I noticed—you'll pardon me for mentioning it—that you seemed struck by one of the girls."

"Yes, for some reason she reminded me of my daughter."

"Her name is Maria Elena Herrera. I know her family. We can go there."

———

As the afternoon sun shifts westward, the two men drive slowly through the narrow streets of a district more impoverished than anything Bensen, despite growing up in a poor neighborhood, has ever seen or even imagined. The unpaved roads are deeply rutted; bone-thin dogs wander the streets and alleys of a sprawling settlement where hundreds of ramshackle huts—ingenious assemblages of wooden factory pallets, sheets of metal, and cardboard—intermingle with small colonies of one- and two-room cinder block dwellings. Bensen's senses are bombarded by a host of sights, sounds, and smells, pleasant and unpleasant—the cries of babies and shouts of children; play-songs sung live mixed with occasional music from a radio; the pungent smells of spicy and exotic foods being prepared; garbage and waste products piled up waiting for pickup by an apparently non-existent local authority; people burning their trash; odd-colored water wending its way through ditches and trenches.

"I believe these canals run past the factories, where they dump their waste straight into the water; some of it is pesticides and toxic by-products," Juan Ramon ventures. "Fortunately, our plant has very little toxic waste," he says with noticeable pride in his voice. Nowhere to be seen is a store larger than a corner *bodega;* nowhere a bank, service station, pharmacy, or medical clinic; nowhere any signs of the amenities of civilization that Bensen takes completely for granted. "And yet, life goes on," he thinks, watching a group of boys passionately kicking a soccer ball back and forth across a dusty vacant lot devoid of even a patch of grass.

When they reach their destination, a tiny cinder block house among a cluster of others, they are greeted at the door by Maria Elena's mother, Rosa, a woman in her mid-thirties. The entire dwelling comprises two small rooms: a back bedroom and a larger living quarter that includes the kitchen. Ushered into this room, Bensen and Juan Ramon join several grandparents and half a dozen children ranging in age from about four to twelve. Through the doorway Bensen catches a glimpse of a small black and white TV, playing reruns of Woody Woodpecker and the Roadrunner; he smiles at the familiar voices. Maria Elena is still at work, Rosa tells them, and is not expected home for some time, perhaps many hours if she is "offered" an overtime shift tonight. Through a window into the dust-blown patio central to a dozen of these cement-block structures, he can see laundry drying on crisscrossed ropes and a single outhouse, situated right next to a lone spigot, apparently the sole source of water for all the families in this *colonia*.

The furniture in the larger room consists of woven mats placed directly on the bare concrete floor, and a pair of upside-down wooden packing crates; his hosts insist that Bensen sit on one of these. The children gather excitedly around the visitors, while at least three generations of women draw and boil water, prepare rich-smelling coffee, and arrange a wooden tray with *dulces,* sweets quickly rounded up from neighbors for the special occasion.

When all have gathered in a loose circle on the floor, Juan Ramon speaks briefly to them, then turns to Bensen and says, "I told them you are a visitor from North America, an important person from the *maquila* where Maria Elena works." He lowers his voice a little as he adds, "Fernando, the girl's grandfather, said he felt nervous that a wealthy gringo would be in his house, but that he will try to make you comfortable here."

Bensen smiles and nods graciously at the assembled group, but he is far from comfortable. His body soon grows weary of the backless, bare wooden seat. And the little houses are built so close together that the racket is almost as bad as in the factory, with the blare of numerous radios and televisions playing different stations, popular music introduced by excited announcers, babies crying, children shouting, mothers trying to maintain a semblance of discipline. Privacy, he realizes, is completely nonexistent.

Nevertheless, the next hour passes most agreeably for Bensen. With Juan Ramon serving as translator, the people question him about life in America. "Is everyone really as wealthy as they look on TV, and as you appear to be, dressed in such fine clothing? What are the chances that people like us could find work in *el norte?*" Bensen in turn asks them about their family, and how they came to live in this *maquila* town. Rosa, with two of her children now nestled against her and a baby in her arms, tells him that life has been difficult for them since they left their village in the foothills of the central mountains.

"*Claro, esta dificil en la sierra.* Of course, it was also difficult there," she admits. "We had no running water and no electricity. From the time I was a young girl, I spent three or four hours every day, starting at dawn, walking up and down the hill to the well in the village center, filling a water bucket and carrying it back on my head. It was the only way to get water for cooking, drinking, bathing, laundry, washing dishes. I wanted to escape, and when I was old enough to marry, my husband also wanted to leave. There were no jobs for us there; only difficult work in the fields, and for what? Barely to survive.

"So," she continues, "we managed to save enough pesos to take a bus to the border. After weeks of waiting on long lines for work, my prayers were answered: I got a job in a *maquiladora,* and my husband also got work day to day as a laborer, building new factories or putting up houses, like the one we live in."

But even two salaries have never been enough at the wages they receive, she tells Bensen. "*No alcanza*—it doesn't reach. That was nearly fourteen years ago. I am already too old for the *maquilas;* they favor young women in their teens and early twenties. When they hire workers, the company always asks for women "*no mayores de veinte y seis anos*"—no older than twenty-six years old—or maybe twenty-seven or twenty-eight; I was lucky to keep my job until I was thirty. I could never get one now. So the children have to work. Otherwise, we would have nothing to eat. The way it is now with us, some nights we don't have very much. But we live."

Their parents have joined them here in the *colonia,* she says, although "maybe it was a mistake. They are no longer able to grow vegetables—nothing grows in this dry, dusty ground—or keep a goat for milk. We used to have mango trees, and oranges that we could pick. We used to have flowers all around us. Now . . . if there ever were flowers and trees here, they've all been cut down, they're gone." There is genuine sadness in her voice. Bensen grasps how ugly and desolate these barren surroundings must feel to people who've known the natural beauty of the countryside. "I think our parents have the most difficult time, because they were used to hard work, and they have not been able to get jobs here; it is painful for them not to contribute to the family's economic well-being. But they help in other ways." She glances toward a corner where one of the older women is seated on a mat, embroidering flowers onto a white blouse like the one Maria Elena was wearing in the factory.

"Despite all that I have told you," Rosa continues, "essentially we are a happy family. My eldest child—Juan Ramon tells me you saw her—earns money at the *maquila*. My husband is strong and a good worker; people like to hire him. Most days we eat. We have electric light," she says, pointing up at the single, bare light bulb dangling in the center of the room, "and TV for the children. And none of us has to walk for hours to collect water. We are fortunate. My family is together. We have food and a place to sleep, things that many people do not have."

She pauses and a shadow passes briefly across her face. "Like all parents, we want our children to have a better life than we have. I would like my children to eat healthier food to make them strong. I dream that they might be able to go to school, learn to read, and be able to earn more money. But right now it is no more than a dream.

"Still, we are not unhappy. When we were about to leave our village, suddenly I became afraid, and started crying. What was I doing? Was I crazy to leave my childhood friends, my family, the land that I knew? What did I think I would find? My grandmother held me and said, 'Have courage, Rosa. Even though life may be difficult and filled with problems, it is still possible to be at peace. *Confía en Dios y la Virgen,*' that's what she told me, 'Trust in God and the Virgin.' I try to do that."

Listening to her speak, Bensen's heart fills with a disquieting mix of compassion, pity, and embarrassment for the abundance of his life and the role his company appears to be playing in perpetuating the scarcity that marks theirs. How right Katie had been to question him about conditions here—and how wrong of him to reject her!

He had flung the word *idealistic* in her face, as if it was somehow stupid and wrongheaded, or at least naive, to have ideals, something only foolish young people would do. Now he feels proud of her for caring about people, for being morally outraged, and for taking a stand, even at the risk of arousing his disapproval and anger. "How can it happen," he asks himself, "that someone gets so caught up in the pursuit of money and success that all other values—and even the most important people in your life—become secondary? Is that what business is inevitably about?"

When Juan Ramon finishes translating Rosa's words, Bensen says, "Thank you for telling me your story. I see that it is hard for you. But you know, things are changing in the world. It may be possible for your children to go to school, and for all of you to have a better life." He longs to add, "And I will help you! I will make it happen," but he holds back, knowing it will not be easy, and he does not want to make idle promises.

"Señor," Rosa's father, Fernando, suddenly interjects, "We are very rude. We asked you about your country, but not about yourself. Tell us, are you married? Do you have children?"

"Yes," says Bensen. "I am happily married. And I have a child. A daughter." He wants to say more, but is unable to go on. They all wait silently. Finally, fighting off his emotions, he manages to say, "She is very sick. She is in the hospital."

Abruptly, Fernando stands up, goes into the back room, and returns with a print, framed in carved wood, of a brown-skinned Virgin Mary. "*Pide a la Virgen Maria,* pray to the Mother of God," he says earnestly, holding the picture out before Bensen. "She will help your daughter. Pray to her every day!"

Bensen again has to fight back tears. That these people, living in the humblest of circumstances, are ready to be so generous to a stranger, is overwhelming to him. He tries to resist. "I cannot take this from you! It's your family's picture!"

"You must, señor! She will help your daughter," Juan Ramon translates, then says quietly, "Accept it, sir. They will be offended if you do not."

"Thank you," Bensen says, holding out his hands to receive it. "*Muchas gracias,*" he manages, and they all smile.

"This is what she promised, señor," says Fernando, and with eyes closed, recites musically in Spanish, pausing for Juan Ramon to translate. The words of love and sweet promises of help and healing are strangely moving and reassuring to Bensen. "These beautiful words, and your faith, mean a lot to me," he tells them.

Soon Juan Ramon indicates that Bensen must leave for an important meeting at the factory. All rise and stand together in the room, savoring the moment, like dear friends gathered at the door after a pleasant evening, reluctant to part. Bensen says, with all sincerity, that he is sorry to have to go, and grateful for their hospitality and friendship. "Thank you," he says, looking at each one, "I hope some day to repay your kindness."

———

Back at the *maquila,* Jim Morris is sitting behind the desk in one of the production offices with a stack of papers in front of him when Bensen walks in for their meeting. He stands and takes a step toward Bensen to greet him, but

Bensen turns away and promptly sits down. Because Jim is such a good friend, Bensen's had to psych himself up for the confrontation. He can't allow himself to be soft when he expects to terminate Jim's employment.

"So, what did you think about our factory, Mr. Davis?" Jim asks, trying to lighten the air for their meeting. He moves his chair out from behind the desk.

"The factory can wait," Bensen says coldly, ignoring the joking tone and getting right down to business. "I want to talk about these charges against you. How could you possibly put us in this kind of situation?"

"Bensen, hang on a minute here, we haven't looked at the whole picture. You know who I am, you know what I stand for."

"Yeah, but how did these things come up?" Bensen demands. "It seems like it's more than just a vindictive employee or a one-time deal. There's substantial evidence that you've been doing this kind of thing repeatedly. Is that true? Have you been bribing people?"

"I told you, Bensen, I've given some gifts. It's the way it's done. We'd never have the numbers we've generated without those gifts."

"The numbers are good. I've been very pleased. But what the hell are we going to do when this comes out on CNN?"

"Can we take this one step at a time, please?"

"Fine," says Bensen. "You talk."

"Okay," Jim says. "First, no money changed hands. To my mind, bribery means cash, and there was no cash. Ever."

"Your definition of what constitutes bribery may not hold, either in court or in the press. What else?"

"I admit that I broke company policy. I admit that I may have been . . . I was . . . too lavish with gifts, to make things happen, to get preferred status in negotiating contracts. But the real question, Bensen, is this: Why did I do it?"

"Does it matter? It's done."

"It matters to me. And if it doesn't matter to you as CEO, at least you could listen as my friend."

Some of Bensen's tension has been dissipating as Jim has spoken candidly about his behavior. "I'm listening," he says.

"Thanks. Now, I gathered this morning, when you called me, that you've started to recognize how bad conditions are here. And by the way, it's not just here, it's throughout Latin America."

"Conditions are appalling," Bensen acknowledges. "That's the second issue I wanted to take up with you."

"Well, I've been wanting to get resources to do at least some of the things that ought to be done down here, and every time I try to get the funds allocated, *you* tell me it's going to lower the earnings per share and hit the stock price, so we can't do this and we can't do that."

He pauses for effect, and Bensen does take in the point. Then Jim continues, "Bensen, these are sweatshops, pure and simple. It's going to be serious business when that comes out in the media, a helluva lot worse than the story of my misdemeanors trying to round up a little business."

"It *is* coming out," Bensen says, and tells him about the *New York Times* series. "You may be right about the relative severity or seriousness," he concedes. "But if they hit us with both at once, it'll hurt."

"I'm sorry about my part in it," Jim says. "But if you had only listened when I tried to tell you about the factories, we might have been able to avert some of this."

Bensen reflects on Jim's remark for a moment, then he says, "So, correct me if I'm wrong here, but I think you're suggesting that one of the reasons you felt you had to push for more business any way you could was that I wasn't giving you the support you needed."

"That's right," Jim says, and quickly adds, "I'm not saying that what I did was in any way your fault, Bensen. I'm not trying to pass it off on you. The decisions I made, and the actions I took, were my own. But the motivation was to increase business in the hope of generating resources for my territory."

"And you wanted more resources for . . . ?"

"Well, to grow the business, of course. But also for some bare-bones community development. For a wage boost. For some rudimentary health services for employees. Nothing spectacular. I thought if expansion and earnings growth were substantial enough in my territory, that I'd have more leverage with you."

"Not a bad strategy."

"Yeah, but it didn't work! When you don't want to open the door, you don't give an inch. Not a damn inch, Bensen!"

Again Bensen is quiet. Then he responds, "All right. I hear what you're saying. Maybe we both screwed up here. You should probably not have done your gift-giving, and I should have listened to you and not been so bullheaded. I think you're right, we might have been able to head off this attack about the factories if we had acted earlier. And more importantly, maybe we should have cleaned up our act because it was the right thing, not just to avoid trouble. That's what you had in mind, isn't it?"

"It's exactly what I had in mind."

"Well," Bensen says, glancing at his watch, "let's take this further soon. No, I mean it! But I've got a plane to catch. What about you?"

"I'm staying a few more hours."

Both men stand, and this time Bensen moves toward his friend, takes Jim by the shoulders, and looks him in the eyes. "You know, don't you, that I'll probably have to give you notice of termination?"

"I knew it was the likely outcome."

"The thing is, we could try to ride it out. Maybe it won't break in the major media. But even if it doesn't, people are going to be looking to me and asking, 'Bensen, can we all do that kind of stuff? Is it okay?' If it's okay for you, it's got to be okay for everybody. And my opinion is, it's not okay."

"I accept that. Personally, I never liked it. In fact, I can honestly say I hated it. But it was good business; it worked."

"Yeah," Bensen says. "Maybe that's the problem right there."

———

Jim's cell phone rings as the two men walk out the door to the parking lot. He glances at the screen, punches the air with a "thumbs up" sign and says, "Rafael Gutierrez, president of Alessandro, the men's clothing chain. Hundred sixty-two stores and growing. I should probably take it."

"No problem," Benson replies.

Jim clicks on the phone. "Rafael, *momentito por favor.*" Holding the phone away from his face he says, "I wanted to hear about Katie, and Emily . . ."

"It's okay. We'll talk. No change yet with Katie . . . I'll call you." He holds out a hand; Jim grasps it with one hand while he lifts the phone to his ear with the other and turns to go back to his desk.

As Benson approaches his rental car, he hears Juan Ramon Hernandez call out, "Mr. Davis?"

"Yes?"

"Sir," Juan Ramon says, catching up with him, "you told me this morning that you wanted to go over the precise numbers detailing our operation. I'm afraid we never got to that."

"That's all right, Juan Ramon. What I needed to learn here is not about numbers."

Juan Ramon walks with him to the rental car, and the two men stand together, chatting for a few moments before Bensen's departure for the airport.

Sensing that there is something more to be said but unsure of what it is, Bensen delays driving off.

What is troubling him, he realizes, is a feeling of guilt for deceiving Juan Ramon about his identity. With everything to lose, this man has been direct, helpful, and courageous, risking his job by revealing dark secrets about the factory and its management to a visitor from corporate headquarters, while he, with nothing to lose, has been concealing the truth about himself. As they shake hands, he retains Juan Ramon's hand in his grip for a moment and says, a little hesitantly, "I want to thank you not only for helping me, but for your efforts on behalf of these people. I may be in a position to help them quite a lot."

Juan Ramon looks into Bensen's eyes, then squeezes his hand warmly. Before he can reply, Bensen adds, "But one thing puzzles me. Please tell me how you can be two things at once—a top manager at a plant that takes unfair advantage of thousands of people, and yet a man who cares about those people enough to risk his position by revealing the truth."

As the two men stand face to face, hands still locked in a tight grip, Juan Ramon looks deeply into his eyes and replies, "You will know the answer when you can tell me, Mr. Quinn, how you can be chairman and CEO of a company that pays these people less than a dollar an hour while you accept millions of dollars every year—and at the same time, a man with a good heart, who wants to do what is right."

Bensen is flabbergasted. "You knew all along who I am?"

"I knew. I recognized you from pictures in annual reports and company literature. When I saw that you were concealing your identity, I asked myself, 'Why would he do this?' Right away I felt that your purpose was not to harm us, but to know the truth. I hoped that what you learned would help you decide to do the right thing."

"I did want to know the truth. And I am going to act on it."

"Thank you, Mr. Quinn. Thank you very much."

Deeply moved, Bensen relaxes his grip, and turns to go. Then he looks back for a moment and says, "Juan Ramon, I can assure you your courage and integrity will not be forgotten. Thank you once again."

On the flight home, Bensen resolves to dramatically improve conditions at this and other company plants. "If, God forbid, I have blown it with Katie," he thinks, "if it's too late to set things straight between us, I am *not* going to let the opportunity slip away to help these people have a better life." He'll call a special staff meeting to explain what he wants to do, and launch a study of what changes to make and how to implement them. He knows there will be opposition from most of his top people and from the Board, but he's determined to overcome any resistance and move ahead. His mind charged with excitement, he covers page after page in his yellow pad with ideas for a new direction for the company.

Wake-Up Call . . .

Leadership sheds light on the shadows to reveal the way to a more purposeful future. As leaders, before we can project a meaningful vision, we must first examine personal and organizational shadows. As Bensen casts a light on the parts of himself and his business he didn't want to look at, a new, more life-enriching vision emerges.

What are the personal shadows you have been avoiding looking at? _____

_____

_____

*What are the organizational shadows that need examination?*_____

_____

_____

If you dealt with these shadows, what new energy, conviction, and purpose might come into your life? _____

_____

_____

Walking the Talk . . . With Baby Steps 19

"Anne, it's Bensen."

"Ben, you sound like you're on the moon."

"Close. I'm on a plane. Sorry to call you at home, but it's important."

"That's okay. Where are you?"

"On my way back from one of our factories. I wanted to see for myself how things really are before those articles come out."

"And?"

"It's bad, worse than my worst-case scenario."

"Where did you go?"

"Mexico, one of the *maquiladoras* near the border, south of San Diego. A place called Las Flores."

"Who's with you? How come I didn't hear about it?"

"I went by myself."

"No!"

"Yes."

"You're crazier than I thought," she says, and laughs. "Hey, I've got a great job offer, I can say that!"

Bensen laughs too, happy to be talking to her. "Actually," she continues, "I admire your courage. It can be dangerous down there. So I hear."

"I didn't even think of that, before I went."

"So, what did you learn? Aside from the fact that things are bad."

"Oh, way too much to tell you on the phone. I can tell you this, though: The time has definitely arrived to transform the way we do business. There are going to be big changes in this company."

"What kind of changes?" she asks.

"I don't want to get too specific yet," he says, then adds, "To be honest, I'm still thinking it through, but the ideas I'm working with are in the direction I believe you'd want to go. I've been mentally reviewing some of the conversations we've had over the last year or so and I'm seeing better what you've been trying to tell me."

"Like what?"

"For example, that we've got to cultivate a more comprehensive vision. You've talked about how important it is to consider long-term sustainability, not just short-term profit, and how that requires serving the different constituencies we interact with."

"Yes."

"I see your point, now. We should be creating value not only for owners and investors, but for our employees—all of them, not just executives and management—as well as for our customers, suppliers, and the community. I think if we start putting our attention on having a positive impact in these areas, that will speak to another of your concerns: that our work should be more meaningful."

"It definitely would."

"Now that I'm ready to start moving on all this," Bensen says, "I hope it's not too late to keep you on board. I value your input. And your friendship."

"I'd sure like to know some specifics. And what sparked this for you."

"A lot of things have been leading up to it. The immediate catalyst was the factory, the conditions there, and the people I met. They have an unbelievably hard life. I had no idea. I was shocked by it, Anne. I wasn't exactly born with a silver spoon in my mouth, but I've never seen anything like this. We're talking about eight or ten people living in a couple of small rooms, with no plumbing, no running water, industrial waste and raw sewage floating by in open ditches, no medical care for children or anyone else, not a tree in sight, children having to go to bed hungry. To jump from my comfortable life into the midst of that bleak existence was a major wake-up call for me."

"You didn't know things like that were going on in the world? Come on, Bensen. . . ."

"Of course I knew, but I didn't think it was going on so close to home. And I don't just mean distance-wise. I mean, *in my company!* I'm ashamed to admit this, but until today I've thought of the workers on the production floor in our factories more like numbers than human beings, costs to control rather than lives we touch. Of course, that's very convenient. If we don't see them as people, with faces, voices, dreams, and concerns like the 'real' human beings in our lives, we can use them for our own purposes, like commodities, the way we use up natural resources, and not worry about the effect we're having on them. But if you *connect* to them, and to the parts in you that are alive with feeling, the whole picture changes. Today they became people to me—fine people, honorable people who deserve to be treated as such."

"Sounds like it really affected you, Bensen."

"Very much. I used to congratulate myself for all the jobs we provide. I no longer feel so proud. Of course, we *do* provide jobs. But life could be much better for these people with just a little attention and a minimal investment from our side. We're going to do it. And I'm certain—though I haven't figured this part out yet—that we don't have to compromise profitability to accomplish this. My intuition tells me we'll actually be able to improve it, in the long run."

When Bensen stops talking, the silence on the line lasts a long time. "Anne? Are you still there? Did I put you to sleep with all that?"

"I'm here. Ben—first of all, this is amazing. I can't believe I'm hearing this from you."

"You're the first. But everyone will hear it soon."

"Then let me ask you—why *are* you telling this to me, before anyone else?"

"Because you're the only one in the company who's had the guts to try to get through to me about this stuff. Or maybe you're the only one who saw it. Anyway, I thought you'd care. And I don't want to lose you. I need your help."

"Ben, you know I care. I'm sure you remember that I grew up with a Hispanic mother and an English father; most of my relatives on my mother's side live in Mexico, some of them just a few miles from where you were. If you want to do something for those people, I'll help you. If you will really do it."

"I'll really do it," Bensen says. "Of course, it won't be only those people. We have to think about our facilities in the rest of Latin America, and in Asia. But we can start there. In fact, if you'll stick around, we can make that plant our prototype. We'll try things out there, see what works, and then take the best ideas companywide."

"I'm listening."

"Let's brainstorm after I'm back. How are you coming with your vision for the company?"

"I've outlined quite a bit. I'd love to start talking about it."

"Great! How about tomorrow morning, early?"

"Fine," she agrees, "I'll be in your office at what, seven, seven-thirty?"

"Let's say seven-thirty. I'm getting in pretty late tonight."

"Bensen—what about the Board of Directors? Will they buy it?"

"We'll soon find out. I'm going to call Bill Jordan as soon as we hang up. If

I can show him the merit of what I want to do, if he'll look at it, I think we can take it the rest of the way."

"Good luck," she offers.

"I'll need it. But I'm on fire with this. It's important. It needs to happen. See you in the morning."

———

Bensen immediately phones William Jordan, his longtime mentor and a good friend since their college days, who's now a key figure on his Board of Directors. He feels that Jordan, an African American who has been enormously successful in business, is more likely than the other Board members to resonate personally with his ideas.

"Bill," Benson begins when Jordan's secretary puts him through, "I've got some important ideas I'd like to run by you as soon as possible."

"Fire away," Jordan says, "I've got a little time right now, if you do. But first, how's Katie? Any improvement?"

"The last I heard, nothing has changed. It's been a couple of hours since I talked to Emily."

"Let me know, will you? I'm praying for her every day."

"Thank you, Bill."

"So, what's on your mind?"

Knowing he will need a face-to-face meeting if he has any chance of persuading Jordan to go along with him, Bensen doesn't want to reveal anything concrete on the phone. "I think this is something that would be better in person," he says. "Besides, we haven't seen each other for awhile; it's a good excuse to get together."

He's gratified when Jordan says, "Well, the gods are smiling on you; my lunch for tomorrow canceled. Let's do it."

———

Early the next morning, Bensen arrives at his office suite to find a handwritten note from Anne taped to the outer door: "Bensen, please come down to my office, I have something to show you." When he gets there, she's at her desk in front of her computer screen. "Look at this," she says without looking up. "This is going to blow your mind." Then she turns to him and says, "Let me get you a chair," but he is already sliding one over and places it next to hers.

"What have you got?" he says.

"Watch this," she answers, clicking away at the keyboard. "When you challenged me to formulate my vision statement about the company, it struck me that maybe other people were thinking along the same lines I was. And *voilà!*" A search engine comes on screen, with responses to her keywords. "These, Bensen, are some of the people and organizations thinking about how to restructure the way we do business, to take better care of people and the planet.

"Take a look at the top of the page," she continues excitedly. "These are the first ten of 14,319 entries on this search engine! I've been here since five-thirty visiting some of the sites. I thought we were on the cutting edge, but it turns out that hundreds of thousands of people all over the world are involved in this stuff. There are consultants, corporate officers, entire companies committed to a more principles-driven way of doing business. Some of these concepts are really great: 'balanced scorecard,' 'triple bottom line'—and here, look at this," she says, opening to a web page on which one of the organizations has posted, "the mindset of society is changing, from competition, focus on short-term goals, and exploitation of labor and resources, toward sustainability, long-term growth, cooperation, connectedness, and recognition of the responsibility that business has for society. The effects are widespread and highly practical, but the core transformation is personal and spiritual: People are feeling their interconnectedness with each other and the broader global community."

"Yeah, that's pretty much it," Bensen says.

"So it means we don't have to reinvent the wheel," Anne says excitedly. "We can just plug in to some of this visionary intelligence, and figure out how it applies here."

"This is reassuring," Bensen says. "I just wonder . . . you've been looking at their material; how do these people deal with profit in relation to these ideals?"

"Everyone wants profits, Bensen. The idea is to integrate profitability with values."

"Good! I'd like to see some of their suggestions for doing just that. But first, I want to hear what you've been working on. Tell me the idea you're most excited about."

"I'm developing a new index to measure the performance of a business—starting with us, of course. I'm tentatively calling it the Value Creation Index. The key idea is that the impact or value of a company lies in more than just its financial success or failure. The stock price would remain as the measure of shareholder value, but there would be maybe a half-dozen other factors."

"Good," Bensen says emphatically. "Once you think about it for even ten seconds—with an open mind, that is—it's obvious that the financial measure is insufficient to gauge how a company is truly doing, in the big picture. So what are the other index components?"

"One would be an evaluation of employee satisfaction and motivation," Anne begins, "to determine how they feel about their jobs, the company, the corporate culture. This would be done through periodic questionnaires and employee interviews by an outside organization."

"Sounds appropriate," Bensen says, nodding with interest. "What else? Something for customer satisfaction?"

"Yes. There would have to be an assessment of whether customers are satisfied with the company's products. This would probably be tied in with measures of quality. Is quality being maintained or compromised? Are customers receiving proper value?"

"And of course you'll have a Green index," Bensen contributes.

"Right. What impact does the company have on the environment? Is it taking irreplaceable resources and giving back toxic by-products, polluting the water and air and filling landfills with unnecessary waste? Or has it worked out a way to consume less, pollute less, recycle more?"

"I was just thinking," Bensen says, "that if this catches on and hundreds of corporations start using your index, it will create a new industry, to assess how corporations are doing and to get the information out to investors and the public in a coherent way."

"Exactly," says Anne. "Standards will have to be determined, such as how much employee satisfaction gives you a 'one' rating and what gives you a 'ten'? Investors will want to know how a company is really doing, what its policies are, and how it's performing on social and environmental issues, what grades it receives in these periodic evaluations. Instruments will have to be developed to rate companies in each area."

"Then," Bensen throws in, "the question comes up, how much weight to assign each area."

"Right," Anne agrees. "Does environment count equally with quality issues? How do you balance and combine the factors to come out with a meaningful total score, your Value Creation Index rating?"

"This is going to be very interesting. Anyway, sorry for the interruption, I got you off track. What next?"

Anne looks at Bensen silently for a moment, then says, "I *would* miss this kind of brainstorming, Bensen. It's exciting."

"I'd miss it too," he says. "But I won't have to, because you're staying, right?"

"Let's just move ahead here; we'll see how things unfold, okay?"

"Okay," he says. "What else do you have?"

"Another factor that would have to be included is the relationship of the company to the community," Anne continues. "With a global corporation, of course, you'd have to consider multiple communities—corporate headquarters, production facilities, service centers, retail outlets. Does the presence of the company provide a steady and secure source of varied employment? Or does it offer mainly low-skill, low-wage work that fluctuates with hirings and firings tied to the ups and downs of the stock price? In general, does the organization enrich the quality of life in the locations in which it operates?"

"What about an overall ethics mark?" Bensen queries. "Does the company market cigarettes or unsafe products to children, or knowingly sell tires that blow out when they overheat? Does it run sweatshops in Mexico? Are its accounting practices not just legal but ethical and fair?"

Bensen leans back in his chair and beams at her. "It's an outstanding idea, Anne. And it provides a kind of master key to understanding the range of issues that have to be dealt with by each company."

"Would you do it?"

"I *will* do it," he says emphatically, then laughs.

"What's so funny?" she asks.

"Can you imagine the change this will represent in Board rooms? Once a few big companies take the lead on this, others will feel obliged to follow. It'll catch on. I can see it. In light of recent business events, the public and the investors will demand it."

Now Anne leans back too, smiling with satisfaction. "I'm pleased that you like this, Bensen."

"It's just what I needed," he tells her, "to start clarifying my own thinking. But I'd bet anything, now that you've shown me the tip of the iceberg on the web, that other people are working on creating something like this. Shall we do

The Seed of Value Creation: Serving Parts and Whole

a search for other index ideas? Or why don't you tell me what else you're work-ing on. . . ."

———

A few hours after the meeting with Anne, Bensen walks into the restaurant for his meeting with Bill Jordan highly charged, his determination to move for-ward with major changes significantly reinforced. He's armed more with rough ideas and enthusiasm than with a well-delineated plan of action, but he's eager to present his vision to Jordan and build it together. After shaking hands and spending a few minutes catching up on mutual friends and family members they order their meals. To their amusement, both men order chicken salads—albeit with exotic names and flavorings, but chicken salads nonetheless—and iced tea.

"Times have changed, haven't they, Ben?" Jordan says with a laugh. "The days of steaks and martinis are over. At least for most of us."

"It's true," Bensen replies. "And that, thank you very much, gives me a per-fect opening for what I want to talk about. We've changed how we eat because we know a lot more about the impact of diet on health. And we want to be healthy. When we were thirty, we figured we were invincible and could get away with anything. Now we know we have to be diligent and take responsi-bility."

"And?"

"I think the time has come to change the way we do business, because of what we know about our impact on other people and on the environment—that is, if we want our company to be healthy, with sustainable growth over the long term."

"We've taken some steps to be more environmentally aware in the business. Thanks to you, I might add."

"Yes, we have. But remember, you didn't want to; Peter Kim, Tom Wilson, and the rest of the board didn't want to. In truth, even though I pushed for it and I could see that it was important, I didn't really *want* to. We all felt that we'd have to spend too much to restructure systems and procedures—to enable recycling, to redesign for products with more acceptable, natural materials, to search out new suppliers—and we'd have to put out more money than we wanted for some new equipment. But we did it. And you know the end result is that we're actu-ally saving money, and people like the products. We'll make up our costs in an-other fourteen to sixteen months, and after that it will all be gravy."

"True enough. But what I gather you're looking at now is different. Or is it?"

"It's not that different. I think you'll agree that the recycling and energy efficiency we instituted were, from a values perspective, the right thing. We just didn't see it as good business. But it turned out that it was."

"Okay."

"I think we're in a similar situation."

"There's something you want to do that's the right thing, but it's going to cost?"

"Something like that. But first let me tell you the back story, so you'll know why I'm thinking this way."

Bensen recounts his trip to Mexico: his eye-opening walk through the factory, what he learned in his discussion with Juan Ramon Hernandez, and his poignant meeting with the Herrera family, describing in detail their tiny, scantily furnished home and their daily struggle for survival. "They have a daughter who reminds me of Katie," he tells Jordan, "a young girl, maybe fifteen, who works in the factory. Looking at her and at the other girls working there, I couldn't help thinking, 'I would *never* want this to happen to my daughter; why should I accept it for anyone else's child?'"

Then he begins to enthusiastically lay out the foundation of his plan: upgrade working conditions in the factories, raise wages for production workers, and allocate corporate funds for infrastructure improvement and community redevelopment in areas surrounding the plants. "They deserve better education, proper sanitation, clean water—we take these things for granted and they don't have them."

Instead of hearing him out and then critiquing his presentation, Jordan immediately cuts him short. "Ben, you can't go in that direction. Your compassion for that family, your concern for the workers—that's all fine. It's admirable, Bensen. But those are your personal feelings. They have nothing to do with business. We're in business to make money, not to help poor families. If you want to donate money to their community, fine. If you think making a contribution in the name of HighQuest would be helpful—as well as good PR—then do it that way. But don't let it affect your thinking about how we do business."

"Bill, I . . ."

"Let me finish. I don't want you to misunderstand. I'm not suggesting that you should be hard-hearted, Bensen, believe me. What I am saying is, don't confuse your business responsibilities and your personal values. It's two different worlds. I volunteer as a tutor in a literacy program—you know that, right?—and Jill and I support the symphony and several adoption programs. But that's our personal lives, and our personal funds. From a business standpoint, the measures you're considering are not the concern of the company. They're not feasible. They would cut too deeply into profits. And you know what that means, not only for the company you've worked so hard to build up, but also for your own career. You have to forget it."

"Bill, I've barely begun to spell out my ideas," Bensen protests. "You haven't heard any specifics."

"I don't need details to know that the whole direction is wrongheaded. I don't think I have to remind you that corporate officers, notably the Chief Executive Officer, are obligated by law to set aside personal values in favor of the financial interests of the organization and its shareholders. Your job is to maximize profits, not to be a humanitarian. What are you thinking? As I said, personally I applaud your concerns. But I cannot and I will not support you in pursuing these notions if they would endanger corporate profitability, as it is clear to me they would."

Then, lowering his voice and leaning forward across the table, he adds, "Ben, if you don't mind an old friend speaking frankly, I think you're exhausted, and your emotions are all churned up over Katie. Your thinking's not clear here. Give it a rest for a couple of days, and I'm sure you'll agree with me."

Despite his strong sense of purpose and habitual bullheadedness, Bensen is politic enough to know when to back off, and he does. But this unreceptive and unsympathetic response from Jordan, a trusted friend and an older, more experienced executive, crushes his exuberant mood. The conversation continues on a different track, and Bensen leaves the meeting conflicted about what to do.

He knows that Bill is right about his corporate responsibilities. But still he questions whether there couldn't be a way to maintain or increase profitability and growth, and at the same time offer all HighQuest employees, at every level, a more positive, life-enriching work experience.

For the remainder of the day, and throughout a restless night, Bensen swings back and forth. When he contemplates the new direction he envisions for the company, a direction he feels deeply is the right way to go, he is resolved to press forward, to act on his vision no matter what. But then the voice of his long-established way of thinking and acting speaks up: "Why do I imagine I can single-handedly change the way business is done? It'll be too hard. And too risky. I can't jeopardize the company's profitability for some idealistic dream."

He wants to overcome what he views as Jordan's conventional wisdom, yet he's caught in it himself, his mind readily slipping into its familiar ruts.

By the time he encounters Kenji in the garden early the next morning, he's worn out by the internal conflict and on the verge of acquiescing to the pressure of Jordan's demands. "Kenji," he says after updating him on the trip and the meeting with Jordan, "I'm known for my bottom-line practicality. I don't know what got into me. I must be going soft."

"Yes, Bensen," Kenji quietly replies; "you *are* going soft—in the heart. That is not necessarily a bad thing."

The remark is enough to stop Bensen's slide. "So you think I'm correct? That I should forge ahead?"

"What I think doesn't matter. What do *you* think, Bensen? Why do you want to take this new direction?"

"It's just the right thing. It's the human thing to do."

"So, that's your reason: It's the right thing?"

"It's the right thing," Bensen says with conviction.

"Leading with integrity means that you put your values into play."

"Yes, I believe that."

"And what does it mean to you, in this case?"

"That I shouldn't separate my business values from my life values, the way Bill Jordan wants me to. I don't agree with him. I didn't realize it till recently. Even last week, when Anne Holmes told me she was fed up with living two different lives, that she wanted to tear down the wall between her personal values and her professional values and start working at something that expresses what is truly meaningful to her—even then, I'm not sure I completely understood. But now I do. At the production facility, I saw that my friend Jim's personal values were such that he thought bribery was a bad thing. He said he hated it. But when it came to business, he went right ahead and gave gifts to get contracts. This whole question reminds me of something you once said to me, Kenji. You said, 'Seek integration.'"

"Ah, you remember!" Kenji replies. "Do you also remember how you reacted to what I said?"

"No, I'm afraid I don't."

"You were a bit dismayed! You said, though not in so many words, 'That may not be so easy to do!'"

"Well," says Bensen with a laugh, "I'll give myself credit for being right on that one!"

"Yes, what you're setting out to do will not be easy. Many will oppose you. You'll have to be definite about what you aim to do, and why you want to do it."

"I feel clear about it," Bensen says. "And I know I'm in for a battle. I've never shied away from one before."

"What do you think has happened to make you change your point of reference so radically?" Kenji asks him.

"What do you mean?"

"What do I mean?" Kenji puts his hands on his hips and looks at Bensen, his dark eyes twinkling. "I mean, last year at this time, how focused were you on investing more resources to improve the lives of your employees and their communities?"

"You're right," Bensen says. "I'm turned around one hundred eighty degrees. For twenty years I've been intent on bolstering profits, slashing expenditures, raising production efficiency."

"What happened? Was it only your visit to Mexico?"

Bensen quietly reflects for a minute or so. "No, I think it's a combination of things," he says. "Certainly, one factor is Katie. Her accident forced me to see that I was not living my life, shall we say, from the heart. Even where I thought I was, with my family, I really wasn't; I was hardly there."

"You poured all your passion into your work."

"Yes, I did. The place for personal love in my life was pretty small. With the pain I've felt about Katie, the possible loss—it was like crashing into a wall and not being able to continue in the same way. Or looking into a mirror and seeing things about myself I'm not happy about, and wanting to change. So that's one factor."

"And how would you define it?"

"Like what you said before, about 'heart.' Giving space for more human feeling, more caring. Goals like increasing market share and boosting profits lose some of their charm when your child's life is in danger! My sense of priorities, of what really matters, made a shift."

"That makes sense. What else?"

"Watching Katie hover at the edge of death has made me face my own mortality and vulnerability in a much deeper, more realistic way. As long as I didn't acknowledge that my time here is limited, I could get away with doing things that didn't genuinely matter, or that were expedient but not meaningful—even of dubious morality. I can't do that any more. I need to live a life of service, based more on what I believe."

"And do you know what you believe?"

"Not entirely, but each day it becomes a little clearer. I believe in the preciousness of every human life, and of life itself; I believe in the necessity of people having freedom, so they can grow and express who they are. I believe in living authentically, from our deepest essence. I believe we are all much, much more than we think we are, and that life is mostly about discovering and uncovering all that we have the potential to be."

"That's beautiful, Bensen."

"Yes, it is, isn't it?" he replies, a bit astonished at the spontaneous outpouring of his deepest convictions.

"What else has contributed to your new vision and priorities?"

"Well, the trip to Mexico. What I saw in that factory—the pressure being put on those young girls, the heat, the dust, the indignity of it all—and then what I learned about their lives . . ."

"Many people live that way," Kenji quietly interrupts.

"That's just the point!" Bensen fires back. "They don't have to. At least not so many. It isn't right!"

"So, we're back to your first point: caring about it, wanting to serve, because it's the right thing. But why is it that you see these things now, and you never did before? Or if you did see them, you didn't care? Or if you cared, you didn't care enough to take any action?"

"I think the truth is that I didn't want to see it. My job as CEO is to make my company profitable and keep it growing, and that means keeping costs down and maximizing productivity. It also means cultivating our image, marketing aggressively, and all that—but that's in a different area than we're discussing. Like all companies that make things, we're—to put it crudely—chasing the availability of cheap materials and cheap labor around the world. I've always believed we were doing a favor to those communities by bringing in thousands of jobs. Now that I've experienced the factory firsthand, I see that it's not so simple. We *are* contributing by providing jobs, but our responsibility doesn't end there. At least, it shouldn't."

"And you didn't want to see that because . . . ?"

"Because I didn't want to deal with it. It was comfortable to believe that we were doing all we could, that the effect of our business was positive. If that turned out to be not true, well, I'd either have to live with feeling guilty about what we were doing, or launch significant changes."

"Neither of which would be easy."

"No, they wouldn't."

Bensen looks off into space, and after a minute Kenji says, "What are you thinking, Bensen?"

"You might think this is strange, but ever since the morning in the garden when you taught me how to connect to Essence, I've been feeling . . . different."

"In what way?" Kenji asks.

"More peaceful. Contented in a way I wasn't used to."

Kenji nods. "Yes, I understand that."

"I've begun to feel that I have everything a man could want. I have material abundance, health, a beautiful family, career success. So why am I running so hard, pushing myself so hard, always moving toward the next horizon, taking on the next challenge? What do I want? When I ask myself that, the answer that comes is—I don't really want *anything*. It's just a habit I've had for a long time, a mind-set that drives me.

"Maybe at one point it was valid. When I didn't have those things, working for them was meaningful. But now, I don't need anything more for myself, I have enough and more than enough. When I realized this, at the same moment I felt, 'What I do want, what would give my life meaning, is to do what I can for others.' It was a simple feeling, but it was powerful."

Kenji regards him affectionately. "You are in a position to do very much," he says.

"Yes, I am." At that moment, Bensen recalls the words of the university president, Dr. Reynolds, who had advised him so long ago to "get inside the walls," where he could exercise power. "I do have a position of influence," he says to Kenji, smiling at the memory, "and I intend to use it, not solely for myself any more."

"This is your next horizon, Bensen, your next challenge," Kenji says, his eyes sparkling playfully.

"You mean, that habit of pushing forward isn't going to change?" Bensen says.

"Not very likely, I'm afraid. It's your nature. You have a gift for leadership and achievement that isn't going to go away. Now you'll use it for a more far-reaching purpose—more authentic to who you are, and more valuable to others."

"I feel that," Bensen says, "and I will work to make it true." Then he adds, "Of course, I didn't mention this when I was listing the reasons for the transformation in me, but obviously, there's also you, Kenji. You have had a tremendous influence on me. These conversations, the questions you've asked me to consider—starting with whether I'm happy with the music I'm playing, the contributions I'm making—they've had a huge impact on me."

"I'm glad, Bensen. That means very much to me," Kenji says, then immediately inquires, "So, what do you see as your options now?"

"My friend Bill Jordan made it sound like a black-and-white choice: either do my job as CEO, which means putting shareholder value ahead of all other considerations, or become some kind of mushy-headed, misguided humanitarian and lose my job."

"How do you see it?"

"There does appear to be an incompatibility between maximizing profits and what I would consider compassionate, ethical action. Right now I don't know how to reconcile them. I acknowledge that my responsibility as a corporate officer is to grow the company, to increase earnings. But I would be denying what I know is right if I abandoned this strong desire not only to help these good people, but also to restructure the way we do business."

"Restructure the business? No wonder your friend Jordan was worried."

Bensen laughs. "He was worried *before* I got a chance to say that!"

"What are you planning?"

"Well, I don't have a specific plan yet. But the basic principles are clear."

"Principles are seeds for the tree," Kenji says with a smile.

"Yes, they'll grow into something."

"Are you ready to talk about it?" Kenji asks. "I mean, since it's still in the seed stage. Seeds are tender when they first begin to sprout; sometimes they need to be nurtured in silence."

"The main thing," Bensen says, "the guiding principle, if you like, is that people's work should give their lives dignity, increased freedom, and expanded opportunity. I expect my job to give that to me. It should be true for everyone, and it's not. For most people, work is not a joyful, meaningful, growth-producing experience; it's drudgery—or worse. This says to me that business, as we conduct it, as it's operating today, stands in opposition to the full living and unfoldment of life. That has to change.

"I assume that what I saw in Mexico is representative of the living and working conditions of millions of people around the world. I accept that I may never be able to change things for most of them. But there's no reason people have to live like that in places where we, and other successful companies, do business. If the people who work for us live so poorly, then we're not doing *our* job. We should set things up so their jobs can contribute to their health, their happiness, and their children's future, and we can make our profits too. Real leadership demands no less!"

"What about that man you met in Mexico?" Kenji inquires.

"Juan Ramon? What about him?"

"He has a good job," Kenji says. "Probably, his children are going to school, and he has a comfortable home for his family. Your company gives that to him. There must be many people in his situation."

"That's a good point," Bensen says. "It reminds me that it's not all one way or the other, that we're neither the great benefactors that I used to think we were, nor some evil force oppressing people. We definitely contribute value. . . ."

"But you feel you could do more."

"Yes, much more." Again Bensen looks pensive, and stares off into space. Then he says, in a quiet voice, "When Juan Ramon and I were saying goodbye, he looked at me and said he didn't understand how I could take home a huge salary, pay people a few cents an hour, and still be a good man, yet he implied that he thought I *was* a good man, because I was there, and I seemed to care."

"You are a very good man, Bensen."

"Well, then I'm a good man trapped in a dilemma, especially if I can't find a way to make the changes my spirit is crying out to make. I truly don't see how to do it and still maintain our competitive edge and our profitability."

"What if you can't do it? What if it isn't possible, and you have to choose?"

"It has to be possible."

"You say that with such conviction, even though you can't see it."

"What I see is that it's something that needs to be done. My job as a leader is to find a way, and make it happen."

"Sounds like you're committed to this path," Kenji states. "Are you?"

"I'm committed. If I try and fail, at least I'll have done my best to accomplish what I believe is right. As you said, integrity means putting your values into play. If I don't try, I'll know that I caved in, that I acted according to what *others* believe. That's not acceptable to me. It's not leadership."

———

As they are about to part, Bensen has an afterthought, and he notices that Kenji is quietly waiting. "I said before that I felt contented, and there was nothing I wanted for myself. That's not true. There is one thing I want with all my heart. I want my daughter to recover. I know it may never happen, but I want it like I've never wanted anything before. Of course I want it for *her;* she deserves to live a long and full life. But I can't deny that it is a very personal, perhaps selfish desire."

His voice rich with affection, Kenji replies, "You are beginning to expand the range of your compassion and concern to embrace many others. The entire world is becoming your family. But let me assure you, my friend, that even as your concern for other people grows, the love you feel for your child will have no equal."

Wake-Up Call . . .

Awareness without commitment is an empty promise. It's knowing that something important in us or in our organization needs to change, but not doing anything about it. It's knowing, for example, that we ought to show more interpersonal warmth, but never practicing it. Awareness engages the head of the leader; commitment captures the heart.

What is something you are aware of in your organization that needs to change but that you haven't had the courage or commitment to do anything about? _____
_____

What is something you are aware of in your own life that needs to change but that you haven't had the courage or commitment to do anything about? _____
_____

What are the negative consequences for you and others if you don't do anything? _____
_____
_____

What are the positive consequences if you take action? _____
_____
_____
_____

What are you going to do? By when? _____
_____
_____

20 Awakening Together

The moment Bensen steps across the threshold of his daughter's room in the hospital, he is overcome by a feeling of shock and dread. Not that anything seems worse, or even different. Just the opposite. Except for softer lighting, a few vases filled with flowers, and the balloons and colorful cards on the walls and tables sent by Katie's classmates and friends, it all looks the same.

By contrast, he has just come back from a life-changing experience in what seems like another planet, another universe. His life is moving rapidly forward: Every day seems to bring new revelations, most of them positive. He's excited about the challenges facing him as he gears up to pilot the company into uncharted waters. He feels a reinvigorated and passionate sense of purpose.

Yet here's his beloved daughter, lying in the same position, with the identical monitors recording the pulsations of her heart and the slow, steady breathing. Some of the bandages have been removed from her face, and he can see that the bruises are beginning to fade, a sign that life is still coursing through her. But she remains pale and motionless, sustained by oxygen flowing through a tube to her nostrils and the plastic sacks of artificial nourishment that still hang on their stainless steel trees.

He has discussed with the doctors the possibility that Katie might not pull through. He's spoken of it with Emily. But at this time of renewed hope and awakening in his own life, he won't give in to those thoughts. Instead, he reaches out to her.

"Sweetie," he says, sitting beside her and taking her hand in his, "the last time I saw you, I was about to leave on a trip. I promised to tell you about it, and there's quite a story to tell. . . ." He begins tentatively, still uncomfortable speaking out loud when there's no apparent listener. By the time he nears the end of the tale, his natural exuberance and optimistic spirit have dispelled his self-consciousness and he's no longer holding her hand, but pacing the room as he speaks.

"When I was in Mexico, it struck me that conditions there, in the factory and in the home and the neighborhood I visited, were similar to the kind of circumstances I objected to when I was in college—and now I'm the one responsible for creating them! Okay, not entirely responsible, but I'm the CEO: The buck stops with me.

"When I saw how upset it made me, I understood that the same values that have been meaningful to me in the past are still alive in me, very much what I care about and want to stand up for. Something deep inside me is waking up, and it's very important to me to do something more meaningful and positive with my life and with my company. I'm determined to transform my organization into a force that helps everyone connected to it to build excellence.

"I see so many ways I can make a very different kind of impact. Did you know that if you add up all our employees plus their family members, we directly affect the lives of at least 50,000 people? Then there are all the people in their communities, everywhere we have a factory, all around the world. We have some real power. Granted, it's still only a tiny corner of the universe, a few hundred thousand people, but we ought to use that power for a good purpose."

His story told, he sits down again at the side of her bed, takes his daughter's hand and gently presses it, hoping for some glimmer of response, of life returning. After a while he lets it go. Leaning back in the chair with a sigh and closing his eyes, he almost inadvertently slips into the familiar meditation practice Kenji taught him.

As usual at the start of his practice, a jumble of thoughts and imagery— sounds, sights, memories, undone tasks—vie for attention in his mind. This time, perhaps because he is so exhausted, his meditation feels more like a series of dreams. Drifting here and there, he has discussions with Juan Ramon that never happened, signs HighQuest checks for large sums of money to build parks adjoining company factories. On a hazy morning he and Katie hike a trail in the woods, among pine and gleaming white birch trees high above a dark blue lake. The trail ahead of them leads into a dense thicket, but Bensen, wanting to have a better view of the water, skirts the brush while Katie takes the easier path, and they lose sight of each other. He clambers over some rocks, coming close to the edge, and a few small stones break loose and tumble over the side, dislodging a few larger ones that go clattering downhill.

"Dad, are you there?" Katie calls out.

"I'm here, Honey, I'll catch up to you in a second," he replies.

But then he hears again, "Dad, are you there?" and he realizes—*it's not a dream!*

He opens his eyes and sees her eyelids fluttering as she struggles to come out of her long sleep. She squints and tries to focus, and again faintly cries out, "Daddy? Is that you? Are you there?"

"I'm here, Sweetie. I'm here!" he says, leaping to his feet and leaning over so she can see him.

"Where am I? What's going on?"

"You're in the hospital. You had an accident."

"I did?"

"Yes, Sweetheart."

"It must have been bad . . . if I'm in the hospital," she says haltingly, looking around.

"You broke some things, and you have a lot of bruises. And—you were unconscious for a little while. But you're going to be okay. You'll heal up and be dancing in no time. Everything is going to be okay."

"What about my *face*?" she asks with panic in her voice, now aware of the bandages.

"Only some bruises," he lies, not really knowing. "You'll be as good as new."

"Was I alone? Did anybody get hurt?"

"Nobody except you got hurt. You were with Jessica and Joe, but they were just shaken up. Some . . . guy went through a stop sign and skidded into you," he says, on the verge of rage, but catches himself. "It was very foggy and the road was wet."

"Was it my fault?"

"No, Honey, you weren't driving. It was Jessica's car. And if she saw the guy, it would only have been at the last second."

"I don't remember. . . ." she says, then asks, "How are *you*, Dad? How's Mom? You guys must have been worried about me."

Bensen bursts out laughing, the relief spilling out, long-held tension releasing.

"What's so funny?" Katie asks.

"Sweetie, we weren't worried. We were *terrified!* But not any more. Anyhow, your mother is fine. And we need to call her right now!" he says, and steps away from the bed toward his briefcase, resting on the floor on the opposite wall.

"Of course she was worried," he adds, lifting out his cell phone, "but she knew you would be okay."

"And you, Dad? Are you still mad at me?"

Bensen is shocked at the concept, and freezes in the middle of the room. He has no idea what she's talking about. "Mad at you? About what?"

"About that meeting I went to, about sweatshops. The last thing I remember is that you were mad at me, and you yelled at me."

Tears come to Bensen's eyes. That this could have been his daughter's last memory, the last experience she remembered! He is ashamed.

"No, Sweetie, I'm not mad at you," he says softly, returning to her side. "Not at all. In fact, I'm proud of you."

"You are?"

"Yes. I know I wasn't supportive of you about that, but the truth is, I'm *glad* you're the way you are, that you care about the things you do."

"Really?"

"Yes, really. And I've got a lot to tell you about. I've been away too, in more ways than one."

"You're always away!"

"Well, I'm here now, with you." He sits again in the chair, punches Emily's number on his automatic dialer, then puts the phone in Katie's hand. "Can you hold this okay?"

"I think so," she says, lifting the phone to her ear.

"Good," Bensen says. "I hope she's sitting down when she hears your voice!" he adds, wishing he could see his wife's face.

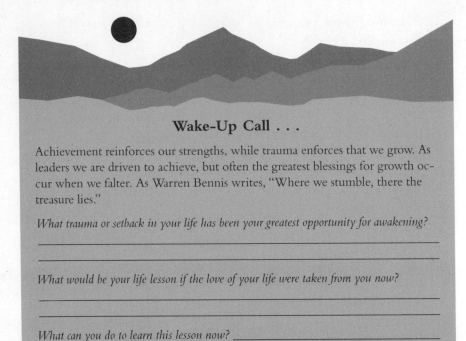

Wake-Up Call . . .

Achievement reinforces our strengths, while trauma enforces that we grow. As leaders we are driven to achieve, but often the greatest blessings for growth occur when we falter. As Warren Bennis writes, "Where we stumble, there the treasure lies."

What trauma or setback in your life has been your greatest opportunity for awakening?

_____

_____

What would be your life lesson if the love of your life were taken from you now?

_____

_____

What can you do to learn this lesson now? _____

_____

_____

Where do you stumble as a leader? What treasure awaits you there? _____

_____

Facing the Demons of Doubt 21

For the first time since the accident, Bensen is in his exercise room before dawn, lifting weights, working the ski machine, sweat pouring off his face and soaking through his dark green T-shirt.

The doctors have confirmed that Katie is going to make a complete recovery. She's had no brain injury. Her mental powers are undiminished, and physically she should be perfectly intact once her bruises and broken bones have healed. No longer bogged down by the constant, nagging worry about her that sapped his vitality and disrupted his concentration, he feels like Superman, bursting with energy and eager to plunge into action to fulfill his plan. Only— what *is* his plan?

He moves to the treadmill and soon falls into a steady jogging rhythm that frees his mind to drift toward an answer.

Emily, clad in bright lemon-yellow sweats—from a competitor, Bensen notices with amusement—comes in to join him, sets the stationary bike to her less demanding level of exertion, and starts to pedal. It's the first time they've been in this room together in years, and both of them feel it is symbolic of the rekindled vibrance and intimacy in their relationship. "It's a new beginning for us, isn't it, Ben, with Katie coming back to us," she says.

"Most definitely," her husband replies as their eyes meet across the room and a warm current of love flows between them. For a while they hardly talk, but this is a silence not of alienation and longing, but of communion.

After a shower and hasty breakfast, Bensen steps out a back door to greet Kenji before leaving for work. He's surprised to see the gardener, about one hundred feet away, talking to a stocky, middle-aged, red-headed man in a business suit. Kenji raises a hand in greeting and motions for Bensen to join them.

"I'd like you to meet a friend of mine, Mick Callaway from Callaway Building Materials," he says as Bensen approaches. Bensen extends his hand and Callaway clasps it enthusiastically. After getting over his surprise that Callaway is a friend of his gardener, Bensen quickly scans through his mental files. Callaway Building is one of the world's largest building supply companies, perhaps *the* largest, and Mick is the founder and president. Anne had mentioned the company in their early-morning brainstorming session a few days ago. They were doing good things for the environment, she said, shifting to recyclable materials instead of petroleum-based, non-degradable and toxic stuff, changes that had required a lot of initial capital and irritated suppliers; but customers loved the changes, and their profits had climbed steadily. She had also enumerated some employee benefits Callaway was offering: stress management, conflict resolution training, prevention and wellness seminars, and other programs for personal and professional development.

"Mick introduced policies at his company that address some of the concerns you and I discussed yesterday," Kenji says, "so without telling him anything specific, I asked him to come talk with you about it. I hope you don't object. I thought it might help you out of your quandary."

"Kenji tells me you're leaning toward some employee-centered innovations," Callaway says, getting right to the point. "I've gotta tell you, Bensen, you'll be happy you went that way, if you do it carefully."

"I've heard something about what you've done at your place," Bensen remarks. "How did you—and how do you now—justify the extra costs? It seems that it would be counterproductive to do the things I'm considering; that's the dilemma Kenji's talking about. The way I see it, if our costs go higher—even if we hike wages up just a notch or two and pour a modest amount of funds into improvements at the factories—then we either maintain competitive pricing and face reduced profit, or we raise prices and price ourselves right out of the market, while our competitors cut our throats. *They* will not increase wages, *they* won't go along with factory upgrades, so they'll gain a competitive edge, our sales will drop, profits will drop, the stock price will drop, and before I know it, the ax will drop—on my neck! I'll be looking for a job, my successor will reverse the policies I initiated, and in the end nothing will have been accomplished."

By the time he finishes his gloomy recitation, Callaway is laughing hard. "Bensen, you're telling it just the way I told it to myself. Frankly, at the time I jumped into making these innovations, I'm not sure I had myself fully convinced I could justify doing it. I did it, as I'll tell you in a second, because it felt like the only way I could look at myself in the mirror. I . . ."

"I understand that," Bensen interrupts.

"I was frightened about it, I have to admit."

"And I understand *that,* too!" Bensen says emphatically.

"I think your analysis is correct," Callaway says, "but it's incomplete. It *is* going to cost you more up front. But you'll see—the entire corporate culture will change. When people are treated with respect and generosity, when they feel that they're part of something good, a team, an organization they can be proud of, their motivation takes a quantum leap upward. This isn't just business-school theorizing, it's real. People work harder and more productively when they're proud of what they're doing, not merely putting in time in order to collect a paycheck."

Callaway's words remind Bensen of the recent HighQuest employee survey and his brief conversation with Hari Rao. Meaningful work, and a sense of participation in company decisions, were more important than money, the young man had said.

"I can promise you," Callaway continues, "based on our experience, that you won't have nearly so much absenteeism, and your employee turnover will be cut in half or even better than that. I don't have to tell you how much money that will save you on executive searches, training new people, and so forth. And here's another thing. I don't have numbers yet to substantiate it—we're still pretty new at this—but it looks to me like there's a lot less stress-related illness. That means your health care costs, and related expenses involving lost time, temporary workers and all that, can drop significantly. I haven't been able to translate this into lower insurance rates yet, but I'm working on it."

"So," Bensen says, "you're saying that from your experience, it's ultimately *beneficial* to the bottom line to take better care of employees?"

"Oh, without question. It's beneficial to the bottom line, and to the entire experience of going to work and being at work! It's so much more enjoyable to be around people who truly want to be there. For myself, I've always loved what I do—the long hours, total involvement, the process of building a company and guiding it, taking an abstract vision, a bunch of ideas, and manifesting it into buildings, employees, products—I'm sure you can relate. But this is a new ball game for me. I feel like I'm leading the company into a new way of doing business."

"That's exactly what I want to do at HighQuest," Bensen says, amazed at what he's hearing. "Let me ask you something else. The other day, one of my top people said that you consider your employees to be a primary constituency, on a par with shareholders. Is this true?"

"That's exactly right, Bensen, exactly right. I know it's politically correct to say that employees are our greatest asset, but how many companies actually act on that idea? The thing is, they *are* our most important asset, and that's why it's so important to invest in them. It's an investment, and it pays off. But if I read you right, you're not thinking of doing this for the payoff. That's where my story comes in, so I might as well tell it to you now. And don't worry," he adds, glancing at his watch, "it's short. I've got a lot of appointments today, too!"

"I'm very grateful for this," Bensen responds. "I have time to listen."

"Good! Well, several years ago, I was kind of toying with these ideas. I was getting an uneasy feeling that times were changing, but business practices weren't—or, to say it better, they *were* changing, sure, but not in what I'd consider a leadership way. They were evolving for the purpose of maintaining growth and profitability, chasing the cheapest labor from country to country, setting up international trade agreements that favored the big players, but all of that wasn't helping people live better lives, and it was devastating the environment.

"I started to see that the company's long-term best interest was different from the short-term goal of showing profit and growth in every quarter. 'I'm a leader,' I said to myself, 'and leaders ought to have a longer-range, more comprehensive view. One that not only benefits ownership, but also brings value to customers, employees, the community, and the environment.'"

"This is very right thinking," Kenji says, joining the conversation for the first time. "Life is an interconnected whole. If you create harm in one place, it affects everything negatively. Poison one finger, you poison the whole body. Similarly, good done anywhere is good done for the whole.'"

Callaway turns to Kenji. "Yes, Kenji. That's exactly the point, clearly stated. Thank you."

Kenji smiles and nods, and Callaway then continues:

"I was feeling that it wouldn't do to look after the interests of a few—in this case, my family and my investors; we're not a public company, you know—while selling products made from nonrenewable natural resources and chemically intensive synthetics that would end up stuffing the earth with thousands of tons of discarded building materials, in utter disregard for the future. I was complying with the regulations about production by-products, but you know how lax the rules are, Bensen. Complying didn't mean a thing; we, and our suppliers, were spewing tons of toxins into the water and the air. How could that be okay?

"I don't remember when I started dwelling on these things, but I found myself caring about it more and more, not wanting to be a contributor to the problem, but not seeing my way clear to doing anything about it, either."

As Callaway speaks, Bensen finds himself nodding in agreement, increasingly drawn into the tale that resonates so closely with his own.

"I guess my dad must have instilled some of that 'old-time religion' of business ethics into me," Callaway continues. "You know, the idea that business is about providing a service, something people need, and that making a profit is legitimate but not the only *raison d'être* for a business enterprise. Anyway, I was thinking about all those things. Then something happened. Do you remember when there was a fire at a New England textile factory, and the plant burned to the ground?"

"Malden Mills," Bensen recalls.

"Exactly. And I presume you remember the rest of the story—how the owner, instead of taking the opportunity to lay off the employees and move operations offshore, where he could save God knows how many millions of dollars, not only committed to rebuilding the facility in the same spot, but also kept the employees, every last one of them, on the payroll the entire time the factory was being rebuilt."

"I remember," Bensen says. "He even gave each of them a Christmas bonus so they could buy presents for their kids. It was a story every cost-conscious CEO in America hated to hear!"

"Yes," Callaway agrees, nodding his head. "Except for me, and maybe a few others. I thought, 'My God, if this guy is willing to spend several million dollars, out of his own pocket and his children's inheritance, to do the right thing, I can risk it too.' That's the moment I understood that without my employees I'd be nowhere, so I'd better start treating them right. And without my integrity, I'd also be nowhere, so it was time to act on what I believed."

"What did you do?" Bensen asks. "How did you start?"

"Well, I wanted to move on two fronts simultaneously. The first—which I don't think applies much to you, so I won't go into it at length—was ecological sustainability. It doesn't take a genius to see that we're mortgaging our children's future. They're the ones who are going to have to pay for the damage we are doing to the earth; they'll have to clean up the pesticides and fertilizers, the radioactive waste; they'll have to suffer and pay for the diseases caused by those unnatural substances. They'll have to pay to get clean water, and a lot more of them are likely to go hungry because of the soil we've depleted and the species we've destroyed. You've read the science, you know as well as I do that all of this is on its way."

"Well, frankly, I haven't looked into it as thoroughly as I should," Bensen admits. "But I understand it enough to get the picture."

"I wanted to redesign how we ran our business so that we took the smallest possible amount from the earth that was not renewable, and put back, as waste products, as little as possible that was toxic or harmful," Callaway explains. "So we studied the materials we used and replaced many of them with natural products made from renewable resources instead of petrochemicals. We implemented massive recycling, which cut down on waste dumped into landfills and decreased the need to purchase new materials. And we retooled our factories to reduce harmful emissions. All of this, of course, didn't come free, but we've already made back our expenses and we're in the black on it; starting next year and on into the foreseeable future, we'll be benefiting by at least eighty million dollars annually."

"Very impressive," Bensen says. "What was the other front? Employee benefits?"

"Right," says Callaway. "What I did there was start talking to people. I asked them what they wanted, what we could do at Callaway Building to make it a place they wanted to come to and spend their day. I listened personally, I gave people some time to meet in groups and come up with ideas, and I assigned qualified staff to interview others. Then we investigated to find out which of the ideas on the table made sense—could we afford it, was there any research supporting it so we could comfortably get behind it—and then we made some choices and started implementing."

"What kinds of things did you do?" Bensen asks.

"Well, right from the start I told them that the lower the cost to us, the more likely it would be that we could make it happen for them, and they responded to that. One thing they definitely wanted was staggered work hours: Some people wanted to come in early, so they could go home and look after their kids when they came home from school. Others of course preferred working later, or in home offices a day or two a week."

"That sounds easy enough."

"It was. And the people affected by those changes were extremely grateful. Another thing we did, which turned out to be great for us, was that some people who commuted a long distance wanted to cut down on travel time. They proposed four ten-hour work days. We asked if it mattered to them which days they worked, if they could be flexible on that. We had a little juggling to do between those who wanted to stick with five eight-hour days and the ten-hour people, but the end result is that we have a fifty-hour work week at corporate headquarters and flexible shifts at our main North American plant, without having to pay overtime, and everybody is happy."

"And it doesn't cost you an extra cent," Bensen remarks. "Except keeping the lights on a little longer."

"Right. It's a win-win situation for all of us."

"I understand that you've also got a lot of programs going—human potential–type stuff."

"Quite a lot," Callaway responds. "Not all at the same time, but available. People come through, facilitators, trainers. I wasn't a big believer in all that—there's a lot of hokum floating around—but we sorted out the ones that make sense for us."

"And you feel—sorry for asking again—you believe it's not money down the drain to keep employees happy, but it has a positive effect on profits?"

"It's not just a belief. I'm sure of it. Actually, I believe that doing what it takes to keep our employees happy is important just for itself, but that's another story. From a purely business standpoint, happy, healthy workers are more productive. They have fewer health and personal problems, and they *create* fewer problems, because they're more reliable, they make fewer mistakes, and they get along better with other people. Their teams are stronger. They do better work. They know we care about them, so they care about us: They gladly give us extra when we need them to. Every penny we put in comes back multiplied."

Bensen is as encouraged by this account as he had been discouraged by Bill Jordan's hasty rejection of his ideas. It's exactly what he needs to hear, and in gratitude he turns to Kenji, who meets his gaze calmly, a slight smile curving his lips, his dark eyes sparkling as ever.

"Profit. Now there's an interesting word, isn't it, gentlemen?" Kenji says. "It usually means *my* profit, *my* gain. What a narrow view! How powerless a man must feel, to be always running after his own welfare, his own 'profit.' How powerful to be free of grasping, and to give from abundance, to have enough to share."

Both men nod enthusiastically, and Callaway adds, "Don't I remember something from the Bible about this—'What does it profit a man to gain the whole world but lose his soul?' or something to that effect?" Kenji's few words of wisdom have taken the conversation from the purely practical to a higher level.

And yet, even Callaway's story and Kenji's sage remarks are not enough to solidify Bensen's resolve. Instead, they activate all the opposing arguments he's been struggling with; a dozen objections rise up and crowd together in his mind. Almost as if anticipating them, Callaway says, "Of course, because we aren't a publicly traded operation, it was easier for me to implement my ideas. Sure, I had to worry about profitability, and about losing employees if my ideas were a bust and the company got in trouble, but I didn't have to worry about my job! I didn't have a conservative Board of Directors putting the brakes on, or a bunch of investment bankers looking to score a short-term gain. I feel for you, having to blast through all that!"

"Thanks," Bensen says, pleased that Callaway acknowledges the difficulty and complexity of his predicament. "But let me ask you this: I can understand how these reforms we're talking about could be cost-effective at corporate headquarters, or at a one-horse operation involving only one or two factories, where finding qualified people takes a long time and training can be a big investment. But I'm dealing with dozens of offshore plants in third world countries, where the supply of cheap labor is endless; people stand in line from before dawn day after day to get a job that pays thirty-five cents an hour. And training takes a few hours or a few days. Why shouldn't I take advantage of that labor supply? And what more am I required to do for them? After all, we're providing jobs for those people. My main responsibility is to my shareholders, and it's to accelerate growth and profitability."

"Let me answer that one point at a time, if you don't mind," Callaway replies. "First, it's true that we don't operate under quite the same conditions as you. Most of our work is done in North America, though some of our factories and suppliers are in other countries. Wherever our production facilities are, we've definitely found that making improvements pays off in greater productivity. Things like investing in new, more efficient machinery, upgrading or installing ventilation and cooling systems, even little things like buying back braces for workers who do heavy lifting. Again, these do cost something up front, but they pay for themselves in a short time."

"Let me ask another question," Bensen says. "I've been feeling that I want to contribute more to the well-being of the workers. I'm seeing that they are not just replaceable parts of a production mechanism, they are human beings, who create the products that make our company successful. They spend more time under the wing of the company than they do with their families.

"So here's the question: Am I here to take advantage of their labor in order to make myself and a few other people rich? Or am I in the privileged position of being able to make a lot of lives better, by serving them and their needs? When I look at it from this perspective, I get excited about raising their standard of living, helping them earn enough money to send their kids to school instead of to the factories; I think of how their neighborhoods could be transformed from slums and dusty wastelands to surroundings even one-tenth as nice as how I live, with trees, beautiful parks and gardens, adequate medical care, maybe a library or a community center for the kids. We expect that our jobs will allow us to provide those basic things for our families. Shouldn't they expect the same?"

Callaway is nodding. "Yes, of course."

"But," Bensen goes on, "then some little devil sits on my shoulder and talks to me in the language of my twenty years of corporate experience, and I think, 'Come off it, Bensen! Get real! Surely those people are already better off because we're there. We're giving them jobs. We're putting food on their plates and a roof over their heads. How far must we go? I can't be responsible for their lives. I can't save the world. Besides, I'm a businessman, not a philanthropist.'" But even as Bensen hears himself speak, he knows he doesn't believe what he's saying.

Kenji, who had been silent for some time, quietly interjects, "Then it comes down to the question of what contribution you want to make, what legacy you want to leave behind you, doesn't it, Bensen? You, like all of us, are part of the continuum of humanity and the great interconnected web of life. When the end comes for you, what you did with your days will either have hurt that continuum and injured the web, or nourished them. It's up to you. Do you want to be known as a driven executive who made lots of money for himself, his company, and a handful of shareholders and bankers, or as a leader who decided to create value for many people?"

Without giving Bensen time to reply, Kenji continues, "Creating jobs is a good thing, Bensen. But it is not enough. People should have jobs that lift them to a better life, just as yours did for you. They should have work in which they are treated with dignity, that helps them use and develop their creative powers. The factories they work in should not pollute the neighborhoods their families live in and create new slums. That is not so hard to do. Why not do it?"

Bensen is chastened by these strong words from his teacher. "Yes, Kenji," he responds. "Why not do it? After all, what has driven me to look at all these things is *not* the question of how to maximize profits. I've been doing that well enough."

"And you can keep doing it," says Callaway. "That's the point of our discussion. Workers work hard for employers who prove by their actions that they care about them. Customers respond to companies that serve their best interests. Think about it: How many times will you keep going to a bank that makes you stand on a long line, or keeps you on hold when you call up for service, while their recorded message continues to say, 'You are very important to us'?"

"True enough," Bensen says. "But people will put up with it for a bargain."

"Oh, I don't know. Do you always buy the least expensive product? I think people are looking for quality, too. And service. And a product they can feel good about buying. If it turns out that adding to your costs necessitates a slight price increase, I'm sure that if you let the world know what you're doing and why, you'll find that many people will buy it, even if it costs a little more.

"That happened for us," he continues. "When we made our master plan for all the changes we were going to make, we allocated a substantial budget for educating our customers, our retailers, even our suppliers, so they'd understand why we were doing what we were doing. We developed written materials, trained our sales force, and pulled out some of our most eloquent employees to act as speakers, to explain how vital it is to stop polluting the environment and using up nonrenewable resources if we are going to leave a sustainable world for our children and grandchildren, a world that can meet the needs of future generations as well as our own. And people understood. I can't tell you how many letters we get, every day, from around the world, from customers thanking us for our courageous policies and our earth-healthy products. People care more than you might think, Bensen. But they don't know what to do about these huge macro-problems. We are leaders. We have the chance."

With those words from Callaway, all three simultaneously feel that the meeting has accomplished its purpose and it is time to end it. "Thank you so much," Bensen says, turning to Callaway, "for your time and your insights, and the inspiration of what you've accomplished. I don't know how many people can appreciate the courage it must have taken for you to do what you did, but I do! And thanks for coming over so early in the morning."

"Think nothing of it," Callaway responds. "Kenji asked me to come. It's a pleasure to do something for him. He asks so little, and gives so much."

Though he's never thought about it before, Bensen realizes the deep truth that has just been spoken. At that moment Kenji says with a chuckle, "So, shall I ask more of you, gentlemen?"

"Anything," Callaway replies.

"Are you sure about that?" Kenji says. "There's an old proverb, 'Be careful what you ask for, lest it be granted!'" he adds, breaking out into full laughter.

———

The reassuring conversation with Callaway, and Kenji's pointed reminder that his time on this planet is limited, so if he is ever going to live up to his values and ideals, now is the time, carry Bensen over the line toward decisive action. But the demon on his shoulder won't give up, and by late afternoon and evening, another set of objections thrusts him back into conflict and indecision.

He sees that if he tries to overhaul the company's way of doing business without first making an open-and-shut case that the proposed innovations will increase market share, profit, and growth, his days at HighQuest are numbered. The Board of Directors will force him out. From their point of view, they would be entirely justified. Looking at the situation from the mindset that has guided him for more than two decades, he's not certain he doesn't agree with them.

Even more bewildering and disturbing are his insights about the factory system that his company is tied into. The more he thinks about it, the more he sinks into despair about even the *possibility* of making positive changes. "Suppose I decide to take the risk and pay the workers more. The owners of the contract facilities, where most of our products are made, would laugh at me. 'High-Quest is only one of our customers,' they would say. 'If the other companies don't want to pay higher wages, how can we make a distinction? The workers work for all of you. We can't pay them thirty-five cents from eight o'clock until nine to sew jackets for your competitors, then sixty cents to do the same tasks for you. How could we manage that?' Or they could say, 'Okay, we'll pay what you want, write us a check' and then keep the money and falsify the books, as Juan Ramon explained. How would we ever know the truth or insure that what we want actually happened?"

The scope and complexity of the situation are daunting, and Bensen, as smart and knowledgeable as he is, hits the wall trying to figure it all out. Should he risk initiating radical change, knowing that he would be putting his career on the line? Is it *worth* the risk, considering that he may not be able to accomplish many of his objectives?

After several days of turmoil, he sees Kenji again. Still struggling with indecisiveness, he bares his heart and begins to reveal the depth of his conflict. To his complete astonishment, for the first time since Bensen has known Kenji, the old man appears irritated. "You've gone over this again and again, Bensen," he snaps. "Are you ready to do it, or aren't you?"

Shocked into momentary silence, Bensen doesn't respond. Kenji asks, "Are you still convinced of the rightness of your motivation—that it's the right thing to do?"

"Yes, I am," Bensen replies.

"Do you believe, after talking with Mick Callaway, that you could implement your ideas in a cost-effective way?"

"Yes. Of course, I can't be certain, but I'm not asking for that. I believe it's possible."

"Then what is holding you back?"

When Bensen fails to answer, Kenji probes again. "Are you afraid to confront the Board?"

"Maybe. I don't know. I'm moving into new territory."

For a few minutes the men fall into one of their not-unusual silences. Finally, risking Kenji's renewed displeasure, Bensen quietly asks, "Have you any suggestions for me, Kenji? You know I never ask; somehow, the questions you pose get me thinking, and seem to generate the insights I need. But I feel truly stuck right now."

"I have only one suggestion," Kenji replies, all traces of annoyance gone. "If you are truly unsure of how to proceed, go deep into your heart. If you remain tangled in the brambles of the intellect, you will never resolve it. Look within to find your true conviction, what you believe, what you stand for."

Kenji pauses after these words, then says with added power, "But once you know, Bensen, that is the time to act with courage. Courage is not the absence of fear: It is doing what is important and meaningful even in the presence of fear. Feel the answer in your heart, have courage, and take action—go the way of a true leader."

———

Early the next morning, before anyone but the janitors has arrived, Bensen is at corporate headquarters, staring out the wall of windows across from his desk at the tops of the trees, ignoring Kenji's suggestions. Instead, he's mentally replaying the factors he wants to consider. He wants to take bold action to pro-

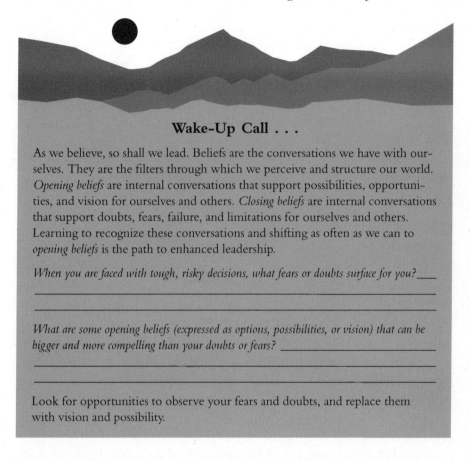

Wake-Up Call . . .

As we believe, so shall we lead. Beliefs are the conversations we have with ourselves. They are the filters through which we perceive and structure our world. *Opening beliefs* are internal conversations that support possibilities, opportunities, and vision for ourselves and others. *Closing beliefs* are internal conversations that support doubts, fears, failure, and limitations for ourselves and others. Learning to recognize these conversations and shifting as often as we can to *opening beliefs* is the path to enhanced leadership.

When you are faced with tough, risky decisions, what fears or doubts surface for you? ____
_____
_____

What are some opening beliefs (expressed as options, possibilities, or vision) that can be bigger and more compelling than your doubts or fears? _____
_____
_____

Look for opportunities to observe your fears and doubts, and replace them with vision and possibility.

vide a higher quality of life for the thousands of workers who make HighQuest products. He wants to take reasonable measures to uplift their communities. And yet, at the same time, he is intent on preserving the dominance of his company in its industry, making a good product, and achieving continued financial success for himself and his family. Is it possible?

Last night, after a day of vacillation, he had gathered Emily and Katie in the living room for a family meeting and asked them how they felt about his decision. If he pushed for the reforms he believed in, and eventually was forced out of HighQuest, would they be upset? Katie, in her direct way, simply said, "Dad, isn't life more than your job?"

Emily at first laughed. "Ben, we already have all the money we'll need for the rest of our lives. And besides, I have my consulting business. Holding on to your position is the last thing we have to worry about."

Later, when the two of them were alone, she added, "Since when do you consult Katie and me about decisions you need to make in the business? We appreciate that you're asking our opinion and checking in with us, but I hope you're not looking for an excuse not to act on what you know is the right thing. It seems to me that leadership is about going beyond what is, having a vision of something better and moving to manifest it, and that's exactly what you want to do here. It's exciting!"

And then this morning, when he went into the kitchen to prepare his coffee, he found this note from her on the kitchen table:

> "Do not go where the path may lead, go instead where there is no path and leave a trail." —Emerson

He finds himself gazing idly at the picture the Mexican family had given him, now sitting on a corner of his desk. In the car on the short drive back from the family's home to the factory, Juan Ramon had explained that it was a painting of the Virgin of Guadeloupe, beloved of the Mexican people since an Aztec, newly converted to Christianity, saw her in a vision near what is now Mexico City in the early 1500s. The pale brown skin, downcast eyes, and gentle expression of her beautiful, youthful face move him deeply. Draped over her head and around her shoulders she wears a dark blue shawl, a night sky sprinkled with stars; rays of golden light stream from her form. Her hands are clasped together in a gesture of prayer and blessing.

As Juan Ramon recited from memory some of the words legend attributes to her, Bensen had been so moved that he took out a notebook and wrote down a few lines. "I am the Mother of the true God, through whom everything lives, the Lord of all things near and far," this lovely apparition had declared. "I am your merciful Mother, the Mother of all who live united in this land, and of all humankind. I will give all my love, my compassion, my help, and my protection to the people. I will hear their weeping and their sorrow, and I will alleviate their many sufferings, needs, and misfortunes."

Dwelling on those words, Bensen is again stirred as he was then, and this time it's not because he's overtired or Katie is in the hospital. For the first time in many years, the doors of his own heart have swung open wide enough for him to hear "the weeping of the world"—not only the suffering of its people, but the cries of its polluted oceans and waterways, its burning forests, its dying species. He sees that what the world requires is an influx of service, of love and compassion, so perfectly symbolized by the tender young mother.

He remembers Kenji telling him to live a life of wholeness. Looking honestly at himself, he's forced to acknowledge that while he has been extraordinarily effective in the realms of action and achievement, moving comfortably in the familiar "masculine" territory of reason, order, and control, he's been sadly deficient in the nourishing qualities of the "feminine," qualities he has long looked upon as weak or inappropriate for a businessman and a leader. Far from being balanced and whole, he has been one-sided. He feels that this image of the mother, so revered by the people of his neighboring country, is somehow asking him to become a more complete human being, and a more effective, authentic leader, by opening his awareness to the deeper values of life and opening his arms to those in need. "Those of us who are blessed with abundance and good fortune," he feels, "have a responsibility to be of service to those who don't have as much."

The picture also reminds him of the people who gave it to him, and of the unspoken but firm commitment to help them that he had made, sitting on the wooden crate in their tiny living room. "Rosa and her husband had the courage to give up the life they knew in search of something better for themselves and their children. Juan Ramon had the courage to risk his job by blowing the whistle on problems in the factory—and to no less than the CEO and Chairman of the Board! Why can't I muster up the guts to do what I feel is right? They had their security to lose, their comfort in a family and a familiar home, a secure job. Is that what I'm afraid of? Losing that? Or of striking out into the new and unknown?

"I've never backed away from a challenge before. But I've always been on a familiar track, the all-American 'success' track, and this is different. This is going beyond the prevailing model, forging a new path. But it's a path that *must* be forged!"

Late in the morning, as he is jotting down points for the staff meeting he has called for early afternoon, Marie buzzes him and says, "There's a woman from an organization called Global Watch on the line. They must be calling for your comments, but why do you suppose they're calling *today,* before that *Times* article I've been hearing about comes out? Do you think they could have heard about it?"

"Well, if *we've* heard about it, why couldn't they?" Bensen responds in a lighthearted way. "I'll take the call."

"You really want to talk with them? I could send her to public relations. She *said* she was returning your call, but I'm afraid I actually laughed when she told me that, I'm sorry."

"It's okay. I *did* call them, though, and I do want to talk with them."

Pressing the flashing light on his phone bank, he says crisply, "Bensen Quinn."

"Mr. Quinn, this is Marcie Lowenthal returning your call. You *did* call, right?"

Bensen laughs. "That I did. You spoke at my daughter's school a few weeks back. Westport High School in Connecticut."

"Yes, a couple of us were there."

"Well, I *wasn't* there, as you might expect. But your message has caught up to me nevertheless. I've looked on your web site and I'm impressed by what you've found out, and what you want to do about it, what you stand for."

"Thank you."

"I've decided to take the initiative in creating an independent factory monitoring system, one that fairly and equally represents the interests of both business and labor, and I'd like to discuss partnering with you on it."

"I'm listening," says Ms. Lowenthal.

"And you're skeptical," Bensen says.

"I shouldn't be?"

He laughs, but then says, "If this is going to work, we're going to have to trust each other's motivations and intentions. But that will come in time. We need to get together and talk it through, and you can judge for yourself."

Bensen can practically feel the disbelief and suspicion on the other end of the line, but he moves ahead. "Here's my idea: If those of us who want a fair inspection system can take the lead in setting it up, then, when my competitors and other companies who do not want this to happen try to disrupt it, we can pressure them—shame them if necessary—into compliance by applying public pressure that we, with the power of our combined forces, can generate. They will try to take control by putting their own people onto the monitoring board, to outnumber us. We've got to be on the lookout for that, and keep it from happening if we want anything real to come of this."

"It sounds like you've given this some thought," Ms. Lowenthal offers.

"Only recently. But—"

"Mr. Quinn," she interrupts, "if you're serious, name the time and place and we'll be there."

"I'll give you back to my assistant to set up a meeting time. But there's one condition I need us to work with at the outset: no inspections for at least six months. HighQuest will be taking unilateral action to begin improvements at our facilities, but I wouldn't want anyone looking at our factories until we've at least gotten started."

It's Ms. Lowenthal's turn to laugh. "I can tell you right now, Mr. Quinn, that your facilities wouldn't have any surprises for us. But we are more than willing to honor your request if you are sincerely going to help make this happen."

"I want to get the wheels turning as quickly as possible, Ms. Lowenthal," Bensen says emphatically. "As quickly as possible."

———

"Ladies and gentlemen," Bensen says to his assembled team of executives and senior managers, "I know there are some urgent matters for us to consider, but I'm preempting them for the moment. I have something important to discuss with you. We won't be able to go into it deeply today, but I want to kick it off this afternoon and then carry it further over the next few days." He pauses, regards them seriously, then grins and says, "When I tell you what I want to do, I know you'll think, 'Poor Bensen's gone around the bend.' Maybe I have. But I've seen something there, a new vision of what could be up ahead for our company, that I must share with you."

In the next half hour, Bensen shocks the group by recounting his trip to *Las Flores maquiladora* and what he saw and felt there. "I am not exaggerating at all," he says, "I'm simply describing to you what factory conditions are like, and how people live. I see that it is making you uncomfortable. Well, it made me more than uncomfortable; it made me resolute to do something about it. I am determined to change both factory conditions and living conditions for the better.

"If I am going to succeed, it will have to be a team effort. I will need you. You know me. When I want something, I am a bulldog. But I can't do it without you. So over the next several days, I want you to free up enough time to discuss this with me, first to hear me out—and to try to talk me out of it, if you want—and then to create a plan together. These sessions will be a prototype for one of the changes I want to make, to some extent at the factories but definitely here at headquarters, toward more employee engagement on all levels of planning and decision making."

He pauses a moment to look at each person in turn, then says, "I would like you to consider this type of thinking in your decisions, strategies, and plans as we move forward."

Again he pauses, considering whether there is anything more he wants to tell them. "There's one more item on my list today," he says. "It's a confession. For the better part of a year, Jim Morris, our Director of Operations for Latin America, tried to get my attention about conditions in those factories. He saw firsthand what was going on, and he didn't like it. But each time he brought it up, I brushed him off. 'Too expensive,' I said. 'It would have a negative impact on share price.' Well, he was right to bring it up, and I was wrong not to listen. I hope I've learned my lesson. In practical terms, that means, if you see something that you think is important, bring it to me. I have a long-standing habit of not listening . . ."

Cautious laughter in the group makes him stop a moment. "But I am going to do my best to turn over a new leaf.

"Okay," he says, "now let's move on to the business at hand. Bob?"

"Bensen, I hope we haven't procrastinated too long on preparing how we're going to respond to the *Times* article. This is our last chance—it's coming out tomorrow."

"I accept full responsibility for the delay," Bensen replies. "Let's tackle our response right now."

"The first piece in their series about globalization," Bob says, "the article featuring our offshore operations, is scheduled for the front page *and* the business section. They're making a very big deal out of it. You know it'll get picked up by the financial networks and everybody else. Everyone loves a scandal. We've got to act decisively. We've drafted a press packet, outlined a Q and A sheet for responding to media inquiries, and written scripts for a couple of TV commercials. We just need approval so we can start printing and shooting. We need you to either sign off on it or add your input." He looks expectantly at Bensen.

"What's the gist?" the CEO inquires.

"The idea is to take a proactive stance," Bob replies, and explains that the company will launch an aggressive PR campaign to put a positive spin on their industry leadership. "Essentially, we'll say we're committed to running a quality operation at our factories, but we don't have complete control because many of the production plants are run by subcontractors rather than the corporation. But now that we know, we're taking care of it. We're proud of our products and the way we've always cared for our employees, and now we'll do even better."

Bensen listens and sees that it would be effective—and that, to a large extent, it is true. But he cannot do it. The intended smokescreen is unacceptable to his awakened conscience; it convinces him even more strongly that he must lead the company in a new direction.

"No," he says. "We can use some of that approach, the part that's true. But what we're going to do is seize leadership of the industry by admitting our mistakes and trying honestly to figure out what to do to improve things."

"That's exactly the spin," says Bob. "That's what we're going to say."

"No, you don't get it," Bensen says. "We're not just going to *say* it, we're going to *do* it."

"Okay, we can do that, Ben," Bob says energetically. "We can clean up one factory, or a couple of them, then invite the media and human rights teams to come see what we've done. It'll be terrific!"

Again Bensen stands firm. "No. This is what I was talking about a few minutes ago. I know it's hard to switch from our usual way of covering our butts and maintaining our image. But that's not going to cut it any more. The truth is, I want to make real changes. In our own factories we can do it more quickly, once we figure out what we can afford and set up a timetable to make incremental changes. In the factories run by contractors, we will have to bear some of the costs, but our contractors will have to pay their share, too. We're a big customer. If we pull out our business, it will hurt. They'll have to at least listen. We'll work with them to get the modifications we want. If that doesn't work, if they won't do it, we'll open more of our own factories, where we can be in control, organize things to our own satisfaction and monitor compliance."

He looks from one to another, engaging each person with his gaze. "Can you see where we are headed?" he says.

"We're starting to," the answer comes.

"Good," Bensen says and beams at his team. "Then in this spirit, let's dig in together and prepare our response to the article."

22 Passing on the Torch

"I wish I had been able to play my role in *Our Town,*" Katie had remarked to a group of friends visiting her in the hospital. Before she was released, and long before she could stand and walk, they had spoken to the drama teacher, chosen a date for a special performance, resurrected the costumes and sets, and reserved the high school auditorium for a one-night-only performance at the beginning of the new school year, "featuring Katie Quinn and the original cast."

As the lights dim, Emily takes Bensen's hand and whispers, "I'm so happy for her tonight."

The community response has been gratifying. Even though most of the parents in attendance had already seen the play at the end of the previous semester, they have turned out again, and when Katie makes her first appearance on stage early in act 1, they pour out their applause so generously that Bensen can see her visibly blush and momentarily stumble over her opening lines. But she picks up and carries on successfully, and the play proceeds.

At the first intermission, community members lavish unusual attention on Emily and Bensen, coming up to them individually and in small groups.

"I'm so happy for you," Brooke Kingsley says, giving Emily a warm hug.

"She seems to be completely recovered," her husband Duane observes.

"Oh yes," Emily concurs. "Her physical therapy sessions are finished now; she's dancing again, back on the soccer team, totally immersed in her *very* active life. We couldn't keep up with her if we tried."

"I shudder to think of what you went through," Brooke remarks, shaking her head.

"It was no fun," Emily replies. "We thank God every day for her now."

Bensen chuckles and addresses the small circle of friends gathered around them in the lobby. "It's amazing. The exact same things that worried us—and irritated the hell out of us!—before the accident, things like her clothes, her choice of music, the posters on the walls of her room, all have a completely different meaning."

Brooke nods knowingly, but Duane asks, "How do you mean?"

"Well," Bensen says, "we're so grateful to have her back, to have her with us, where we can see her, hug her. . . ." His voice breaks off.

"What my husband is trying to say," Emily continues, "is that when she was in the coma, we realized that all of the things that used to bother us were absolutely unimportant; what mattered was that she recover, and get to live her life."

"Well, I hope you can hold on to that when she *plays* that music, or stays out too late," Duane says, only half joking.

"It's a bit of a challenge," Bensen acknowledges. "It's easy to fall back into old patterns. But our bottom line now, which we never forget, is that we love her and we're thankful to have her unique and wonderful spirit in our lives and our home."

"Bravo!" Brooke says. "It's a lesson for all of us, a great reminder of what really matters."

The third act of the play opens in a cemetery on a hill above the town of Grover's Corners, and Bensen, already emotionally stirred by Katie's acting and the response of his friends and acquaintances, is further shaken when the narrator says, "People wild with grief have brought their relatives up to this hill. . . ." He feels how close he came to experiencing that ultimate grief with his daughter.

Then, as the narrator continues, some beautiful lines remind him of an awareness that is opening up to him, a ripening fruit of Kenji's teachings:

> Now there are some things we all know, but we don't take'm out and look at'm very often. We all know that *something* is eternal. And it ain't houses and it ain't names, and it ain't earth, and it ain't even the stars . . . everybody knows in their bones that *something* is eternal . . . All the greatest people ever lived have been telling us that for five thousand years and yet you'd be surprised how people are always losing hold of it. There's something way down deep that's eternal about every human being.

Feeling the truth of that, Bensen feels grateful for his teacher, and resolves to thank him directly, next time he sees him, for his help and the insights he has offered. "But where is he?" Bensen wonders, drifting away from the play for a moment. "I haven't seen him for a long time, it seems." He turns to Emily and almost asks her about it, but she is absorbed in the play.

The character that Katie is playing has died as a young mother, giving birth to her second child. Arriving in the town cemetery still attached to her husband and children, to her farm and home, she asks to go back from the dead to the living, and is allowed to do so. But what she finds deeply upsets her. It seems that people are living very superficial lives, not feeling truly alive, not genuinely relating with one another. "Oh Mama," she laments, "just look at me one minute as though you really saw me."

"They're sort of shut up in little boxes," she remarks. "How in the dark live persons are."

Now for the first time she truly appreciates how wonderful life is, and how beautiful her parents were: "They're so young and beautiful. Why did they ever have to get old? . . . I love you all, everything.—I can't look at everything hard enough."

Finally, she can't bear the poignancy of it, and she asks to return to the world of the dead. "I can't go on," she cries. "It goes so fast. We don't have time to look at one another . . . I didn't realize. All that was going on and we never noticed. Take me back—up the hill—to my grave. But first: Wait! One more look.

> Good-by, Good-by world. Good-by, Grover's Corners . . . Oh, earth, you're too wonderful for anybody to realize you.
>
> Do any human beings ever realize life while they live it?—every, every minute?

In this moment, Bensen realizes it, and feels grateful and content.

———

The satisfaction and quiet joy of the evening are still with him the following morning. Arising, as usual, before the others in his small household, he goes to his workout room, but instead of tuning in to the usual bombardment of media information while exercising, he spends the time taking stock of his life. As he looks at how things are unfolding, he realizes that he has every reason to feel satisfied.

At work, despite ongoing problems in the broader economy, HighQuest is continuing to do well. Earnings aren't matching the high-water marks of a few years back, but they are sufficient to generate substantial profits. And equally important, the wheels are turning rapidly on the factory restructuring he has initiated. The work groups he has set up, to study what could realistically be done to fulfill his new vision for the company, are coming in with ideas for implementation. His senior executives are not yet solidly committed to his new approach, but they are increasingly open; several have come to him privately and pledged their support.

The partnership with Global Watch, the corporate watchdog organization, is taking shape. Their fierce antibusiness attitude has sometimes angered him and several times made him almost walk out of negotiations and drop the whole idea, but he reached a critical turning point when he understood that their viewpoint came from years of observing and trying to combat corporate abuses. In their zeal for reform, Marcie Lowenthal and the others in her organization had been as blind to the positive aspects of business as he had been unwilling to see the dark side. Gradually they've hammered out a middle ground, and, he feels, grown as individuals, developing a more tolerant, universal view as they've structured an action plan to help insure that companies they monitor will operate in a fair and balanced way.

On the home front, Katie is, as she was as a little girl, the joy of his life, but now she is also becoming a friend. She has responded enthusiastically to the turnaround she perceives in her father. Between his sincere efforts to stay connected with her life and concerns, and his passion to bring a more values-driven approach to the company and contribute more meaningfully to the community—motivations entirely foreign to the Bensen Quinn she grew up with—the gap between them has all but disappeared.

Bensen and Emily are closer than they've been in years, having come through the crisis with greater love and appreciation for one another. Emily is beginning to trust that the changes in him are real and permanent, and is opening up to reconnection and a renewal of their love. Like Katie, she is delighted at the direction his energies have taken, but for her own reasons. Though her respect for her husband's character and exceptional level of achievement never wavered, at times she wondered if she had misread his nature: Could it be that his humanitarian impulse, so important in drawing them together, did not go deep, but was only a youthful phase? She had hoped expectantly for a revival of it, and felt sad when that renewal did not come. Now that it has, she is contemplating a more active partnership role in his work, drawing upon what she's learned in her career as a consultant.

The icing on Bensen's cake is that, unknown to anyone else, unseen but profoundly meaningful, the spiritual dimension of his life—completely outside the borders of his concern until a few short months ago—has blossomed, putting him in touch with a place in his own being that is both stable and full of joy, peaceful yet a surprising wellspring of creative inspiration. It was this that he was reminded of last night, when the lines about the "eternal in us all" were spoken.

It's a crisp autumn morning, and after his workout and a shower he goes to the kitchen for his morning coffee-making ritual, then carries his mug out to the garden. As always in these early hours that he loves, it is quiet and serene. Many of the flowers are gone now, and the chorus of birds has thinned, but the turning leaves are creating a new panorama of color, rich with orange, red, and gold.

His thoughts turn to Kenji, who has not only manifested this visible sanctuary of beauty, but has also given him the tools to build an invisible *inner* sanctuary that he now carries with him into all he does. Once again he feels an upsurge of gratitude to this man for the lessons he has taught him, and for their friendship. But then he remembers his thoughts at the play: Where *is* Kenji? It seems he hasn't been here for quite a few days.

Bensen walks to a wilder, less cultivated part of the property, among a stand of old oak trees, where Kenji had fashioned a small shed to house his tools and supplies. The shed is closed and no one is around. Concerned, he goes back into the house. Emily is downstairs now, and he asks her, "Isn't Kenji supposed to come today?"

"Yes, it's one of his regular days; he should be here."

"He's not around anywhere. I'm feeling a little concerned."

"Maybe he just didn't feel like coming over so early. He's getting older, you know. Don't worry, he'll show up."

She has hardly finished speaking when the telephone rings. "Mr. Quinn?" the voice at the other end inquires. "This is Shichiro, Kenji Ueki's son. My father asked me to call and tell you that he isn't able to come over today; he's feeling quite ill."

"Oh, I'm sorry to hear that. It's nothing serious, is it?"

"Oh. You don't know."

"Know what?"

"About my father's cancer. I guess he never told you."

"*Cancer?*"

"He's actually exceeded the doctors' predictions by quite a long period. Four years ago, they gave him no more than a year to live."

Bensen is stunned. "I'm so sorry to hear this news. I didn't know. I had no idea. Is there anything I can do?"

"No, thank you. He's in bed now, resting. If his strength comes back, I'm sure you'll see him. You know how much he loves his work. He'll want to continue if he's able."

"Would you mind if I call to see how he's doing?"

"That would be fine."

"And if there's anything I can do, please let me know."

Dazed, Bensen stares out the window, barely able to convey to Emily what he has just learned. Suddenly the garden looks more barren than beautiful; dried leaves are blowing off in the chill wind, and some of the branches are already bare.

As he sits in silence, the events, revelations, and transformations of the past few months pass before his awareness, and he realizes how important this man has become to him in such a short time, how much he has influenced his life. He feels that Kenji's wisdom and compassion, and his willingness to patiently listen and to talk, have come as a priceless gift, a kind of blessing at a difficult time. With clarity and force the thought comes, "This man gave me back my life as he was losing his . . . and I didn't even know it. What can I do to repay him?"

He feels a compelling desire to connect with Kenji, if for no other reason than to show his appreciation and gratitude before it's too late. He reaches for the phone and returns the call to Kenji's house.

"I know there may be nothing I can do," he tells Shichiro, "but your father has been very important to me. I would like to come over and express my gratitude to him, if that would be all right."

"I know that you have also meant much to him. I'll ask him. Please hold on."

After a minute, the son returns. "My father would be delighted to see you. But please be aware—even though it's only a few days since you've seen him, he is quite weak."

"I won't stay long," Bensen promises.

———

After reshuffling his morning responsibilities, Bensen drives to the part of town where Kenji lives, glancing occasionally at the directions scribbled on a square of paper he has stuck to the dashboard. The modest residential neighborhood is away from the route he takes to work, and unfamiliar to him. The houses are small and simple, mostly older, wood-frame structures with their front yards neglected, their porches cluttered with an assortment of toys and tricycles. As he makes the turn onto Kenji's street, a house down the block captures his attention. It's not visually compelling, neither flashy nor discernibly different from the others. Yet it seems to have a kind of aura, a special quality he can't see, and he knows: That's Kenji's house. He drives up and parks in front without even looking at the number, then sits for a moment before getting out, captivated by the feeling of the house, appreciating the tidiness of the front yard, the carefully cropped hedges and orderly flower beds. "This is what he's about," Bensen thinks, "this simple elegance, this gracefulness."

As he's about to put his finger to the bell, the door swings open and a tiny gray-haired Asian woman is standing before him. "Mr. Quinn?"

"Yes."

"I'm Ueki-San's wife. Please come in." As he steps over the threshold she says warmly, "I've heard so much about you from my husband."

"Really, he spoke of me?"

"Oh yes. He has enormous respect for you."

"He has respect for *me*? He's helped me so much. Your husband has been very important to me, and I am grateful to him. Deeply grateful."

She smiles and bows slightly, her face lighting up.

"I had no idea he was ill," Bensen says.

"He does not speak of it much. It is, it seems, of no great consequence to him. Even the pain he takes in stride." After a pause, she surprises Bensen by confiding, "But it is not easy for me. We're life partners. Even though we married late, we've been together for forty-seven years. I will miss him."

"Perhaps he'll regain his strength and surprise everyone, and you will have more good years together," he says in an effort to comfort her.

"Perhaps," she replies. "But come, I'll take you to him." As they walk through the living room toward the bedrooms at the back of the house, Bensen eagerly soaks up the atmosphere, wanting to make both the observable beauty and the subtle feeling of the place part of himself. The home is furnished in a simple Japanese style, uncluttered, with strong, clean lines and much empty space. The floors are beautiful hardwood, and most of the furniture is also made of richly textured, exquisitely crafted wood. A few subtly colored ink-brush landscape paintings of pine trees and mist-shrouded mountains, and two or three energetic, spontaneously drawn calligraphy panels hang on the walls. A large hand-thrown ceramic platter stands upright on a wooden shelf; graceful vases support large bouquets or a few simple flowers artfully arranged. Bright light pours in through the many windows, through which he can see gardens more elaborate and whimsical than in the small, more conventional front yard. Inside and out, a sense of order and harmony prevails.

Kenji's wife escorts him to the threshold of her husband's room, leans toward him and whispers, "Please have regard for his strength," and leaves him. As he stands at the threshold a palpable silence washes over him like a soft wave. Kenji is in bed, half propped up by pillows so that he is almost sitting. His eyes are closed and he looks entirely serene. Katie also looked peaceful, Bensen thinks, but she was gone, her consciousness shut down or, perhaps, in some faraway place, out of reach; by contrast, Kenji is an extremely alive presence. Even though the eyes are closed, Bensen can feel the liveliness of his teacher's spirit.

Unsure whether to disturb him, Bensen continues standing silently at the threshold. Without moving or opening his eyes, Kenji says softly, "Thank you for coming, Bensen. I've been waiting for you."

Surprised, Bensen steps into the room. "How did you know it was me?"

"I've always known who you are," Kenji replies in the same quiet voice, "even when you did not."

"That's so true, Kenji. You always knew how to bring out my best. I've been thinking about that, and wanting to tell you how grateful I am."

Kenji looks pleased, but makes no reply. Bensen, unsure how to continue, says, "I was glad for the chance to meet your wife. She seems like an extraordinary person."

At this remark Kenji opens his eyes, looks at his visitor and says, "I've had many teachers in my life, but Keiko has been the most important."

Once more, silence takes over. Then Bensen says, "Katie's started dancing again. She's completely fine, just as you said she would be. We went to see her in a play last night, at the high school."

"I'm very happy for you. For all of you," Kenji responds.

"When you told me that she would recover, I was too frightened and traumatized to trust," Bensen says. For another minute, no one speaks. Bensen floats in memory to that first conversation with Kenji, and when he recalls his teacher's words—"She will be okay. And *you* will be okay, too"—he feels the same surge of electric power in his body that he had felt then.

"Bensen, please sit down," says Kenji, glancing toward a chair at the side of the bed farthest from the door. Bensen crosses the room, and as he sits down and looks around, a feeling of discomfort comes over him. Kenji seems so alive and his mind so clear, but on some deep, instinctive level Bensen knows that he is approaching his end, that this is very likely his deathbed and these his final days or weeks. Even though he's thought about death a lot in recent weeks, he's had little actual contact with it, or with the process of dying, and he feels unprepared and unsure of himself.

"What is it, Bensen?"

Bensen laughs self-consciously. "How do you always know what I'm thinking?"

"I don't always know," Kenji says. "But"—turning to Bensen with a playful grin—"what is it that you want to say?"

Bensen can see that although *he* is feeling ill at ease, Kenji is his usual self, unperturbed, even-minded, and even now full of the joy of life. He feels emboldened to ask, "Kenji, are you afraid to die?"

This seems to amuse Kenji, who chuckles and replies, "You know, Bensen, we're all like perennials—those flowers that bloom, fade, and come back the following year. We sprout, we blossom as fully as we are able, then our bodies decline and decay, and we go away. I know that my nature, my essence, is the same as the enduring life in those perennials. Forms come and go; Essence never dies. So, to answer your question, no, I am not afraid."

"I'm glad to hear it. Perhaps I'm more afraid than you are. Whenever the end comes for you, I will miss you very much."

"I cherish our friendship too, Bensen," Kenji says, and holds out his hand. Bensen takes it, realizing that this is the first time, in all the years they have known each other, that they have physically touched. Kenji's hand is warm, but his grip, for a man accustomed to physical labor, has little strength. For a full minute, perhaps more, they remain like that.

"But to speak to your concern," Kenji says, picking up where they had left off, "it is not the end, it is just a passing stage. This Kenji body that you see before you, *that* will have an end. But I—who I truly am—will always be with you."

"Then permit me to ask you something else," Bensen says. "You know how well off I am." He pauses. "This is difficult to do graciously. I simply want to offer to help you in any way I can, including financially. If you could use some assistance, with medical bills, extra care, hospital costs, anything—I would be more than happy to help, and I beg you to accept the offer."

Kenji laughs a hearty laugh, which puzzles Bensen, who fails to see the humor in it. "I mean it sincerely," he says.

"Your offer is very kind, my friend. But we are financially comfortable. There will be no need of help. Your generosity is appreciated, I assure you." Then he continues, "Bensen, thank you for coming to see me, for sharing your joy about your daughter, and for offering to share your means with me. I have something important to share with you, too."

"What could that be? You've given me everything."

"I know *your* story, Bensen. But you don't know mine. I think it's important now that you know my story. Please listen, I want to talk to you for a while."

"Do you have enough energy? I promised your family I wouldn't tire you out."

Again Kenji laughs. "I have as much energy as I need," he says.

———

"I have not always been a gardener," he begins. "Nor have I always been a guide, a gardener of souls. My life was much like yours when I was a young man." Closing his eyes as if to look into the past unencumbered by his present surroundings, Kenji says, "I was born in nineteen hundred and twenty-three and grew up in a village of farmers and simple country people. My parents had a tiny house and a small plot of ground, where they grew most of our food. Both of them worked in the community's rice paddies and took their allotted portion of the yield. We lived close enough to the sea to exchange rice and vegetables for freshly caught fish. So, although we were certainly poor, I don't remember ever being aware of it. If I had to go to bed hungry once in a while, it didn't seem to matter. My parents were there, and my two sisters; there were fields to play in, frogs to catch, and friends to join me in all sorts of mischief.

"Of course, all the children had many chores. We didn't have hours every day to idle away with games and television; there was always work to be done. I was fortunate in that most of what I was asked to do, I enjoyed. My greatest pleasure was working with the garden. Every part of it was satisfying: preparing the ground, digging out rocks, planting seeds or placing the seedlings my father would carefully nurture, removing weeds. I loved watching things grow.

"My father must have loved it too. I am grateful to him for initiating me into the mysteries of the garden, not as some necessary drudgery, but carefully protecting my child's sense of the miraculous. I distinctly remember the spring morning he first took me out to work with him. I was very small, perhaps only three or four years old. He knelt in the garden next to me—I can still smell the freshly turned soil, and see the worms wriggling in the black earth. He had one hand conspicuously closed in a fist, and I knew he wanted me to ask him about it, so I said, 'What do you have in your hand?'

"'Melons,' he said, and I laughed, because no hand, not even a giant's, was big enough to hold melons! Then he unclasped his hand and showed me about a dozen seeds.

"'We will plant these,' he said, 'and you will see: they are really melons. *They* know what they are; they only need a little help from us and they will grow.' Every day I watched the little mounds of earth he had built up for those melon seeds; I ran to him when the first sprouts appeared; and at the end of summer, when the melons were ripe and too heavy for me to carry, I sat with him in the grass at the edge of the garden plot, watched him slice open the first one, and shared with him the cool, sweet, miraculous fruit, carefully saving the precious seeds.

"I also remember vividly all the fruit trees that grew in front of our house and around the village. I recall the joy I felt each and every spring, when the plum blossoms came out, white and pink, or the apple blossoms, and the air was filled with their delicate fragrance. It was like living in heaven."

Kenji stops talking, his eyes still closed, savoring the memories. Then his mood seems to shift. "By the time I was eleven or twelve," he says, "the Great Depression that swept across the world had reached our little village, too. I don't believe it was as bad for us as it was in the cities: There were no factories or big businesses for people to lose jobs, and most everyone had a place to live or family to take them in. But we were aware of it, and we were also aware, as the decade progressed, of the feverish, nationalistic buildup toward expansion of the Empire. Some of the boys my age, of course, got caught up in the fervor of it; boys always do. They are led to believe that war is some grand and glorious celebration, and they are always shocked when they come face to face with its brutality and unrelenting horror."

"You speak of it like someone who saw it," Bensen says.

"I saw it. But I knew before I saw. I don't understand why everyone doesn't; it seems so obvious. Yet always people are surprised. In our case, they were more than surprised, they were stunned and disbelieving. No one thought we could lose the war, or even that it could come to our shores, our cities; no one foresaw the horrible devastation, the misery and destruction, the demolished buildings and torn-up streets, the horrible smell of the dead, the mothers and young widows wailing for their lost. . . ."

Kenji pauses in his recollections, and looks Bensen in the eyes. "I don't know why no one saw it coming. Every tradition teaches the law of cause and effect, 'as you sow, so shall you reap.' Your Jesus made it even more clear: 'Those who live by the sword shall perish by the sword.' What did we expect would happen?"

Again Kenji pauses. "Perhaps we will always have war, we humans," he says. "But we must always do what we can to prevent it."

Bensen is stirred by the force of Kenji's words, and his ardent resolve to live up to them. He also sees that behind the bright, clear eyes the memory of suffering—his own and others'—still remains, and casts a shadow on his joyful spirit. With sadness, he perceives his teacher's age and his fragility, his mortality, his vulnerability. He had grown accustomed to seeing only his wisdom and power.

"When the war ended," Kenji says, continuing with the tale of his life, "I made a mistake, the worst mistake of my life. I'm ashamed of it now. How did I react to the horror that I experienced? Did I vow to do my part, so that war would never again happen? Did I, in recognition of the inevitable pain and suffering of human life, seek a spiritual life? That way, I could at least try to save my own soul, and perhaps, if I turned out to be a good student, I might gain enough insight to help lead humanity out of the cycle of delusion, violence, and destruction. No, I did neither. I became afraid for myself and insecure about my future, and I clutched at the raft of material success.

"Like so many people, I was desperately poor at the end of the war. I determined to go to the opposite extreme, to become wealthy, so that I would never suffer want again. Through a distant relative, I made contact with a man who had a prominent position in the automobile industry. This man got me a modest office job, but he kept his eye on me, and if I earned it, he saw to it that I was rapidly promoted. In quite a short time, I rose to a high level and began to make a substantial income.

"I thrived on the accomplishment and on the energy of success building on success. I was astute at making deals and expanding the business, so I did a lot of international traveling, met many powerful people. I had lots of subordinates.

I was well known and admired. I also invested in the Tokyo stock market, which, as I'm sure you remember, enjoyed tremendous growth before its decline in recent times. My fortune quickly grew. Everyone thought I was a big success.

"But I began to feel, deep in my heart, that something was missing, that my work wasn't connected to my essence and to my true values. In terms of our conversations, Bensen, I would say that I wasn't building a legacy I could look at with pride. Oh, I was proud of my accomplishments, day to day; it always feels good to do things well and to meet challenges successfully. But where was it all going, what was it for? It didn't appear to be leading to anything meaningful or worthwhile. Selling more and more cars? So what? It wasn't what *I* wanted to create. It wasn't the music of my soul or my heart. It wasn't authentic.

"I won't trouble you with the whole story of my internal struggles and my decision to leave my position. It was difficult enough to reach that conclusion—it was completely impractical and against all the values and standards of the culture—but when I did, the people around me made it virtually impossible to follow through. Back then, you see, a top position like mine was considered a lifetime commitment, by the company as well as the individual. No one wanted me to step down, and they practically forced me to take a leave of absence rather than submit my resignation. But I knew I would never go back.

"Being retired was, at first, even more difficult than reporting for a job I didn't feel enthusiastic about. After working twelve to fourteen hours a day, suddenly I had no focus, and I didn't know what to do with myself. I was still a relatively young man, in my mid-forties, and I knew I had years ahead of me. I wanted to do something meaningful with them, but I didn't know what.

"Then, one summer day, sitting outside on the terrace of my house, I was served some sliced fruit and melon for an afternoon refreshment, and in an instant I was back kneeling in the earth of the garden with my father, planting seeds. In that moment, I knew what I wanted to do. I wanted a simpler life, connected to my roots, if you'll pardon the expression. I wanted to get back in touch with the earth and the feel of being surrounded by growing things, the smells and textures of plants, the songs of birds, the sounds of the wind and water.

"When I told this to my friends, they laughed. They thought, 'Kenji has a few loose wires, but let him try. He'll soon get tired of having dirt under his fingernails, and he'll be back at his desk.' But I found that creating beautiful gardens enlivened the music of my soul.

"The more I studied the art of gardening and landscape design, the more I realized that I could create sanctuaries for people like you, sanctuaries for people's souls to come forward. Having the courage to take that first step opened everything for me. Working with plants became the gateway to living my *true* purpose: working with people as a gardener of souls, a cultivator of the spirit, so their full potential can blossom and unfold.

"I was very, very fortunate that, when I was going through my crisis, I met a man who was a true spiritual teacher. He was a simple monk, not a priest or a scholar, and he was completely invisible to the public. But people knew that he was a man of great realization; he knew the truth about things. He was my guide through those months of turmoil and indecision, and it was he who set me on the path of living a spiritual life."

"Kenji," Benson breaks in, "do you think that a simple life—a life with less stress and strain—is necessary to lead a more spiritual life?"

"It can definitely help. A simpler life carries fewer distractions, and one doesn't get as tired. Most everybody these days is busy with endless tasks and concerns, bills and mortgage payments, family members to worry about, office intrigues—even you, with your secretaries and assistants to help you, don't you often find yourself too preoccupied to think about important things, too busy to settle down even for a few minutes?"

"Yes, I do. Even though I've found the wisdom you've given me immensely valuable, it takes great determination to carve out time to put it into practice each day. That's why I'm bringing up the question."

"The short answer is that simplicity is good," Kenji says. "But we each have our own path. For some people, a quieter, more circumscribed life would be boring, and they'd feel restless and constrained; that could be stressful in itself, don't you think? I'm sure that's how I would have felt, when I was a young man full of ambition. What I needed was a way to maintain equilibrium inside while I was spinning in the whirlwinds of business."

"Like the calm at the eye of the storm," says Bensen. "Yes, I can think of many, many days when that ability would have served me well!"

"And you will have it, more and more."

"I asked you about simplicity because I've been wondering about something," Bensen ventures somewhat hesitantly. "You know I've been going through a crisis of meaning in my life, like the one you just related to me. Maybe I've come to the wrong conclusion about how to resolve it, with my grand plans to revolutionize the company and all that. Maybe I should cash in my stock options, get out of the business, and create a simple, beautiful life like yours. I also love to grow things; maybe I should even become a gardener."

At these words from his student, Kenji's smile unfurls into a roar of laughter. He laughs so hard that his wife and son come to the doorway, thinking something is wrong. "I'm fine," he says, waving them off. "And don't blame Mr. Quinn! I'm just a silly old fool, I laugh at everything."

Turning back to Bensen he says, "The thing is, you *are* a gardener, Bensen. But you're a different gardener from me, with a very different garden. Your garden is the family you have now, the business you have now, and the broader world that the business affects. Tend to that. Nurture that. My teaching is not about cultivating a different life, it's about standing fully awake in *your* life."

Kenji closes his eyes, takes a deep breath, and becomes still. It seems like several minutes before he speaks again. "Decades ago, when I was going through my spiritual crisis," he says, "my 'crisis of meaning' as you aptly put it a moment ago, it was considered acceptable for someone with my feelings of disquiet and discontent to go off to a monastery in quest of enlightenment. People understood that material existence—ordinary daily life—cannot possibly bring the fulfillment we human beings seek. There's nothing wrong with it, of course, it's just incomplete; trying to be satisfied with it is like trying to be nourished and satisfied with the outer skin of the orange without ever getting to the sweet, juicy fruit inside.

"I believe many people are waking up to this awareness today. They're not sure what they are looking for, or even precisely what it is that they're missing, but they know intuitively, instinctively, that they need something more, that life is far greater than the daily grind. Of course, you and I know that what they long for is to penetrate the skin of the orange; they need to connect with their inmost being and deepest purpose."

"Yes," says Bensen. "Then even the daily grind lights up with the glow of that inner richness."

Kenji responds with pleasure to Bensen's comment. "Yes, Bensen. And that's why I'm telling you this story. My natural reaction, when my teacher helped me open to the deeper truth of my nature, was to think of becoming a monk, too, like him; I thought it might help me pursue the path more devotedly. But he wouldn't hear of it. He helped me see that my mission was *to live a spiritual life in the world*. And I believe I've found a way to do that."

"You certainly have, Kenji."

"I believe it is the way for most people. I do not see many lining up at the monastery gates!"

"Nor are they likely to," Bensen concurs.

"So what I want to ensure—the one important task I have left to perform—is that others will have the opportunity to find this way, too, and benefit from it."

Again Kenji grows silent and looks thoughtful. "Bensen, right now your growth is exhilarating. New horizons are opening up to you quickly, both inwardly and everywhere you turn. Quite naturally, you feel grateful for it all—for your daughter's recovery, your fortunate marriage, the opportunities you have created for yourself in the business world. And not least of all, you are grateful to me—I know, I feel it—for the seeds I have sown in your heart.

"Your pace of growth and transformation will not slow down. Soon—very soon, I believe—you will find yourself living a life of great fullness. It is already happening. A few days ago you told me that sometimes you feel you have everything a man could want."

Bensen nods in agreement, and Kenji continues: "Not everyone who has material abundance feels that way."

"That's for sure!" Bensen snorts.

"It is a product of inner contentment," Kenji says. "As you said then, the more contented and fulfilled you become, the less you feel driven to seek anything for yourself."

"Yes," Bensen affirms. "It's very liberating."

"As this becomes your natural state, your values and concerns will shift. What you will come to cherish and appreciate above all, what will give your life meaning and purpose, will be the opportunity to give to others, to use your leadership to serve.

"You are not fully there yet, and I do not mean to rush you. As a gardener, I know that all things ripen and blossom in their own time. But the day is coming when you will experience a joy deeper than anything you have ever known, when you see other people start to wake up in the garden of their lives, as you have done. And you will be the catalyst, the instrument for their awakening, a true leader of life.

"When you first came into the room this morning, and you thanked me for helping to bring out the best in you, I didn't say anything, but I assure you, my friend, there is nothing in my life—nothing—that gives me a greater sense of having lived meaningfully.

"You have been unaware of your true destiny, Bensen, but I have not. While you were busy building your business and raising your family, I have been watching you, learning about you."

"You worked at my home for eight years," Bensen says, "and I barely spoke to you, other than to say good morning. And you rarely spoke to me. If you knew I had important lessons to learn, why didn't you approach me?"

Kenji chuckles. "And would Bensen Quinn, CEO, have listened to the wisdom of his old gardener?"

"You're right," Bensen says, looking down in embarrassment. "I wouldn't have paid any attention."

"You weren't ready to hear. There's an old saying, 'When the student is ready, the teacher will come.' Unfortunately, a crisis is usually necessary before people are willing to listen, to be open to something new. Now that you are listening—and you *are* listening, aren't you, Bensen?—now I must tell you that you are destined to be a special kind of gardener. The most precious gardeners are those whose garden is life itself. The ones who grow the ungrowable, without tool, wheelbarrow, or shovel. They neither plant nor water; their medium is spirit, authenticity, purpose. Whatever their presence touches enriches life. You, Bensen, are a gardener of life."

Bensen's heart thrills at his teacher's words. But at the same time, doubt makes him hesitate. "I have so much to learn," he objects, "so far to grow. This is all so new to me."

Kenji doesn't allow him to pursue this line of thought. "I've never asked you to do anything, Bensen," he says, "but now I'm going to. I've passed on to you what my teachers have given me. Now it's your turn. As the seed receives its life from the parent tree, and in turn creates a new tree, which generates new seeds, it's time for you to start handing on what you have learned."

"What would I do?" Bensen asks.

"You have already begun. The plans you are making for your business and the more conscious way you've begun relating to people signal to me that you are integrating this knowledge into your life. These changes are the fruits of the knowledge. Now I would like you to accept responsibility for passing on the knowledge itself: planting the seeds so that others may blossom and bear fruit, too. Will you promise that to me?"

"What makes you think I could do that? I'm a businessman, not a teacher. I do feel more kindly disposed toward others than I have in the past, but I'm not a humanitarian."

"What specifically to do, you will decide, as time and circumstances present themselves to you."

"Time! That's another problem. Where would I find time to do this?"

"What I am asking," Kenji states patiently, "is that you treat all that you have learned as not for you alone, and that you carry on this tradition, the tradition of gardeners of life. Take it, and use it in the service of humanity and the service of a better world, in all that you do."

In his heart, Bensen wants to say "Yes!" to this, or to anything his teacher might ask of him. But he comprehends the magnitude of what is being required of him, and holds back. "This is not about respecting or pleasing him," he thinks. "It's about *being* him, *becoming* a Kenji, a teacher. Can I do this? Am I worthy of it? Am I ready? If I promise, I have to be able to keep the pledge."

Without missing a beat Kenji says, looking him in the eyes, "You *are* ready, Bensen."

Returning his teacher's powerful gaze, Bensen feels a warmth and strength penetrate his body. Suddenly he realizes—and he laughs aloud at his denseness at not realizing it before—that Kenji is not *asking* something of him; he is *offering* something, sharing the most precious part of his own life with him, entrusting him with a sacred task. His resistance melts, and as it dissolves he feels his awareness open and fill with a soft glow, suffusing his body and expanding to fill the room.

"If you wish me to carry on the teachings you have given me, Kenji," he says, "I promise you with all my heart that I will do it."

"Bensen," his teacher says, "your torch has been lit. Now go and spread the light."

Wake-Up Call . . .

Recently a client burst into my office and announced, "I finally get it. I'm a torch!" Amused, I responded, "Well, that's just great . . . and what exactly have you lit lately?" Without hesitation he passionately responded, "People! I'm a catalyst to ignite other people's energy."

Leaders are the torches who simultaneously light the way and ignite others to reach new horizons.

Who were the key people in your life who lit your torch? _____

_____

_____

To whom are you passing on your torch? _____

_____   _____

_____

What are the lessons and principles you want to ignite in them? _____

_____

_____

What do you need to do to make your torch burn more brightly? _____

_____

_____

The moment he receives the call from William Jordan asking for a meeting with him "as soon as possible," Bensen knows this will be the confrontation he has been anticipating.

Promptly at the appointed time, Jordan strides vigorously into the office, shuts the door behind him, and without a handshake or any friendly chitchat, takes a seat and abruptly gets down to business. "Bensen," he says, "there's great concern about where you're headed. I thought I had talked you out of those offbeat ideas of yours."

"You came close," Bensen replies.

"Well, I'm sorry I didn't succeed. I've gotten some phone calls. Listen, you've got to tell me what you're up to here, and we need to straighten it out." He pauses a moment and his expression softens. "Bensen, do I need to remind you of our long friendship, how faithfully I've supported you, and that I've got your best interests at heart?"

"Bill," Bensen says, looking Jordan in the eyes, "we both know you've always been my greatest supporter, both before you were on the Board and since, and you've always been a friend I could count on."

"Well, thank you. In light of that, I urge you to listen to what I have to say. You owe it to me, and I think you owe it to yourself. Don't continue on this path, Bensen."

For a moment, Bensen's mind drifts back to when he and Bill Jordan first connected, during their college days. In addition to his occasional participation in civil rights and antiwar demonstrations, during the summers Bensen volunteered to help build housing for the poor. On one of these projects, he found himself nailing up sheet rock panels next to a young black man with a familiar face.

"I can't help thinking I know you from somewhere," Bensen had said.

"I'm in Leland two-sixteen, right after your two o'clock accounting class," the fellow had said, to Bensen's surprise. "We sometimes pass in the hallway."

Although Jordan didn't say so, Bensen soon discovered that his new acquaintance, a brilliant graduate student, didn't *take* a course in that room, he *taught* one.

Bound together by shared values—both were business students as well as active volunteers for social causes—Bensen and Jordan quickly became good friends. Both were driven by an internal imperative to make something of themselves—hence the business major—yet both had a heart that drew them toward service. In an odd way, they were also linked by their backgrounds. In a reversal of the common story in America, Bensen came from a poor family "on the wrong side of the tracks," while Jordan was the son of two professionals, an educator and a social worker, who grew up in a disciplined, loving home in a comfortable middle-class neighborhood. Yet both of them knew that the obstacles Jordan had to face were greater, his path to success steeper.

Both of them made it to the top. As CEO of an entertainment conglomerate specializing in programming and publications for African Americans, William Jordan was a powerful figure in American life. He and Bensen continued their friendship over more than two decades. Jordan, the older of the two and the first to jump headlong into building his successful career, remained a step or two ahead of Bensen, and occasionally served as the younger man's mentor and guide. But Bensen understood Jordan well, and the older man sometimes turned to the younger to confide a problem he was having and brainstorm a way through. When Bensen became Chairman at HighQuest, he nominated Jordan for a seat on the HighQuest Board.

Now, Jordan felt the need to protect his friend from himself. "Don't screw it up, Bensen," he says. "We're two of the luckiest people on earth; don't jeopardize what you have and what you've achieved."

"What have the phone calls been about?" Bensen asks, bringing his attention back to the moment. "What specifically, I mean."

"Every one of the Board members has called me. For starters, they're distressed about how you handled the *Times* articles."

"Admitting that we had some work to do to clean up our act, instead of throwing up a smoke screen to divert their attention?" Benson responds.

"If you must put it that way. I think they're coming to me because they know you and I are friends; they're hoping I can either find out something to dispel the rumors they've heard, or help you screw your head on straight so they won't have to deal with it."

"And the rumors are?" Bensen inquires.

"That you are getting soft. That you've got employees using company time to research touchy-feely personal development programs, and you're contemplating making substantial investments in some of them. That you're on the verge of implementing business strategies that run counter to approaches that have served us well."

Bensen laughs. "Well, I wouldn't call anything I'm looking at 'touchy-feely,' but they may not be too far wrong on any of the other points. But have they checked our numbers?"

"I know, I know," Jordan responds. "I know the business is doing well. In fact, it's doing better lately. But that's not the point."

"*Not the point?*" Bensen replies sharply. "I thought they'd consider it the *entire* point."

"What people are concerned about is the direction you may be taking. Maybe the numbers are okay this quarter. Fine. But they're interested in preserving a successful strategic approach, a business culture and tradition that work. What they're absolutely not interested in is making wholesale changes. Tom Wilson told me you're in negotiations with a labor organization, that you're moving toward paying higher wages overseas. Well, my God, Bensen, that's suicidal and you know it. You know how competitive it is out there, and it's getting worse day by day. We've got to keep costs down, not look for ways to increase them. That's like axiom number one in the algebra book; everything else depends on it. So what the hell are you even thinking about?"

Before Bensen can reply, Jordan adds, "Several members have suggested that the emotional impact of your daughter's accident may have gotten you off track. You haven't been your old self. Even though the business is going well, maybe you're a little off your game. I think I even said something like that to you, last time we met."

"You did. And in a way, it's true; the accident set off a lot of feelings and reactions. It's changed how I look at things. But that's behind me now."

"I'm glad to hear it. And by the way, I'm very happy for you, about Katie."

Bensen's face brightens. "Thanks," he says. She's doing just great. She's nearly one hundred percent herself again. And she and I are pals like we haven't been since she was a kid. We're having some terrific conversations, and we do something together—a hike, a movie—at least once a week. But if you've finished all you want to tell me, I'd like to explain some things to you. And," he adds, leaning forward with a smile but riveting Jordan with his eyes, "will you please listen to what I have to say, this time?"

"Yes, I'll hear you out. But before you get started, I want to make clear why I'm here. I'm not representing the Board. I am not assigned to deliver a message. I'm here because of our friendship. I'm still in your corner, even though I'm having grave doubts about what you're doing—or thinking of doing. I warn you, Ben: You'd better take a pretty hard look at things. At least a couple of people are already sharpening their hatchets."

"I figured that, and I'm prepared for it. I'm glad you're here, Bill. I would dearly like you to understand what I'm up to before I have to face the Board, which I know is the next step. It's not that I want to use you to head them off. I'm not counting on your help, though of course I'd be grateful for it, if you see merit in my ideas. I think we *need* a Board meeting and a good discussion—and then some decisions about our direction."

"I was hoping it wouldn't have to come to that. But go ahead; I'm listening."

"Well, first of all, in my opinion, I'm not only not off my game, I am *on* my game like never before. The strategies that I'm considering . . ." The phone rings, and he ignores it. Then his assistant's voice comes over the intercom:"Mr. Quinn, I know you said no calls, but it's a Mr. Ueki, if I have the pronunciation right; he said it's an emergency, and that he was certain you'd want to know about it. He wouldn't tell me anything else."

He picks up, and it's Kenji's son. "I'm sorry to bother you at the office," Shichiro says, "but I think the end is near, and my father is asking that you come."

"When?"

"I think you have to come now."

Bensen hangs up the phone, looks at Jordan and says, "Bill, I know how important this meeting is, and I know how far you've come to talk to me. And I know this is going to upset you, but I need to leave, right away. I'm sorry. We'll have to reschedule. Why don't I come meet you in the city so you don't have to travel?"

"Dammit, Bensen, this is exactly the kind of thing people are worried about. Nothing could have pulled you away from a meeting like this in the past. What's happened to your priorities?"

"That's part of what I want to talk about," Bensen says, standing up. He holds out his hand. "Reschedule soon?"

Jordan takes his hand. "Only because it's you, Bensen. I'll work it out with Marie. Now get the hell out of here and do what you need to do."

Pressing his friend's hand tightly, Bensen says, "I'll just say this: What I want to do, if you and the rest of the Board will get behind me, will lead our business into a new era. It's that big, and that's why I'm willing to risk nearly everything to do it."

———

"What in the world is going on here?" Bensen thinks as he approaches Kenji's house. Both sides of the quiet street are lined with late-model Mercedes, Jaguar, Lexus, and other luxury cars; a limousine with a federal government license plate is parked in the shade of an oak tree, a uniformed chauffeur reading the newspaper at the open door.

Bensen walks quickly from his car up the pathway to the house, but when he reaches the front door he stops and takes a moment to breathe deeply and center himself. The door is slightly ajar; he taps lightly, then when no one comes, gently pushes it fully open and steps inside. Immediately, he feels a powerful presence. On his previous visit he had felt a sense of peace permeating the house, but this is different, a subtle but tangible power that seems to be emanating from the bedroom: at every step closer to the room the vibrant energy increases. As he reaches the threshold, the mystery of the cars is solved: In addition to Kenji's wife and son, who are seated at the bedside, about a dozen distinguished-looking men and women, beautifully dressed and groomed, are sitting on chairs packed tightly together in the small space. All have their eyes closed and are absolutely still, in deep silence.

Kenji too is in meditation. Though he's visibly more frail and wan than he was just a few days earlier, he is sitting up in bed, his face radiant with peace.

Bensen sees that one chair close to the bed is empty and a narrow path has been left open to it from the door. Not knowing who else might or might not be expected, he hesitates a moment, then walks in. Once seated, he closes his eyes and slips readily into the pervasive silence. The only thought he has, as his mind settles down, is how much deeper the silence is when it is shared—or generated—by a group.

He is not sure how much time elapses. Then he hears Kenji's voice: "I have a few words to say to you."

Along with everyone else, Bensen slowly opens his eyes. Kenji's face, always serene, always wearing a kind expression, looks exceptionally tender and loving. "I feel blessed to be in such a wonderful garden, with all of these beautiful flowers," the teacher says. "Thank you all so much."

From behind him, Bensen hears a woman's voice tearfully say, "How can you thank *us*—we're all so grateful to *you!*"

"My teachings," Kenji replies, "are seeds that I have planted in you. It is gratifying to the gardener, to see the blossoming." He pauses and slowly scans the room, looking for a moment at each one of them. "It makes me feel that all the time I spent planting these seeds was well worth the effort." Again he waits a moment. "Take these seeds and use them," he says. "Serve yourselves, serve others, serve the whole. Create value that lasts."

Again the teacher closes his eyes. "Is that it?" Bensen wonders. "Were those his last words to us, his farewell message?" Kenji's breathing is shallow and slow, as if he is fading away. But then he surprises them all by opening his eyes and saying, in a voice that is soft yet full of life:

"You have each experienced the depths of your being. You have also seen how good you feel when you act and serve with awakened awareness, with authenticity and clear purpose—and how tired and out of balance you become when you do not. From these experiences you know without a doubt that beneath the surface values of life, beyond the pursuit of money and material abundance, there is something deeper, something richer, something more true, long-lasting, and real, and it is part of your life now.

"Those who are intent on pursuing profits at any cost," Kenji continues, "have generated many problems, both social and environmental. I ask you now to turn your considerable intelligence, will, creativity, and resources to solving those problems. And I ask you to do this as a group. You will find that you have the means at your disposal, and that many of the solutions already exist. While some people were creating problems, others have been working to resolve them, developing healthful products for daily living and innovative systems and technologies for business and industry that can improve the way people live and work.

"Some of you who have visited me may have noticed my son sitting at his computer. For several years, he has been gathering information about these solutions and making contact with the visionary individuals and groups who are developing them."

Kenji's words trigger a memory of the information Anne showed him on the Internet, about broad-visioned, principle-driven business leaders. "That was probably just the tip of the iceberg," he surmises. "How many more individuals and organizations there must be—scientists, engineers, and inventors; educators, religious leaders, and spiritual guides; physicians, city planners, maybe even politicians!—all of them working in their own spheres of influence to improve the quality of life."

"I am feeling quite tired," Kenji is saying. His eyes are closed, and his voice, which had become increasingly faint, is now barely audible even to Bensen, who's sitting in the front. "My son knows my thoughts," Kenji continues; "please listen carefully as he speaks for me." With those words he turns towards Shichiro, who appears surprised and unprepared for his father's request. Nevertheless he stands and turns to face the group.

"My father wishes us to create a foundation," he tells them, "and he has endowed it with some initial seed capital and invites you to donate more. It will have two great tasks. First, to make the principles he has given us available to the public. And second, to study, evaluate, and then support implementation of the best solution-oriented projects from around the world—in education, health care, energy sources, and other critical areas. Most of the innovative technologies, design systems, and management strategies that we have been studying are not yet widely known," he explains. "But they represent the future. They are the direction the world is going. The foundation will seek out those life-enhancing systems and technologies, sponsor research, and fund pilot projects. When something is proven to be effective, the foundation will conduct educational programs to publicize it, and lobby for widescale implementation."

"The thing is," Kenji breaks in, surprisingly animated, "many of the means to create a better world either exist, or are in development and will be ready soon. The time has come for a new crop of leaders to embrace them and bring them rapidly onto the market." Once again he looks around the room, his gaze connecting with each person. "*You are those leaders,*" he says slowly. "Your intelligence, creative energy, ambition, and broad vision have lifted you into positions of leadership and power. Now you also have the knowledge of what is genuinely important. You know that reverence for life, care for the earth, regard for your fellow human beings, and unfolding the enormous potential lying within each of us are what make life worthwhile. You have all declared to me that you want to leave behind a legacy of service, and you have begun to do so in your own spheres of influence and action, often with great courage.

"Now, by joining together, utilizing your positions, your contacts, and your collective resources, you will be able to do much more than I could have done. Working together, you will be able to hasten the transformation that is already taking place on our planet.

"But"—and again he pauses and looks around the room—"always remember that transformation begins with us. What we are inside gets expressed outside. The world we want to create begins with us."

Leaning back against his pillows, Kenji glances again at his son, and closes his eyes. Shichiro, who had sat down, again stands and turns to the group. "One point that my father has been hesitant to convey will make all this feasible for those of you in business. This point is that the innovations we are talking about offer the promise of enormous opportunity. You see, as world consciousness continues to wake up, ever-increasing numbers of people will want to adopt healthier, more sustainable methods and products. And you and your companies will be there with them, because you will have seen ahead. As he said, you will be the true leaders, guiding humanity to a new stage in its long evolution.

"Now is the period for research and development," he tells the group, "but we must move quickly from that stage. Time is short. The world is at risk, and we need to take action now."

Kenji opens his eyes and nods approvingly at his son. "I can tell you with confidence that what my son said is true: This is the wave of the future, both for the good of the planet, and for creating wealth. You have the opportunity to better serve all your constituencies and add value to our world. Everyone will benefit and prosper."

Kenji once more lapses into silence. Bensen feels strongly that someone should speak, to reassure him that the foundation, and all that he has asked of them, will quickly move toward realization. He is just about to say something when a deep voice from the back of the room, a voice Bensen recognizes but cannot place, says, "Mr. Kenji, I know I speak on behalf of all of us here when I say that we will work together to quickly accomplish what you have asked."

"Good!" Kenji says emphatically. Again he looks around the room, meeting each person's eyes with his steady gaze. "My friends," he says at last, "all this talking has tired me. It's time for me to depart this place, and for you to bless and tend to all the gardens of your lives. I place my trust in you. I know I shall not be disappointed!"

Still sitting upright, Kenji leans against the pillows behind him and closes his eyes. In a minute or two, his breathing becomes shallow and continues to diminish. The assembled students watch and wait, anticipating the end. Suddenly his eyes pop open and he says, in a resonant voice that seems to come from another dimension, "My name was Kenji Ueki. I was a Gardener of Souls. My life's work was to bring out the best in you to enrich the world. Live my legacy! And always . . . always . . . remember the seeds!"

After these words, the master gardener becomes completely still. His eyes roll up in his head, and the aged body goes limp as the spirit departs.

But the death of the body does nothing to diminish the powerful presence of this great being. The silence in the room intensifies, becoming so thick and rich that spontaneously they all close their eyes and offer the support of their gratitude, love, and prayers for the journey they know their teacher has begun. A sense of holiness, of spiritual blessing, pervades the atmosphere.

"If this is death," Bensen muses, still sitting with eyes closed, "then what is there to be afraid of?" He opens his eyes and gazes upon the tiny, shrunken body on the bed, and almost laughs aloud. "This little, frail old man," he thinks, "a gardener—even in death his power far exceeds that of all of us!"

For a long time, no one moves or speaks. Eventually, one at a time, they leave their seats and go forward to the bed. Some stand for a moment for a final look; a few others kneel before their teacher and gently and respectfully touch his feet or his hand. One by one they say their personal farewell, leave the bedroom, and step out the back door of the house, into Kenji's garden.

———

Bensen, the latest arrival at the house, is also the last to leave the room. His feelings are deeply stirred, gratitude and grief, sadness and love dancing together in his heart. He wants to be alone, yet he is also drawn toward the garden and the people gathered there. He feels a solidarity with them, even though they are strangers. Did any of them know that the others existed, or were they all, like him, astonished to find each other when they arrived at the house? He is more than curious to know who they are. And he feels Kenji's commission compelling him: that they work to solve the problems of society together, as a group.

This directive from his teacher has given him enormous relief. Since the time, a few days ago, when Kenji extracted a promise to carry on his work, Bensen has been anxiously pondering what that meant. What was he to do? Where to begin? Kenji had said, "You will know what to do," but he has felt inadequate to the task, and very much alone with it. He realizes now that it was important for him to say "yes" on his own, that accepting the challenge was an important step in his development. But he is comforted and excited to discover that others will be working with him.

Proceeding through the sliding glass doors to the sunlit garden, he sees that a few people are standing alone, appreciating the beauty of the garden or simply wiping away tears and trying to regain composure. Others are gathered in small groups of two or three and are talking. "What an enormous impact he had on my life," he hears a familiar voice saying. "I'll never be the same." He sees that it is Mick Callaway, and walks over.

"Bensen, hello!" Callaway says warmly in greeting. "Do you know Senator Whelan?" Of course the face is immediately familiar to Bensen—the senator from his home state has long earned his admiration for her courageous efforts to enact campaign finance reform and other measures he supports, though she leans a little more toward the conservative position than he does. "Susan Whelan, this is Bensen Quinn; Bensen is Chairman and CEO of one of the state's biggest companies."

"HighQuest, if I am not mistaken," the senator says with a smile, extending her hand to Bensen. "I always liked that name. I'm surprised we've never met."

"I can't think of a better place than this," Bensen replies, returning her smile. But suddenly his smile evaporates as a powerful wave of sadness rises in him. "Sorry," he says, and starts to turn away. But the senator grips his hand more tightly and holds it in both of hers. "There's nothing to be sorry about," she says. "I'm sure we all feel the same way." Looking up, Bensen sees that her eyes are brimming with tears.

"Yes," he says, "it was great good fortune to encounter this man."

"I've met some remarkable people during my career in politics," she says, "some of the world's most distinguished leaders, but none like him. None of his caliber."

Bensen is surprised. "Fascinating," he says. "I've thought of him as a friend, as a mentor, as a wonderful teacher, and even as a great coach. It never occurred to me to see him as a leader. But you're right—he was an exemplary leader, at least for my life. He helped me go beyond what I thought was possible. He helped me become a better leader myself."

"Well put, Bensen. It was the same for me," Senator Whelan says.

"And for me as well," Callaway adds.

"I never quite grasped the connection between growing as a person and growing as a leader," Bensen continues. "I thought Kenji was just helping me on a personal level, to deal with the crises in my life. And I always thought of leadership only as something I *did*. I never saw that the quality and strength of my leadership came from inside, from who I am."

"Kenji helped us to wake up from our narrow definitions of success," Callaway says. "Now it's our turn to help awaken others. But let me ask both of you, did you understand what he meant when he said, 'Remember the seeds'? Was I the only one in the dark about that?"

"I think he referred to the principles he 'planted' in us," says Senator Whelan.

"That makes sense," Callaway concedes. "But his teachings were so informal; I don't know that I'm even aware of any principles."

"Maybe it would be worthwhile for us to discuss that point together," Bensen says. "It seemed very important to him. I propose that we set a date to meet, to talk about that and start moving on what he asked of us."

"Excellent idea," says a tall, silver-haired gentleman standing nearby. This time Bensen recognizes the man behind the resonant voice he had heard at the back of the room—Ron Williams, the network news anchor, looking quite different off camera. "Why don't we spend a few minutes exchanging business cards and getting acquainted," Williams suggests. "We can pick a date, then confirm with each other when we get back to our offices and check our schedules."

At that moment, Shichiro and his mother appear at the patio door, carrying trays filled with steaming cups of tea. All conversation stops and attention shifts to them. "Please have some tea," Shichiro offers. As the group moves to gather around him, he adds, "My father suggested that perhaps you might like to meet here, in his garden, to establish the foundation and formulate plans to carry on his work. My mother and I would be pleased if you would accept this invitation." As people nod in agreement, he adds, "Meeting here will make it easier for my mother to be with us and offer her clear vision and deep wisdom. Except for the monk who set him on his spiritual path when he was a younger man, my father has always honored her as his most important teacher."

All eyes turn in surprised admiration to Keiko, who momentarily bows her head, then looks up with a smile both radiant and powerful.

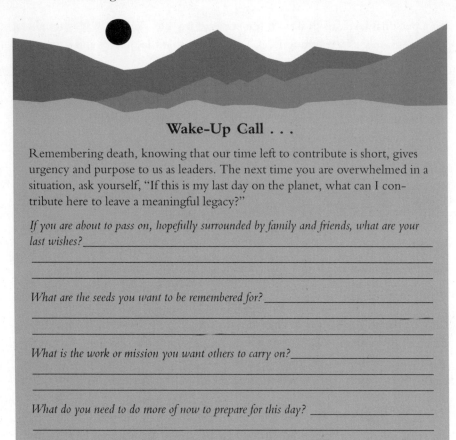

Wake-Up Call . . .

Remembering death, knowing that our time left to contribute is short, gives urgency and purpose to us as leaders. The next time you are overwhelmed in a situation, ask yourself, "If this is my last day on the planet, what can I contribute here to leave a meaningful legacy?"

*If you are about to pass on, hopefully surrounded by family and friends, what are your last wishes?*_____

_____

_____

What are the seeds you want to be remembered for? _____

_____

_____

*What is the work or mission you want others to carry on?*_____

_____

_____

What do you need to do more of now to prepare for this day? _____

_____

_____

Bensen strides confidently under the HighQuest logo spanning the entrance to the Board Room and through the twelve-foot-high oak doors toward his place at the head of the conference table. The discontent and doubts of several Board members notwithstanding, all eight Directors are seated around the U-shaped table, awaiting the Chairman and CEO.

Intently focused on the upcoming meeting, perhaps the most important of his life, he still takes a moment to look around and enjoy the surroundings. This will be the first Board meeting since he had the room redesigned in a bright contemporary style to align with his new thinking. Two walls are now floor-to-ceiling glass, filling the space with natural light and affording a glorious view across the wooded corporate campus to the gently rolling Connecticut hills. The other two walls are paneled in light Norwegian wood, one decorated with contemporary art, the other featuring large photos of models and well-known sports figures, poised on sheer cliffs or with snowy mountain peaks in the background, wearing the latest HighQuest gear for hiking and climbing.

The light-colored, open-ended conference table itself is another of Bensen's recent innovations. The massive old mahogany model no longer looked right, its darkness and bulk belonging to the world he had left behind.

Approaching the podium, he shifts his attention from the surroundings and tries to discern the mood of the group. The room is quiet and charged with tension, far from the jovial and comradely feeling typical at Board meetings over the past nine or ten consecutive quarters, which have largely been a celebration of growth and profitability. Yet it doesn't feel hostile. Bill Jordan meets his eyes and nods. Barbara, Scott, Martin, and most of the others manage cautious smiles. Only Tom Wilson avoids looking directly at him.

Tom, Bensen knows, is his chief opponent. A solid member of the old guard, Tom, the retired CEO of a heavy equipment manufacturer, with his close-cropped white hair, dark pinstripes, and authoritative bearing, tends to be wedded to the old archetype of business that Bensen intends to transform, the paradigm he has lived and justified but has now surpassed. He likes and respects Tom, but he knows that after he's done talking, Tom will be his biggest challenger.

Exactly at 10 A.M., Bensen takes a sip of water, stands at the podium, and smiles at the eight Directors. Looking around at the familiar faces, he is surprised and pleased to find that he feels no defensiveness, but only genuine warmth toward these people, most of whom he has worked with for nearly a decade. In truth, he is grateful for this Board. They're all top quality people, who have helped him make crucial decisions and given him the benefit of their extensive experience. In addition to Tom Wilson and Bill Jordan, two others are CEOs of their own large firms, a third is a CFO, a fourth a high-powered academic in demand around the world as a management consultant. A relatively new face, Peter Kim, is a young entrepreneur whose high-tech product Bensen can barely understand, but he admires Pete's track record of success and the way he handled his company during the technology sell-off around the turn of the millennium. He has learned a lot from this group, and he is well aware of the challenges involved in influencing them.

Over the past two weeks, since his rescheduled meeting with Bill Jordan, he has followed Bill's advice and met one on one with most of them, outlining his vision, getting their input, and attempting to gain their support. They are listening, but most are still adhering rather tightly to the values and strategies that have been successful in their own businesses and that they feel they're entrusted to uphold at HighQuest. He doesn't blame them for wanting to hold on to what has worked; besides, change is not easy, as he appreciates all too well. He knows he's got to walk a thin line between, on the one hand, pushing too hard and alienating them, and on the other, not taking a strong enough stand for his vision.

As he looks around the room, he also feels the presence of unseen others, urging him forward. Kenji, of course, is foremost among them, but there's Mick Callaway, and Senator Susan Whelan, and the other members of his new "family" of Kenji's students. Emily is there, and Katie, now his staunchest cheerleader. The Mexican members of his "family" are there too—Juan Ramon, Rosa Herrera and her daughter Maria Helena, the girls in the factory with their young, tired faces.

"I'm not known for dramatic gestures," Bensen begins. "I'm more of a get-it-done kind of guy, which is why you've all supported my position here. But

I feel the current situation warrants courage, decisiveness, and a willingness to take some risks. So I'll take the first one. I'm going to offer you two alternatives today. If you like the vision I present this morning," and he holds up a thin document, "here is a long-range plan to go forward." Then, holding up a single sheet, he says, "If you don't like it, this is my letter of resignation."

Pausing a moment for effect, he then says, "I appreciate the time most of you have been willing to take, to listen individually to my point of view in recent days, and I thank you for arranging your schedules to attend this special session. I believe there's now a lot more understanding of where I want to go than when Bill Jordan first came to me and, frankly, told me I'd better shape up if I valued my head." Nervous laughter ripples around the table. "But I know there are still enough reservations to warrant our coming together as a group, to air our concerns and get clear on what the direction of this company should be—and whether or not I'm the right person to lead it. So let me lay out for you the course of action I'm proposing, and the rationale behind it, and then let's talk about it together."

He glances down at the notes he had prepared, then turns the pages over, steps away from the podium, and speaks in a direct, informal way. "We live in a new world," he says, "but our vision—the way we look at it—is old. It has become a cliché to say the world will never be the same. That's certainly true. But how will it change? In what direction? We don't know. The only thing that *is* certain is that it's time to see things in a new way.

"For a company like HighQuest, with factories, employees, investors, and markets all around the world, and a desire to continue growing for many years to come, we simply cannot think in the narrow old way about short-term profits. We have to aim for long-term sustainability.

"We live in a world that is intricately interconnected. That means we have to think not only about ourselves, but also about the state of the whole world that we influence and that influences us: about education, about poverty, about the environment, about other cultures and what's good for them, even if it's different from what we value.

"People who are more awake and aware than I was until recently have long been trying to communicate to us that the world is a living system that we're all in together. For our long-term health and prosperity, we have to find a way to take care of the whole as well as the parts. But how well have we been doing our job? If we are honest with ourselves, we have to admit that we're passing on to our children a world filled with some very serious problems. I think we also have to admit that business has been a major contributor to these problems, but the good news is that we can play an equally large role in their solution.

"As we all know, not too long ago it was considered just fine to take and use any and all of the earth's natural resources to produce goods, and it was okay to dump toxic by-products—smoke, fumes, pesticides, radioactivity, mercury, you name it—without regard to the life and health of any species, including mankind. I don't think there was any malice involved here, only ignorance: Nobody considered the long-term effects of what they were doing.

"Little by little, as the consequences of this behavior become obvious, the rules are being rewritten. Now, even as much of the same old behavior of extracting and dumping continues, most businesses would agree that it is irresponsible to harm the environment. Everyone with half a brain knows it's *not* okay, and that this shortsighted vision, and the behaviors it spawns, must eventually be brought to a halt and replaced by an attitude of respect for life and stewardship of the planet. As you know, at HighQuest we have taken significant steps toward running what we might call a clean, green operation, and I think you'll all agree that the changes we made were the right thing to do."

Bensen pauses in his speech to look at each person in the room. "Are you with me so far?" All, even Tom Wilson, nod in the affirmative.

"Just as it is no longer considered okay to disregard the health and sustainability of the environment," Bensen continues, "it should be equally unacceptable to disregard the rights and needs of employees, whether in this country or abroad. The global business community has the power and the means to serve society in ways that are life-affirming, sustainable, and responsible toward the future of humanity and the planet, and it is time for us to step up to the plate and do just that. But to do it successfully means that we'll have to make substantive adjustments in the way we do business."

Glancing for a moment at Tom, then around the room, Bensen says, "I'm sure some of you are thinking, 'Why look for trouble by going into issues that are not our concern?' Well, I've used that line too many times, and it's been used on me too many times, for me to buy it any more. I know you feel the way I do when some employee fails to take responsibility for something by saying, 'It's not my job.' He or she might have been able to solve a problem, save a client, or avert a minor catastrophe by taking an ounce of initiative, but instead: 'It's not my job.' 'It's not my area, not my concern.'

"Have I done it too? You bet. I've told my staff that 'it's not our concern' that thousands of our fellow Americans will be put out of work when we move our factories offshore. I've argued that 'it's not my concern' that the workers in those offshore plants don't make enough money to live decently. There are handy rationalizations for these matters, of course. Globalization—or at least that part of it that involves moving production offshore—means lower costs for our companies, and cheaper goods for us as consumers, two good things. But what about the people who've lost their jobs as we go about cutting our costs?

"Globalization also means that we provide jobs for thousands of people in developing economies—surely another good thing, right?—and we've been assured that the workers there are being paid the 'prevailing wage' for their locale. But if that wage results in continuing hardship, if it's not enough to lift those people out of poverty, hunger, and second-rate housing, shouldn't we set the bar a little higher?

"'It's not my concern' is what we've been saying about far too many things: environmental destruction, social and economic injustice, more than four billion people living in poverty. Well, my friends, it is our concern, whether we like it or not. Our attitudes and actions, especially our business practices, are creating problems that will plague our children and grandchildren, problems that they are going to have to pay for with their money, their health, and perhaps even their lives.

"What's amazing to me is not that we are finally waking up and realizing that we need to be concerned about these things. What's amazing is that we could have fallen asleep and not seen that these issues were our concern all along. We can no longer afford to think that creating value for only one constituency—the shareholder—is the only important measure of success. The world is too small, too interconnected, to do that any more."

Bensen pauses to take a sip of water. He knows that what he's saying is uncomfortable for the Board members to hear, yet he feels they are listening. Encouraged, he moves on to the next phase of his presentation.

"I think you all know that I recently visited one of the offshore factories where some of our products are made. I've realized that in order for you to truly understand what's going on with me, why I'm feeling so strongly that we need to change our way of doing business, I have to take you on that trip."

For the next few minutes, he describes in detail some of the highlights of his visit, beginning with his arrival at the gates of the Las Flores *maquiladora* and his encounter with the armed security guards, through his conversations with Juan Ramon and his visit to the family home. Poignantly, he describes the rows of hard-at-work young women filling the noisy factory under constant pressure from the male floor managers. "We wouldn't consider working under such conditions, or having our kids do so. It's a medieval relic, a leftover from an outmoded world and worldview, and I don't want us to have any part in perpetuating it. It's not in our long-range interest. I don't believe, if you were there and saw what I saw, that you would feel so proud of it, either.

"The thing is, as executives, we deal mostly in abstractions. Market share. Growth. Costs. Sales. Profit margins. But in the factory I didn't see numbers or concepts, I saw people, mostly girls and young women who reminded me of my daughter Katie and her friends. As soon as I started walking through the work stations, it struck me that these were the children of people just like me—and just like you, Marty. Scott. Barbara. Tom. Parents who want the best for their kids. Maybe those parents believe that's just the way life is, and they feel as helpless to change it as to change the weather. But *we* can do something about it.

"Most of those kids ought to be in school, learning and looking to the future with hope. For the few who succeed in becoming supervisors or managers, like my guide there, Juan Ramon, life will be better. *Their* children may have the chance to grow up in a comfortable house, eat enough nourishing food, see a doctor, get an education—and we can take some credit for that. But why not make these things possible for the others? We have the means to do it, so, if we don't, without intending to we're cheating these kids out of their childhood and their future. It may be a profitable short-term strategy for a handful of us, but it's placing real limits on our growth, cheating our companies and our own children out of an expanding global market and a vibrant economy.

"You know, we are all tied to these girls and women, and millions like them in factories around the globe, from China and Pakistan to the Philippines and Eastern Europe, as well as Latin America. Not only because they put together our HighQuest products. They also cut and stitch most of our clothing and our shoes, they make our kids' toys, fabricate our electronic devices and our computers. Without the products they make that we buy and sell, products that make our lives comfortable and our companies profitable, where would we be?

"And how do we thank them? We permit them to work long hours, in unhealthful surroundings where they struggle to meet inexcusably high quotas. They are rushed, harassed, and often humiliated. They have to ask permission to go to the bathroom. They may have to endure beatings if they are slow, or body searches when they leave the factory, which are mortifying to these young girls. We pay them anywhere from twenty-five cents to ninety cents an hour, lock them up in barracks ten or a dozen to a room, work them for five or ten years, then dump them, like a bagful of cloth scrap, without so much as a 'thank you very much.'

"We can no longer do this to our own fellow Americans: it's illegal, and everyone knows it's immoral. Why is it okay to treat people in distant countries, or at our borders, this way?

"You realize, of course, that when I say we do all this, I mean that we allow it. It happens every day, seven days a week, in our factories and the facilities we hire to produce our stuff. By our incessant demand to generate profit at any cost, we condone it and create it. The fact that we're not physically there, directly involved in plant operations, doesn't absolve us of responsibility. It *is* our concern.

"As I said, I believe this is the next phase of a global awakening. Just as pollution is wrong because it does harm to the living systems of our planet, so injustice to our fellow human beings is damaging to every one of us, and I want our company to take the lead in turning it around. Don't misunderstand me. I know that pollution of the earth won't stop overnight, nor will unfairness and exploitation. But those who see the need have to take a stand for what is right."

Bensen pauses a moment to let his impassioned words sink in. Then he adds, with a smile, "And you know what? Doing something about this state of affairs is the best long-term business strategy we could devise. So long as these people are scratching out a miserable living, they will never join the global economic community. They, and millions like them, will never be able to buy any of the stuff we and other companies produce. We are self-limiting our markets. So we don't have to be soft-hearted, just pragmatic, to take a longer view."

Looking at his small audience of powerful leaders, Bensen feels their attention and knows that they are with him. He feels a glow of confidence inside, the same flow of energy he has always felt when he has spoken passionately, whether about social justice or opening up new markets. It feels good to be taking a stand for what he believes.

"Okay, suppose you agree with me," he says. "I don't know that you do, but for a moment let's say we decide we want to do something about all this. How could we do it? Where would we start?

"I put it this way because sometimes it seems that our economic system is like a runaway train. Many people don't like some of the ways it's functioning, but nobody feels they can control it. Look at us. Even though we're the leaders of corporations that are dominating the world's economy and setting much of the world's agenda, we're small potatoes compared to the investment bankers and money managers who move billions of dollars a day from country to country in pursuit of instant profits, or the financial media, who can build us up or destroy our image and decimate our stock price with a paragraph or a thirty-second news piece, whether what they say is accurate or not. In this marketplace, under these conditions, to focus exclusively on short-term gain is futile.

"I know that some people might say just the opposite—that long-term plans and strategies are futile in a fast-changing business climate. In the short and narrow view, they have a point. Long-term strategies require consistent earnings, steady expansion, ethical management, quality control, attention to the customer, things that might not show up in the current quarterly report. But in the long run, they gain respect, customer loyalty, employee loyalty. And we are in it for the long haul. We've seen what happened to the start-up dot-coms of the nineties that were the darlings of the investment community. How many of them are left standing? And how many investors lost their lunch money, or their clients' retirement money, in the debacle? We've seen, at Enron, Arthur Andersen, WorldCom and the others, what happens when character and values get divorced from the pursuit of results.

"We are in business to stay, and to grow. I believe that to stay and grow, we have to build excellence. But we need to expand our definition of excellence, from excellence in management and products, to include excellence in serving our customers, excellence in benefiting the communities in which we operate, excellence in providing our employees with a positive work environment—and most of all, excellence in vision and character.

"I don't know about you, but I've gotten to a point in my life where the contributions I leave behind, and how I feel about those contributions, whether or not I can look myself in the eyes in the mirror, have become very important. I don't want to leave a trail of bodies behind me; I want to leave the world a better place.

"Now, you might say, 'Hey, Quinn, good for you! You've reached the top; this is a good time for you to step down and devote yourself to some do-gooder work in community service or the nonprofit sector, and let us run the company the good old-fashioned way.' But what I propose to you is that we are on the verge of a revolution in business. The old ways are dying out. The command and control model is increasingly obsolete. Running the business solely for the financial bottom line *is* obsolete. It's time to forge a corporate environment that measures success in broader, more intelligent ways. It's time to bring together character, values, and results.

"We may need to do this for our own self-preservation. Business as we know it may not be sustainable for much longer. I don't think the answer, as some critics of globalization propose, is to scale back corporations, to turn back the clock. I don't think that would be possible. Life wants to expand and evolve, it's natural. But what kind of growth? Toward what end? For whose benefit? At whose expense? These are the important questions.

"I've been wrestling with these questions for weeks now. At first I was a little starry-eyed." He sees a roomful of amused smiles, and says, "Yes, it's true. I know it doesn't fit my image. But I felt passionate about making big changes, and all the problems and potential obstacles weren't immediately obvious. You know Bensen Quinn, he just puts his head down and charges ahead! When I did start seeing the problems clearly, for a while I despaired that anything could be done.

"Now, it is my considered opinion that we can make a real contribution to human life, add value to our communities, treat our employees fairly, and help them improve their own lives, *while* we put out great products and continue to increase profits and market share. If we could do that, it would be better, don't you think? And it is necessary now. If we hold to the old ways, we may have a few more good years, but by then we'll be so far behind we'll never catch up. I say, let's move forward now. I want to lead the company into the vanguard of change.

"So, what am I really talking about, specifically?

"First of all, I want to upgrade conditions in our factories and invest in the people who work there. They are, to put it simply and truly, struggling to survive. But that isn't necessary. With a very small expense in dollars—it takes so little money in most of these economies to provide basic services—we can help them rise toward a much better life.

"The picture I'm looking at in my head, that I'd like to convert into a reality, is that these workplaces would become centers of dignity and humanity. Workers would make a living wage. Working conditions would be comfortable and conducive to maximum productivity. We would provide basic medical care, and we would take a genuine interest in promoting growth in the surrounding community, investing in schools and community development projects like parks, or the construction of stores and more substantial homes. I'm not talking about estates and condos. Just livable dwelling places.

"We could also build small libraries, and fund literacy programs. Some of this could take the form of corporate donations, but why not partner with local firms and individuals to create profit-making enterprises, with some of the profit going to us, and the rest staying in the community? Or offer low-interest micro-loans, and let them own it all themselves? Projects like that would open up jobs and generate growth. All of this would quickly uplift a corner of the world.

"Wouldn't that give you a real sense of satisfaction, over and above being able to say, 'HighQuest returned seventeen cents per share this quarter'?

"If a substantial number of multinationals followed our lead, people all over the world would enjoy greater prosperity, and they would look upon us as their friends and benefactors, rather than their oppressors.

"Is this going to cost us? Yes. Up front, it will. But will it cut into long-term profits? I don't think so. We know that it's possible to get a lot of productivity from people by motivating them with fear and coercion over the short term. But we also know that if you treat employees right, give them enough light to see what they're doing, enough ventilation so they have clean air to breathe, time to eat and recoup their strength—and if you go beyond that and give them a sense that this is *their* company, that they are a real and important part of the business and the creation of the product—if you do that, productivity rises. Workers become more loyal. And not just loyal in the long run—that may never be important the way it used to be. But loyal *today:* doing the best they can, because they care about doing the best they can, for the company. I'm certain that innovations of this kind will drive up productivity, reduce losses due to mistakes, and increase our profitability.

"I'm excited about what we can do at the factories. I believe it's the area that calls for the most sweeping changes, and where the effects of our innovations and investments will be most dramatic. But there's a lot I want to do in our corporate offices, too.

"My guiding principle here—and I'd love to have your input on this—is that we will make a genuine attempt to meet the needs people have for meaning, dignity, self-esteem, and community. I believe that if we don't help our people fulfill these legitimate human strivings, they will go elsewhere, to firms that are open to satisfying them.

"To make this happen, we have to start by changing our own attitudes. Even though we always say that people are our greatest asset, our most valuable resource, now we have to do the tough part: We have to *behave* that way.

"I had it easy. My trip to the factory shook me out of my habitual thinking. I was open to change, and suddenly things just looked different to me.

Somehow, we've all got to get new eyes, so we can see our people as they are, with all their human gifts and concerns, and treat them accordingly.

"People on every level of the organization come to work each day for more than money alone. They also show up because it's a chance to meet and learn from other people, to develop friendships, to create products or provide services that have meaning or value to other people and to society. They feel better when they can take pride in doing a good job rather than getting away with just pleasing the boss and going home. They want to feel they are contributing to the growth and success of a company they can believe in.

"We recently conducted an employee survey that indicated that financial rewards take on primary importance only when these other factors—meaning, participation, value creation—are missing. If this is true, then in order to address the deeper needs and interests of the people who work for us, we've got to reinvent ourselves, go beyond our roles as corporate representatives focused solely on financial performance. Along with providing for the material requirements of our employees, we need to become mindful of their inner, spiritual, and psychological well-being. A good place to start would be to acknowledge that work is not merely a method of survival or economic advancement, it's a potential means to fulfillment. After all, *we* love what we do. I would like to make that possible for all our employees.

"I know that these words have been around, and that it's not easy to translate them into action. But we can do it. And it will be worth it.

"One of the things I've learned about change, since Katie's accident, is that in order to move forward, you have to know not only where you want to go, but also where you are. It's common sense. If you don't know where you are on the map, you're truly lost, no matter which direction you try to move.

"So you have to start with a realistic self-assessment: Where am I? What are my strengths, my weaknesses? I've had to do that for myself, and I believe it would be beneficial for us to do it as a company.

"For myself, it became clear that although I have many strong points, I also have more weak or underdeveloped places than I wanted to know about. On the plus side, I make things happen. I don't give up. I have, I believe, a pretty broad vision, and I can often spot trends before they fully manifest. I have a realistic sense of what can be done, and when it's better not to try. And over the years, I've become adept at making acquisitions that are advantageous for the company.

"But when it comes to interpersonal skills—well, when Katie was lying in the hospital, it hit me very hard that she and I had drifted apart. When she came out of her coma and I mentioned that I had been away—meaning in Mexico—she looked at me and said, 'Dad, you're always away.'

"I realized that my relationship with Emily had degenerated, too, largely because of my work habits. And I wasn't exactly Mr. Personality in the office. I needed to learn about all that, and I'm working on it.

"This will be for others to judge, but I believe I am becoming a better leader because I am being honest with myself and with others, showing up with more of who I am. And I believe that for us to be most effective as a company as we move forward, we also need a more complete assessment of our strengths and weaknesses. I want to take an honest look at the things the company has done wrong, as well as identify our strong points.

"I've started on this, but it will have to become a group effort. With the initiative and assistance of Anne Holmes, I've been developing what we call a Value Creation Index. It now consists of half a dozen criteria by which a company's success or failure can be judged. These include financial performance, employee satisfaction, customer satisfaction, human and labor rights, environmental impact, community relations, and overall ethics. For simplicity, we have adopted an expression used in Europe, the 'triple bottom line': financial, employee satisfaction, and customer or community. If we look at ourselves in the light of these criteria, we should be able to make a pretty accurate self-appraisal of where we stand as a business, so we can move forward with energy and power. Instead of looking at one bottom line, we'll establish a multiple-factor bottom line, to gauge the value we are creating for all of our constituencies.

"What we have found so far is detailed in this vision statement," he says, holding up the slim document sitting on the podium. "In brief, HighQuest has a fine reputation with customers for quality products and with distributors and retailers for reliable order fulfillment. Our production processes have been refined to peak efficiency. We've got a highly recognizable and well-respected brand name, great endorsers, and dedicated management, both here and abroad. We've addressed our environmental impact. We're profitable. But we are not currently creating sufficient value for all our constituencies.

"Let me give you an example."

Bensen leans down to open his briefcase, and holds up an item of High-Quest clothing. "This ultra-lightweight, insulated, waterproof jacket sells for one hundred eighty-five dollars in the stores." At this point, he presses a button on his speaker's lectern and the screen behind him lights up. "These are the girls who make these jackets." He clicks his computer keyboard, and a series of photos begins to be displayed, showing the girls bent over their machines, supervisors hovering nearby. "I wish I could convey to you what it *feels* like to be in that factory," he says, "the noise, the dust, the heat, the intimidating shouts of the supervisors. I can only hint at it. But at least you can see what our employees look like. Take a look at some of these faces."

The sequence culminates in several shots of Maria Elena Herrera. "This is the girl whose family I visited." In the final picture, she is looking directly into the camera, her dark eyes rimmed with shadows, but bright with hope. "We pay this fourteen-year-old eighty-seven cents an hour to work on this jacket, which requires about 2.2 hours of labor from several people, none making more than she does. If we look at that fact from the typical business standpoint, we'd all clap and shout and congratulate ourselves for keeping costs so low. But is that what we want to be about? Is that what's going to sustain us into the future? As competition gets ever harsher, is cutting more and more costs out of production going to be the answer? Or are we going to take a stand for quality products that serve people? How about boosting our image, and our market, by paying the best wages in the industry, and letting customers and our shareholders know that's what we're about?

"I invite you all to take a look at some other photographs, on the wall to your left. These models wearing our clothing—this is our public image. But this"—pointing back to the screen with Maria Elena's face still staring at them—"this is what's happening behind the scenes. My desire is to integrate the two, to bring them together."

———

Bensen stands silently for a moment, contemplating his next words. "I've said most of what I wanted to convey," he says, "but I do want to make a couple more points, and I'll make them quickly.

"I believe we're living in a great historical moment for businesses and business leaders. Because business is now the primary influence on society, surpassing family, community, religion, education, and government, the leadership the world so desperately needs must come from the business community. Looking around at the problems and the unsustainable practices, a person could wonder if the necessary leadership is truly there, but I am convinced that it is.

"I believe many people in leadership positions find that the corporate policies they're called upon to enact and uphold are at odds with their personal values. I believe they are more than ready to make a dramatic shift, away from no-holds-barred competition, exploitation of human and natural resources, and one-dimensional focus on short-term profitability, toward sustainability, cooperation, and a sense of responsibility for the billions of people who have less than we do. I am determined that HighQuest will be one of the companies to take that stand.

"As I noted at the outset, it's obvious that many of the world's social and environmental problems have been, and continue to be, created by lack of awareness: short-sighted business practices that disregard the big picture in the pursuit of profit. That's a wrong priority.

"But business also holds the key to the solutions. We have the resources, the international reach, the power in every way. We have the R&D in place to find better ways of doing things. All that is missing is the will. I have the will, and I want to lead this company in the direction of serving the whole as we serve our own interests. When others see that it is possible, profitable, and the only way to be truly sustainable over the long haul, they will follow us. Somebody will eventually take the lead. Why not us? And why not today?

"My vision for the company is that we can serve all the people connected with us: our employees here at home, the factory workers around the world and the communities they live in, our customers, and our stockholders, as well as the environment. In a spirit of stewardship, we need to engage in business with an awareness of our impact. It's time to expand our sense of identity to embrace the well-being of the planet as a whole. This sounds like a lot to ask, but isn't it simply the requirement of authentic leadership today?

"Of the six billion people on the planet, only about two billion are *not* living in poverty. As leaders, we need to ask ourselves, 'Am I a leader who serves the two billion, or am I a leader who serves the entire six billion?'

"I said at the beginning of my talk that the situation calls for courage and commitment. I wasn't talking only about HighQuest. I love this country, and I love this planet, and I want to use the time I have to serve in the best way I can."

Looking around the room, Bensen engages each person's eyes. "Our time together today," he says, "reminds me of a note my wife left for me the other morning, with a quote from a great American writer. It said, 'Do not go where the path may lead; go instead where there is no path, and leave a trail.'"

Pausing for another moment, he gathers his emotions and says, with great heart and depth, "Let's build a new trail together."

For a moment the room falls silent. Concerned, Bensen wonders, "Did I lose them?" Then William Jordan breaks the hush, clapping slowly and deliberately. One by one, each Board member joins him, including Tom Wilson, the last to participate. Jordan then stands and says, "Bensen, you may think our applause represents one hundred percent support of your vision. I'm certain I speak for all of us when I say that we still have some significant reservations about what you are proposing. On the other hand, I'm sure we would all agree that you have led us into the future before—even when many of us were hesitant—and your vision has been on the mark and has paid off handsomely.

"What we *are* applauding is the obvious fact that *Bensen Quinn is back!* Your energy, your passion, your consistent and compelling drive for excellence have always been the force behind HighQuest, and we are excited to see it return. Let's co-create this new vision together!"

Another round of applause tells Bensen that Jordan's remarks do represent a consensus. "I'm glad you think I'm back, and I appreciate that acknowledgement," Bensen says. "But I hope that soon you will realize that we don't need to go back to anything, we need to move forward into a more purposeful, meaningful, value-creating future."

Jordan, in the role as spokesman for the group, responds, "Our final destination may not be precisely what you envision it to be today. But with your passion and our partnership, I'm confident that we will create a great new future."

Applause fills the room again, this time with Bensen joining the group.

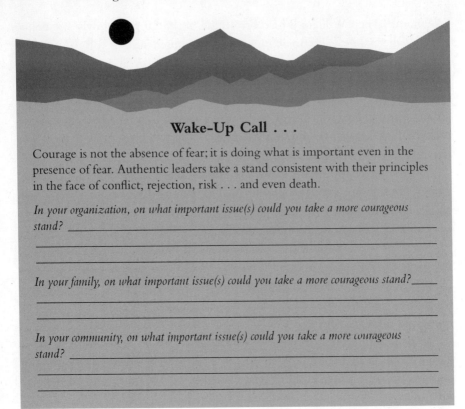

Wake-Up Call . . .

Courage is not the absence of fear; it is doing what is important even in the presence of fear. Authentic leaders take a stand consistent with their principles in the face of conflict, rejection, risk . . . and even death.

In your organization, on what important issue(s) could you take a more courageous stand? _____
_____
_____

In your family, on what important issue(s) could you take a more courageous stand? _____
_____
_____

In your community, on what important issue(s) could you take a more courageous stand? _____
_____
_____

"Remember the Seeds. . . ." 25

Kenji's dying words haunted Bensen. At first, he didn't know what his teacher meant. What seeds? Kenji had said very little to him about seeds.

True, the gardener had referred to them as "the principles I have taught you," but that was not much help. In none of their talks together had he taught any principles that Bensen, looking back over their conversations, could define. Most of the time, it seemed that the two of them had just been chatting like friends. "It was Kenji's *questions*—the things he got me thinking about—that seemed to catalyze change for me," Bensen reflects.

There is a second Kenji-related dilemma that he must resolve. In their last private meeting, Kenji had entrusted Bensen with the task of carrying on his work, sharing with others the teachings he had received. Reluctantly, feeling unsure and unworthy, Bensen had accepted the mission. But despite his pledge, he hasn't been able to pinpoint what those teachings are. How, then, can he honor the trust Kenji had placed in him? If he is to impart knowledge to others, he will have to formulate it, put it down in a structure or format that he can communicate.

That is why, on this bright Sunday afternoon, with the October sun warming the garden, he arms himself with a pen and a new pad of paper and makes his way to the bench where he had often sat with Kenji, determined to define the key points he had learned from his teacher.

He prints in block letters at the top of the page, THE SEEDS. Nothing comes. After a frustrating hour of staring at the page and writing nothing at all, he closes his eyes and settles into himself, as much to relax as to seek inspiration. But still nothing comes.

Bensen repeats this ritual for several days, taking advantage of occasional lulls at the office or sitting quietly at the kitchen table over his morning coffee. On the eighth day, again in the garden, and without any warning, a stream of ideas bubbles forth—clear, powerful, and nonstop—and he writes them down.

Leaning back with a sigh when the flow is over, he feels satisfied that he has captured the core of Kenji's principles.

———

"Excellent, Bensen. I believe these five seed principles contain the essence of my husband's teaching."

Bensen's heart thrills in anticipation of hearing those words from Kenji's widow. Excited by his breakthrough in the garden—it felt like discovering Kenji's teachings fresh, and in a way it was just that—he had wanted to share his insights with Keiko, to verify their accuracy with the woman who had been described as Kenji's "most important teacher." Calling to ask if he might come over and share something with her, he was warmly invited for afternoon tea.

At first, sitting in the living room, they speak politely, almost formally, as they sip the fragrant green tea she has prepared. Bensen is happy to be back in that beautiful home, amidst Kenji's things, speaking with the woman who had shared his life and his knowledge. He has come with a mission, but doesn't mind discussing the lovely autumn colors at the change of seasons, or bragging a little about his daughter's musical talents or her prowess on the soccer field.

Several times a quiet descends on the space in which they are sitting, but, like the silences that had punctuated his conversations with Kenji, they are not uncomfortable, but filled with richness. During one of those quiet moments, the tone of their conversation shifts when Bensen says "I don't wish to make you sad, but I must tell you, I miss your husband very much. Kenji appeared in my life when I needed him the most, and he opened new vistas to me that I didn't dream existed. I will always be deeply grateful to him."

"Mr. Quinn," she replies, looking directly at him now, "one thing you will learn is that the teacher is as grateful for the student as the student is for the teacher. What is a teacher without a student? A potential only, a full water tank waiting for a field to bring to life. The carpenter needs wood; the physician requires a patient; the mother is born with her child: Until then, she is just a woman. In just this way my husband was gratified to find such a fine student so late in his life. He often spoke of you with great joy."

Then she adds, wistfully, "I miss him, too, of course. I know he is all right. He was a very wise, enlightened being. He was no longer merely Kenji; he long ago ceased to identify only with his body or his limited individual nature, so he could let all that fall away. But to me, he was also my husband, and I was his wife. And he is not here to share a cup of tea, to discuss the news of the day, to worry about the grandchildren, to laugh over nothing much."

Again they fall into silence, and sit comfortably in it together. After a while he says, "You know, I was a little puzzled to find Senator Whelan among your husband's students. Her views are quite different from mine and, I believe, from your husband's."

He's surprised at the intensity of her laughter. "My husband's views . . . especially on politics . . . were always changing, I'm afraid. Did you expect all his students to have the same social and political views as you?"

"Well . . ."

"The sun shines its light on everyone," she says. "The sap nourishes the whole tree and all the flowers in the garden. What my husband taught was a way to enliven the sap, to water the root. The principles he imparted to his students were impartial; they were for inner awakening. What you do in your life, how you see things, and what actions you take to improve the world—that is up to you."

With those few words, Benson immediately sees that what he wants to do, and how he wants to do it, is a product of who he is, his background and experiences. Someone else could and would take a very different course of action as they sought to create value.

For a minute or two Bensen digests this important new understanding. Then he blurts out, "Oh! I almost forgot! You remember, I'm sure, that your husband's final words to us were 'Remember the Seeds!' I didn't know what he meant, but I believe I understand now, after some reflection, and I would like to share my insights with you. Would you have time?"

"Mr. Quinn, I would . . ."

"Please call me Bensen, if you wouldn't mind," he says. "Pardon me for interrupting you."

"Bensen, there is nothing I would enjoy more than to discuss these principles with you."

"So you agree that 'the Seeds' are the core principles Kenji was using to guide us?"

"Yes."

"Good. I have formulated five. Let me tell you what I have come up with, and please be so kind as to correct me and help me to improve my understanding."

She laughs. "Bensen, for a CEO and a powerful man of the Western world, you certainly know how to speak to a traditional Japanese person with the proper humility—even if I am a lowly lady!"

Bensen laughs too. "I assure you, I am not being merely polite. I am new to much of this, and I know I have a lot to learn. And to me, you are not a lowly lady, you are my teacher's wife, and, I suspect, a notable teacher in your own right."

"Thank you," she says softly, not looking up. Then, "Please, go ahead, make your points, and we will discuss them and clarify and amplify if there is a need."

Quite succinctly, Bensen explains his understanding of the five Seeds he has identified. It is at this point that Keiko, to his delight, utters almost exactly what he had imagined: "Very, very good, Bensen! I must say you have captured the heart of Ueki-San's teaching quite beautifully. I fully agree with your analysis, and I have little to add. However, there is one more Seed that I think should be included."

"And that is?"

"You have been so perceptive about the others, Bensen. Just give yourself a little more time, I'm sure the sixth one will come." She sits quietly a moment, then adds, "Would you kindly offer to present these principles at the meeting, when we gather all the students to give shape to the foundation? I believe it will be extremely helpful for everyone."

"I would be glad to—especially if I can think of the sixth!"

"You will, I'm certain."

As the evening settles in, the meeting with Keiko ends, except for one more cup of tea.

———

Later, Bensen wonders why Kenji never made any of the seed principles explicit, spelling them out for easy learning or memory. Nor did he give any of his students instructions as to what exactly he wanted them to do with the foundation they were to form.

Then he realizes Kenji had wanted *them* to figure these things out. It was a necessary step in their growth, the final stroke of his teaching. By formulating the principles in their own words, by determining for themselves what kind of value-creating projects they wished to take on at the foundation, they would grow to fully "own" the knowledge he had given them. It was the only way.

"We'll take his principles, and the example of his life, into our own lives, and express them in our own ways." To give them some previously worked-out formulas, like some kind of catechism to memorize, would be to demean them and to deprive them of the growth required as they charted their own direction.

The points he had written had risen from the clear spring of his own understanding; they were the fruit of the seeds Kenji had planted in him. Really, they were only sprouts, or at best, tiny buds. The real fruit, he senses, is yet to come.

26 The New Gardener Begins His Work

"Nice shot, Bensen!" Tom Wilson's voice rings out from a few yards away.

Bensen watches the trajectory of the ball, a white blur disappearing into the blue of the late-October sky, then walks across the still-damp grass to where Tom is stepping back into the golf cart. "I get lucky sometimes," he replies, replacing his driver in the leather bag and climbing in.

As the days grow perceptibly shorter, Bensen is feeling a grateful sense of relief. It seems that the fierce summer storm has finally blown over. And what a storm! Katie's accident, the scandal with Jim, his painful discovery about HighQuest's factories during the trip to Mexico, the death of his beloved teacher, attempting to align his Board with his new vision. . . . Now, with his team cautiously open to his vision of reinventing the company around the principle of balanced value creation, and most of the Board members receptive if not quite as enthusiastic as he might wish, Bensen is feeling that the hardest times are, at least for the moment, behind him. But when Tom Wilson called to invite him for an early-morning round of golf, he immediately accepted the opportunity to cultivate a relationship he knows will be crucial as he attempts to move the vision forward.

The pristine, spacious course at Tom's club is almost empty. Only one foursome is ahead of them, their laughter drifting on the cool autumn breeze.

"It's nice when it's deserted," Bensen remarks.

"Yeah," Tom says, steering the cart up the hill toward the green. "Sometimes I come out alone first thing in the morning. It gives me a chance to think."

"Will it spoil your morning if I ask you how you feel about the last Board meeting?" Bensen asks.

"Not at all. In fact, I've been wanting to tell you my impressions, and that's one reason I wanted us to connect today. I applauded your presentation, Bensen, but as Bill Jordan suggested, it was less because of the content of your plan than the passion behind it. As you know, we often don't see eye to eye on many business issues, and I don't know if I could go as far as you have in this new direction if I lived another hundred years!"

"I know," Bensen responds. "But I think we do see eye to eye on enough principles, and we respect each other's views enough to be complementary parts of a strong team. At least I've always thought so."

"Oh, I totally agree. I will listen to whatever you have to say, but you can bet that I'll also continue to give you a hard time about some things, to challenge you. Fundamentally, I acknowledge what you've done with this company, and I have confidence in your ability to keep moving forward. You just may need a nudge now and then," he says, looking over at Bensen with a friendly grin, "to keep you on the straight and narrow!"

"Okay, here we are," he adds switching gears. The two men stop talking as they assess their upcoming shots, pondering which club and approach to use.

"Now, the other thing I wanted to talk to you about," Tom says as they draw their chosen implements from their golf bags, "is what spurred your turn-around. The last time I looked, you were the same Bensen Quinn I've known for a decade or more. Now you're a new man. Was it what happened with your daughter?"

"That was part of it," Bensen says. "The crisis rearranged my values, showed me what was really important. Put my career into a different perspective." He halts there, wondering if he should mention his conversations with Kenji and how influential they were in shaping his unfolding vision.

He watches as Tom waggles his club and then swings, a nice, fluid swing, with a lot of power for a man in his seventies. "Nice shot yourself," he says as the ball bounces onto the green, maybe twelve, fifteen feet from the hole.

Tom looks up at Bensen and says, "So, Katie. I understand that. The presence of death, the awareness of death, is a great awakener. Being seventy-four, I can't help but think about it quite vividly. Was there anything else?"

"Well . . ." Bensen hesitates. "Yes, actually. While Katie was in the hospital, I met someone who became a kind of mentor or coach. I learned a lot from him."

"Such as?"

Bensen laughs, enjoying Tom's directness, but also because he's feeling a little uncomfortable. He's never spoken to anyone about what he learned from Kenji, and he's just beginning to truly comprehend it; only a short time has passed since he formulated his version of the Seeds and shared them with Keiko.

He stalls for a moment, slowly lining up his own shot. The result is not so satisfying; the ball bounces into a patch of tall grass alongside the green. "Well, it could have been worse," he shrugs. "It could have landed in the pond."

"Were you thinking too much about how to answer my question, and not focusing completely on your swing?"

"Maybe," Bensen replies, a little startled by Tom's perceptiveness.

"Well, don't let me distract you."

"No," Bensen says, "really, what we're talking about is more important. If my score's a little higher today, it won't matter." As they prepare to move on, he says, "The way it all started was when this man asked me if I was content with the contributions I'm making, the legacy I'm leaving behind with what I do and the way I live."

The Seed of Purpose:
Play the Music in Your Heart

"That's a good place to start. Maybe *the* place."

"Why do you say that?"

"Because, to answer that question, you'd have to know who you are, what the meaning of your life is—or what meaning you want to give it."

"Exactly. That's exactly what happened. I saw that my sense of purpose, beyond the pursuit of success—my own and the company's—was almost nonexistent. I mean, there was no higher purpose, very little sense of enriching anyone's life, creating value in the community, serving in a meaningful way."

"Well, Bensen, you served HighQuest admirably, and by doing so, you contributed wealth to thousands of shareholders. And you served your family well; look at the lifestyle you've created for them. And for yourself, by the way. I know your background."

"Thanks, that part is true. But what I saw was that it wasn't enough for me. The context was too small."

"Understood. So okay, you started there, examining your values."

"Yes, that's what got me thinking about my life. Who am I? What am I here to do? I had to look deeply into myself, to find what I truly value, what I care about. I remember thinking that I couldn't create a legacy I'd be proud of, if I didn't know what I wanted to accomplish. But to know what I wanted to accomplish, I had to look even more deeply into who I am."

"And did you?"

"I fought it. I didn't really want to!"

"Understood, I guarantee you," Tom says, laughing. "It can be a painful business, that kind of self-scrutiny. I've been doing it too, lately."

"I wonder if it's easier when we're young," Bensen says reflectively.

"I doubt it. Or if it *is* easier, it may not be as fruitful. When you have a few more years of experience of life, you've got something to look at—patterns of behavior, mistakes, successes. And, I think, more of a desire to get things right, put things right while you have a chance. At least for me, when I was young, I didn't care enough."

"Nor did I. But if I had taken the time . . ."

"Sure! If we had taken the time!" Tom snaps. "But we didn't. And now we are. If I had purchased a few thousand shares of Microsoft when it first came out, I could have been sitting on a bigger pile of money. But I didn't."

"I only meant that I might have made fewer mistakes," Bensen says, "been a better father . . . and husband. Probably a better leader, too."

"I know what you meant. But now you can." Tom's voice is emphatic.

"You're right. I've never been one to look back with regrets. But then, I've never looked that carefully at myself before."

"I think the purpose of looking back is to gain understanding, not to beat ourselves up."

"Agreed," Bensen says. "And not only that, I'd say. I think we're actually more whole, more . . . authentic human beings, if we can own our whole story."

"What do you mean?"

"We all make mistakes. We're not perfect. We never will be."

"What's the news in that?" Tom asks.

"No news. But do we own up to that, as leaders? Or do we try to project some kind of perfect image? Are we willing to admit that we're confused, scared, or, God forbid, wrong? I wasn't. Wasn't willing, I mean. Certainly not as CEO. And . . . not at home, either," he adds, thinking about how he yelled at Katie and told her not to go to meetings about sweatshops, instead of taking an honest look at what she was saying.

"And why do you see this as important?" Tom asks. "I admit that what you're saying rings true."

"I think it's important because honesty, authenticity, being who we are, not only feels better to us, it also gives us a stronger place to stand."

The Seed of Authenticity: Embrace the Flower, Embrace the Thorn

"Like what you said in the Board meeting? About assessing our strengths and weaknesses, so we can move forward with more power?"

"Yes," Bensen affirms. "And another thing. It also breeds trust. People don't trust leaders whom they feel lack self-awareness, who have glaring blind spots about themselves."

"Granted."

"So we can be the kind of leaders that people don't trust but nevertheless have to obey because we hold power over their lives—we can give them promotions or fire them, give or withhold raises. But why not be the kind of leader people want to follow and support because they trust us and are inspired by us, both as people and, to use this word loosely, as visionaries, who have a sense of purpose, a worthwhile goal."

"I totally agree, Bensen. And I don't think you're saying that we have to share our foibles with other people; I don't have to tell 'stupid Tom Wilson' stories, but if I admit *inside myself* that there are those stories, people will pick up that I'm not a hypocrite, not hiding out, from myself or them."

"Exactly. Although, you know, I don't think our position is weakened if we tell a 'stupid me' story once in a while."

"Well, all right. I like this, Bensen."

"Let me tell you something more about this that was an important breakthrough for me. You may find it meaningful."

"Fire away."

"There's a deeper level here. Usually when we talk about being authentic we mean being honest, being true to who we are, being open about strengths and weaknesses and all that."

"Right."

"Okay—but I think there's a higher kind of authenticity. What about being authentic not just to what we are, but to what we can be?"

"Unrealized potential?"

"Exactly. A seed isn't born to remain a seed, but to grow. Puppies are cute, but that's no reason they should stay puppies forever. Growing, Tom, blossoming. We are all so much more than we know."

"I agree, Bensen."

"That's why you and I value freedom so much; maybe that's why wiser people than us have valued it. Not so that we can run around and do whatever we please, but so we can continue growing and becoming who we really are."

For a while, neither man speaks. Bensen had managed to get out of the rough and onto the green, with a good shot that landed his ball within a yard of Wilson's, both of them a mid-range putt from the cup. They focus all their attention on their game. Tom takes only one stroke to put the ball away. Bensen's putt looks perfect, heading straight for the hole, using the slight slope of the ground to advantage. Then, at the last second, it veers just enough to rim the cup and roll beyond, costing him another stroke. "Well, sometimes I *don't* get lucky," he says.

As they set off for the next hole, Tom takes up the thread of their conversation. "You said you had a breakthrough about this. I assumed you meant something personal. Or didn't you?"

"I did," Bensen says, again amused at Tom's directness. "Here's the thing. I realized that I had an unused strength—which in a way becomes a weakness, right? Anyway, I realized that there was something about me that I had buried, because I didn't feel it had any place in the corporate world. Well, that's not exactly true. I don't know that I thought it out. It just happened. But probably I would have explained it that way."

"And it was?"

"A concern for the well-being of people."

"Ah!"

"What do you mean, 'Ah'?"

"I mean, that's the difference I see in you. Between the old Bensen Quinn and the new version."

"Bensen, Version 7.2!"

"No, seriously. I hadn't put my finger on it. But that's it."

Bensen looks amused but says nothing, and Tom, after a moment, inquires, "Are you going to let me in on this?"

"I was just remembering something. When all these changes were just starting to happen, I was nervous about it, and I talked to this mentor I was telling you about. I said something like, 'I feel like I'm going soft.' And he said, 'You're right. You're going soft in the heart—and it's good.'"

They were standing at the start of the seventh hole, and Bensen had only scheduled the time to play nine. The morning was going by too quickly.

"Men of my generation weren't brought up to acknowledge things like soft-heartedness," Tom says, standing still now and looking off over the gently rolling green. "But you get to an age when you realize how important a part of life that is. My wife says I melt into a puddle around the grandchildren, or at least I did when they were little. They can still get anything they want out of me, any time!" He falls silent, but Bensen knows he's got more to say, and keeps quiet.

"When I would go hiking," Tom resumes, turning to face Bensen, "and I'd be out in the woods alone, or with a buddy who was able to keep his mouth shut long enough to enjoy the quiet out there, sometimes I'd feel the beauty of nature so strongly—the leaves fluttering, birds getting used to our being there and flying nearby, singing their songs—it was kind of a holy feeling, how everything was all . . . kind of connected, harmonious. It's hard to describe. . . ."

"I understand," Bensen says quietly.

"And I would feel such love for it all," Tom continues. "If there's any kind of God, and I believe there is, he certainly makes his presence felt out in nature. But the thing is, all of that was in a compartment of its own. The grandchildren, the warm fuzzy feelings. It had no influence, no impact, on my business dealings. I don't know what it is about this business culture that has grown up, Bensen, but it's very one-sided. It rewards hard-heartedness, it almost demands it. It's not a field of generosity and cooperation. Well, I take that back. There are places for that kind of behavior, within a limited sphere. People on a team, for instance. But even there, everyone's got an eye on everyone else, looking for a one-up, for personal advancement, holding on to good ideas to make sure they get the credit for them, that whole game. But I'm getting off my point."

"Actually, you're helping me make mine," Bensen says with a smile. "I'd like to change that culture, transform the way business is done."

"Well," Tom responds, "maybe I'm too old or too cynical to think about reforming the world. I don't know if it's possible to redo the game board in a big way. But one thing I do know is that I don't have to play by those rules any more, and I won't. The game I want to play, if I may say so with you, Bensen, is a game of the heart."

"Meaning?"

"Meaning that I want to serve in the best way I can. It's the only thing that makes sense, now, at this stage of my life."

"Do you think it's age-related?" Bensen inquires.

Tom pauses and looks out across the green, as if the answer is somewhere out there. Then he says, "Well, there's something about being older, having been successful, having played the game and reached a good, high level, that makes it easier to back off and say, 'Okay, enough of that, let me see what I can do with my life that would really make me proud as a human being that I contributed to my community, to my world.' But it wasn't an age thing for you, Bensen, it came to you through other pressures and challenges. So I don't think it's necessarily about age. It's more about when a person's ready to make a wider contribution."

"I have HighQuest as a vehicle for the kind of service I'm intending for myself now," Bensen says. "I have all those factories, and the surrounding communities. That's a big playing field for me to start trying to make a difference, adding value to people's lives. If you don't mind my asking, Tom, what will you do? Or what are you already doing?"

The Seed of Value Creation: Serving Parts and Whole

"I'd like to create value in an across-the-board way that benefits as many people as possible," Tom answers. "But I know I have only so much time left and no more, and I want to use it well."

"And what would that mean to you?"

"Well, at least a couple of things. Since the bulk of my life has been spent in business, I'll focus there. I think I can be useful to a lot of people, particularly through my mentoring foundation."

"Mentoring foundation?"

"Yeah. I told you I agreed with your statement that most of us—maybe all of us—are much more than we believe we are."

"Yes, I remember."

"So here's what happened. A while back, my granddaughter came to dinner, and she brought a college friend. For one of their classes, they're collaborating on a documentary film about the differences in their high school educations. Jessie went to an exclusive private school and her friend attended public school. Jessica's school had carpets on the floor, small classes, assignments designed to help them pass all their college entrance exams with top scores, tutors available if they were having trouble in any subject; they had counselors helping them choose the best colleges and assisting them in preparing their applications; they had frequent guest speakers presenting them with career options, lecturing about new technologies and research. And on and on.

"The other kid had to pass through a metal detector at the front door. She spoke to a counselor once, for five minutes, who told her she ought to be realistic and apply to a community college or a state college that she could afford, and never suggested she might try for a scholarship. The restrooms were so disgusting she felt nauseated when she had to use one. The classes were huge, and geared toward the lowest common denominator, which basically meant keeping the class quiet for fifty minutes.

"Well, I didn't have to see their film to get the message. Kids like that don't get what they need at school, and many of them probably don't get it at home, either. So there should be an additional alternative, which I aim to provide.

"I mentioned that I know your background, Bensen. Mine was quite different. I grew up with money and a not inconsequential degree of privilege. And, mind you, I'm in no rush to give any of it away. But I've come to feel that there's no excuse for the enormous gap between the rich and the poor today. I have it pretty good, as you know. I live in an extremely comfortable home, I own a couple of nice cars, a boat, and a vacation home, I eat far better than kings ever did, I can afford to go anywhere and buy almost anything I might want, while there are literally hundreds of millions of people who live on about a dollar a day—a dollar a day, Bensen, think of it. I'm not planning to give away what I have earned. And I don't believe in supporting people who don't work, who don't take responsibility for their lives. But I am in favor of what the Bible calls being open-handed toward our brothers, and I believe it behooves us to do what we can to feed the hungry, clothe the naked, and all the rest of it. It's our tradition, it's stewardship, taking care of the earth and of our brothers and sisters. It's what we all say we believe in, on Sundays."

Listening to Tom, Bensen is deeply moved. He had no idea all this was going on beneath the tough surface. He senses that it won't be too long before Tom truly understands what he wants to do with the company, and something inside him relaxes about the future.

"I'm not aiming to tackle public education reform," Tom continues. "I don't feel I can rectify all the social evils and the inequality of opportunity. I can just do what I can do. I've concluded that there are things I know, things I've learned, that would be valuable to young people, and I want to spend a good deal of my time mentoring those who could benefit from help and who might be responsive. I'm particularly interested in what we call disadvantaged youth. I'm convinced that plenty of those kids have the ability to shine, if they're given a vision of what might be possible for them, and a little help moving ahead."

"Do you plan to work with them individually, or . . . ?"

"I'll work with some. I already do. But I'm in the process of setting up a foundation to train volunteers in coaching skills, to mentor these kids. That way, I can multiply myself, since my time is so limited."

"That sounds very, very worthwhile," Bensen says.

"Yes, it's very gratifying."

"I'm sure you can line up corporations, and even some smaller businesses, to sponsor your program. We may not be able to contribute HighQuest resources without a conflict-of-interest question, but I will personally be a sponsor."

"Thank you, Bensen. I appreciate that. I'll let you know as soon as we have the procedures in place for donations and sponsorships."

"And here's something else. I may be starting a foundation with some friends of mine; it might be a good fit for you to associate your mentoring program with us. We can talk about it."

———

As Tom guides the cart toward the next hole, Bensen strips off his sweater and Tom pulls off his windbreaker; the autumn chill is giving way as the morning sun climbs higher and warms the air and the ground. "Do you smell the grass, Bensen?"

"I sure do. I love that sweet, earthy smell."

Both are feeling focused and fulfilled in their conversation, and golf has receded far into the background.

"You know, Bensen—and stop me if this is getting too personal—but I'd like to tell you something else that precipitated my thoughts about coaching these younger people. You probably haven't thought about this because you're too young to have experienced it. How old are you now?"

"Turning fifty this year."

"Too young to feel it, but you've probably had to deal with it. It's become an issue with the economic ups and downs we've had over the last several years. Older people are being shoved aside by younger ones, who think we don't have any relevance, we can't keep up."

"Definitely an issue," Bensen says, nodding in agreement.

"Of course, in some ways that assessment is correct." Tom continues. "We'll never keep up with the new and unfolding technologies, for instance. But technology is only a very small part of how life works—and how business works. But I'm jumping ahead here. What I wanted to tell you is that I reached a point where I started to feel obsolete, mostly because of the pressure I was getting to clean out my desk and polish up my golf clubs. This made me very depressed. Luckily, it didn't last long. When I started looking deeply into myself, I saw that even though I may not be conversant with the latest technology, or the latest quality system like Six Sigma, or whatever's in style this year, there's a lot that I do know. And it has to do with having lived a little.

"People who have never seen much of life, even if they're experts in the latest ideas and technologies, don't have a clue about how to deal with hard times. I'm in awe of the know-how of a lot of these younger people, and I won't pretend to compete with them on that field. But that doesn't mean I should be taken to the south pasture and shot. I think there's an important role, a leadership role, for people who have seen a thing or two, who didn't grow up in the nineties boom, who have ridden the ups and downs of the business cycle and know how to move through both, who have the wisdom and the guts to deal with difficult times—and in terms of the mentoring work, who know how to accomplish things and can offer advice to people who have no long-term perspective on how the world works."

"And," Bensen throws in, "who have some idea of how to balance priorities in life, such as the things I'm finally learning about actually spending time with our families instead of just saying they are important."

"Exactly. But I was asking you what you learned from this mentor you encountered, and I've spent a good deal of time going on about myself. Anything else you'd care to mention?"

"Well, there is one more thing that might interest you. It was a totally new idea to me. It's about something he called Essence, the inner spiritual reality. He said that most of the time we operate from our ego, our individual sense of self, but that there's a deeper part of us, usually out of our awareness, that's bigger, more universal. Sometimes he'd talk about it as the underlying intelligence of things."

"Sounds a little too far out for me, Bensen."

"I told you it was totally new for me, too. The thing is, Tom, he taught me a way to sit myself down and connect with it. . . ."

"With what, exactly?"

"Well, all I can say is that it's an aspect of myself that's peaceful, quiet, and expansive. When I touch onto it, I relax. I feel calm. Happy inside. Then, when I get back into activity, I feel centered. Like I'm in the eye of the storm, not blown around by all the craziness that goes with being a leader."

"That part sounds good. I'm not sure I buy the theory."

"No need to buy any of it. But it has had some good benefits for me."

Both focus on their golf game for a few minutes. During that time, Bensen feels as if what he said has confused Tom or made him uncomfortable, and that perhaps he's failed to explain it properly.

"Tom, it occurs to me that this Essence thing is like what you told me you experience when you're out in nature, that sense of oneness pervading things. . . ."

"Correction: what I *sometimes* experience. I wish it happened more often."

"The way he explained it, there really is a oneness at the heart of things, whatever we call it. I once asked him if it was God that he was talking about."

"And what did he say?"

"He said something like, 'Some people may wish to call it that.'"

"That's kind of how I experience it. If indeed we're talking about the same thing."

"I sense that we are," Bensen says. "As I understand it, Essence is the creative intelligence that's conducting all the workings of nature. Because it's so powerful and so all-pervasive, we are better off if we can act in harmony with it, connected to it, like a wave that can rise high because it's supported by remaining in contact with the ocean."

"That makes some sense."

"All I know is that when I take the time to do it, I'm much more effective. I feel more at peace, more like a leader than like a fireman running around putting out fires.

The Seed of Essence: Engage Essence as the Master, Employ Ego as the Servant

The more collected I am inside, the better the results seem to be." And looking around, Bensen announces, "Eighth hole, coming up! I had almost lost track of being on the golf course."

"Yes," Tom says, "this has been a great morning, very stimulating. I wouldn't object to making a habit of this, Bensen. First Tuesday of every month, maybe? The more we talk, the more it seems to me there might be quite a bit of overlap in our work as we go forward; it would be good to keep connected."

"Funny that you should use the word 'connected,'" Bensen says. "It's something else I've found to be important. We were talking before about how we tend not to admit our weaknesses, right? Well, for many years, I had been vaguely aware that I was not renowned for my expertise in relationship skills, but it didn't seem to matter."

"You got away with it, right? I understand," Tom says.

"At work," Bensen continues, "I got things done, the company was thriving, and that's what was important. When the impact of Katie's accident made me examine my priorities and the way I live my life, I saw that I had drifted away from Emily, I had virtually no relationship any more with my daughter, and I tended to treat people in a pretty cold and impersonal way—using them, really, more than relating to them. I had to admit that 'connecting' was an area in which I was not proficient, and that it might actually matter, after all.

"During those very difficult days," he goes on, "somehow the anxiety and grief about Katie stripped away a veneer, and I became kind of vulnerable—much more aware of people, more open with them, and more caring about how I affected them. I started noticing the difference between how I felt when I operated as my old, tough self, and how I felt when I was my new and more open self. Not only did the new style of relating feel good—I was more energetic, happier—but it also evoked a positive response

The Seed of Relationship:
Always Connect

in other people. The obvious conclusion was that connecting is not such a bad thing!"

"I think," Tom begins reflectively, "that people like us fear that it will make us weak, less effective as leaders, if we're too open. I always thought I needed a substantial amount of toughness in order to direct people, to keep things moving."

"And how do you feel about it now?"

"It's not necessary. Not as a steady way of operating." After a pause he laughs and adds, "Sometimes it really does the job, though!"

Bensen chuckles too. "Too true. But I don't want to give you a false impression. Simply understanding the value of connecting, and getting an occasional taste of it, hasn't totally transformed my behavior. I'm still no relationship expert! Even when I try to be more present and open with people, it's not always easy."

"I completely understand," Tom puts in. "I think I'm a lot like you—you may not like to hear that, Bensen, but I'm afraid it's true! It's not built into my character for me to connect, either with myself or with others. I'm so outer-directed, focused on getting things accomplished, it's too easy to be brusque and not even notice."

"Yeah," says Bensen. "I've got a long way to go with this one. . . ."

"Okay, Bensen," Tom interrupts in a strong voice, "this is it: last hole." He sets a ball on the tee and looks up at Bensen with a serious expression. "Now, based on everything we've spoken about today, here's an older man's advice to you: Lean back . . . and knock the crap out of it!"

———

As Bensen drives from the golf course to his office, one sentence of Tom's sticks in his mind. It had come up when the older man was talking about his interest in mentoring. "Plenty of those kids have the ability to shine," Tom had declared with conviction, "if they're given a vision of what might be possible for them, and a little help moving ahead."

Bensen revolves the words in his head, trying to understand why they seem so important. Then it strikes him: "What Tom wants to do with young people is something *everyone* can use: support in drawing out their potential. And it's exactly what Kenji did with me. There I was, a CEO at the top of my career, and yet, after he got done with me, I was a better person as well as a better leader. Plus, he gave me the tools to keep on becoming a better person and a better leader—to continue growing."

Thinking of Kenji in this way brings a glow of physical warmth to his heart. "How did he do it?" he wonders, searching his memory. "What did he actually do? Now that I've formulated five of the Seeds, I know that he helped me understand things, like the importance of authenticity, having a purposeful vision, connecting deeply with myself and with others. But it was all so unobtrusive. At each moment his guidance was so subtle, so masterful that I had no idea what was going on.

"With just a few words, or a simple question, he could generate a new phase of growth for me. Like when he told me the story about his granddaughter. All he actually said was, 'I ask myself if I am playing the music I want other people to remember,' but that was enough to start me thinking about my life and my legacy, the value of the contributions I was making. Or the time I was feeling irritated because the meeting to define the HighQuest 'mission' seemed so absurd, and he said, 'Maybe you need to create a mission statement for your own life.'"

In retrospect, Bensen can see that these probes and prompts were designed to move him, to make him think and feel, to wake him up from the habitual flow of his life. It had all seemed like friendly, spontaneous conversation at the time, but he can see now that Kenji was on top of each and every piece, selflessly serving and guiding.

At this moment, the mystery of the sixth Seed, the Seed Kenji's widow had said was missing from his list, is solved. "Coaching!" he says aloud. "Guidance. Directly serving others by helping them come into their own. It's not only what Kenji did with me; it's the example he set for me as well."

The Seed of Coaching: Drawing Forth Potential

Kenji, Bensen recognizes, *embodied* the Seeds even more than he taught them. "He didn't just impart precepts and principles. Probably his greatest lesson to me was simply being who he was. He never pushed me or lectured me. But he led me forward, steadily and surely, because he saw farther and more deeply than I did.

"He had a clear *purpose*—to help me become my whole, authentic self— and he cared about me. I felt that, so I trusted him.

"He *connected* on all levels: He knew his deepest core; he was in touch with his values; he was a loving friend to everyone around him.

"He *engaged with Essence* as the guiding light of his life, and never seemed to be operating merely from his ego.

"He was deeply *authentic*, honest, and whole, yet he was constantly learning and growing.

"He *created value* with everything he did, whether with the beauty he brought into being through his gardening, the work he did with his students, or just by being so completely present with everyone he touched.

"All these qualities made him a wise and skillful *guide*. So that's yet another thing I have to thank him for—not just for my own personal growth, and the repercussions of that growth in my family and at HighQuest and everything the company touches, but he also gave me a model of how to meaningfully serve other people. . . . He showed me the way to authentic leadership."

Realizing how grateful he is to Kenji, he's amused to remember how he had inwardly struggled when Kenji asked him to carry on his work. "He felt me fighting him, but he persisted. He must have known that if I didn't promise, I might never have considered myself worthy of taking on a task like that. He was too kind to just come out and say, 'What I'm trying to tell you, Bensen, you thick-headed dolt, is that your greatest happiness is going to come from being a coach like me! That's the essential thing I've prepared you for.'"

Closing his eyes for a moment at a red light, Bensen sees Kenji's kind, smiling face, and he realizes that his teacher *did* say that, at one of their last moments together. "The day will come," the master gardener had said, "when you will

find greater happiness in passing on this knowledge, in being the catalyst for another person's awakening, than in anything else you have ever done." After
spending the morning discussing these principles with Tom Wilson, he's had
enough of a taste to know that what Kenji said was the truth, and he is filled
with the silent awareness that his day *has* come.

He laughs silently to himself as he recalls Kenji's unshakable confidence in
him to carry on his work. At the same moment, he senses an impulse deep in
his soul, which whispers, "Bensen, you have indeed remembered the Seeds."

———

If you would like to receive a *free* Awakening the Leader Within
Discussion Group Guide to facilitate team building or general
discussion groups, you can access it at www.leadersource.com.
Just click on "books" and go to "Awakening the Leader Within"
to download this helpful guide.

Awakening the Leader Within

Awakening the Leader Within is designed to be an *interactive coaching experience* that can help you grow toward your full stature as a person and as a leader. To derive optimal benefit from the book, I suggest that you interact with it in three equally important ways:

- **The Story** is crafted to open up feelings and emotions and to inspire you to maximize your capabilities and your contribution; it leverages *the power of the heart*.
- **The "Wake-Up Call" reflection boxes** throughout the book use the power of questions to deepen the key learnings and reveal their relevance to your life and concerns; they leverage *the power of the mind*.
- **The Growth Guide** will help you consolidate what you have learned and focus your heart and mind on the process of commitment and application; it leverages *the power of action*.

If you have only read the story, you are only one-third of the way to gaining the benefits of the book. If this is the case, please *go back* and complete all the Wake-Up Call reflection boxes before embarking on the Growth Guide!

When you are ready to begin using the Growth Guide, review the work you did in each of the Wake-Up Call reflection areas. Take your time walking back through the book. Pause at each box to review your notes and recall the emotions, memories, insights, or commitments that were provoked. Then spend some time organizing and integrating these experiences by responding to the following questions. Don't try to zip through the questions, writing three-word replies. Slow down. Take time to sit quietly. Look deeply. If you work with a journal, use it to write more extensive answers.

What themes consistently arose regarding your personal and leadership development?

_____

_____

_____

Did you find any of the Six Seeds of Awakening or any other principles in the book particularly powerful, insight-provoking, or relevant? Why? What do they mean to you? _____

_____

_____

What stories or scenes in the book had the most emotional impact? Why do you supposed they affected you? _____

_____

_____

_____

Did you relate to the main character, Bensen? In what ways? If you didn't, can you say why? _____

_____

_____

_____

Do you have a Kenji, a profound career/life/leadership coach, in your life? _____ *If not, would you welcome a relationship like that?* _____

If the answer is yes, what will you do to make it happen? _____

_____

Do you think you can be your own coach? _____ *What have you learned from this book that could help you do this?* _____

_____

What qualities would you need to develop, in order to be an effective coach for yourself?

_____

Did any of the other characters strike a positive or negative chord with you? Why?

_____

What can you learn from your reaction? _____

_____

_____

The Three Paths of Coaching

For coaching to have a lasting, transformative impact, three interrelated pathways need to be built: Awareness, Commitment, and Practice. If all three are present and operating, breakthroughs will occur and growth will be sustained. If any one of the three is absent, the results will dissipate over time. You may learn the best techniques and disciplines to practice, but if you lack commitment, you won't continue your efforts. Similarly, all the enthusiasm and commitment in the world won't get you far if you don't adhere to a workable action plan. And without awareness of your strengths and weaknesses, how will you know what to commit to, or what you need to do?

———

Building Awareness is the process of bringing new information about ourselves into our field of view. It might include keeping our attention on a newly discovered gift we have uncovered in ourselves. Or it may involve the more painful process of acknowledging that our behavior is unintentionally self-defeating or affects others in a life-damaging way. Awareness encompasses the *inner discipline* of looking within ourselves to shed light on our strengths and our growth challenges, and the *outer discipline* of observing ourselves as we engage in action and relationships.

Here's one effective approach to building awareness, based on our coaching experience at LeaderSource.

Take some time to make an inventory of your strengths and weaknesses. Look back on your life, and do your best to capture and include in your inventory your finest achievements as well as your blunders. Note the tasks and aspects of life where you excel, where things go easily for you and flow effortlessly toward success and fulfillment, as well as difficult situations (both in relationships and at work) where you struggle and bump into recurring problems, where you just can't seem to get it right. These all shed light on who you are, what your capabilities are, and where you may be in need of some work.

In creating your inventory, make good use of any feedback you can think of, whether a "360-degree assessment" at work or comments people have made over the years about your gifts and developmental needs, your personality, values, and strengths. This feedback may have come from colleagues, bosses, people who work for you, friends, or loved ones. It's important not just to try to figure this out yourself, but to look closely at what others say. Typically there's what is known as a *gap analysis* between how we see ourselves and how others see us, and our intention here is to face the truth, to get a clear and complete picture.

This is not just a good psychological exercise; it's crucial for leadership and for peak performance. In his groundbreaking book *Working With Emotional Intelligence,* Daniel Goleman writes:

> People who are self aware are also better performers. Presumably their self awareness helps them in a process of continuous improvement. . . . Knowing their strengths and weaknesses and approaching their work accordingly, was a competence found in virtually every star performer in a study of several hundred "knowledge workers"—computer scientists, auditors and the like—at companies including AT&T and 3M.

Building Awareness requires the willingness to hold a mirror up to ourselves and take an honest look at the whole person. And it requires courage. To see, to acknowledge, and to embrace both the positive and negative aspects of who we are demands an ongoing act of bravery. But it is well worth the effort. As the French writer Anais Nin said, "Life shrinks or expands in proportion to one's courage." *Building Awareness is the path of courage.*

———

Building Commitment begins with fully comprehending the consequences of our actions. However, it's not enough simply to understand intellectually that if we continue on the path we're on, we're going to fall short of our goals or hurt ourselves or others. We have to feel it. When we have a deep enough *emotional experience* of the impact of a behavior, our life changes permanently. This is why trauma can be such a great transformative teacher. I've seen executives who repeatedly ignore their fitness and self-care needs until they are in a hospital bed fighting for their life. Once they clearly perceive and emotionally experience the consequences of their behavior, meaningful commitment to transformation can begin.

This includes things we don't do that we would like to, as well as things we do that we wish we didn't! It's certainly important to recognize the consequences of any life-damaging behaviors we may have, but it's equally valuable to perceive the inevitable outcome of what we *don't* do, such as gifts and talents we fail to develop and use, or deeply held values we don't express. In the story, Bensen Quinn gradually becomes aware of the consequences of not honoring values that were important to him earlier in his life. As he considers his legacy and starts to see how his life will end up if he ignores these inner soul yearnings, his transformation begins.

Kenji serves as Bensen's coach from their first meeting in chapter 6. By asking "What music do you want to be remembered for?" he initiates Bensen into a process of self-reflection that helps him discover his core values and commit to living by them. This process culminates in chapter 19, where Bensen says firmly, "I'm committed. If I try and fail, at least I'll have done my best to accomplish what I believe is right. . . . If I don't try, I'll know that I caved in, that I acted according to what *others* believe. That's not acceptable to me."

If you would like to begin strengthening your "commitment muscle," you might try this exercise, which we use with clients at LeaderSource. Start by identifying several things you would like to do more of, or less of, in order to improve your life. Make a list of the most important items, and from this list, pick *one*. (If you immediately know the one thing you would like to do or not do, you don't need to bother with the list-making process.)

Then envision your future in a two-part drama. In part one, you have successfully mastered that new habit or behavior and made it part of your life. What does your life look like? How have your surroundings changed? How do you feel? How do people respond to you? What have you gained—materially, spiritually, socially—by making this commitment and honoring it? Don't just look at this picture from the outside: Immerse yourself in it, in the sights and sounds. Try to put yourself completely into your life as it would be. Feel it in your body, feel it in your heart, feel it in your cells.

In part two—and this may not be so much fun, but it's an extremely important part of the process—envision your life *without* the new behavior. You didn't choose it. Or you decided to do it but didn't follow through. How do you feel about yourself? How are others perceiving you? What have you failed to accomplish, how have you failed to grow, because you did not commit and follow through? Again, don't be an outside observer and just analyze it intellectually, but really feel it. Let your imagination go and get into the picture.

Then make your choice. Commit to doing or not doing it. Tell yourself, this is what I'm going to gain if I commit to this course of action, and what I'm going to give up if I don't. This is what I stand to gain; this is what I stand to lose.

I'd suggest going for something really substantial here. For example: If you didn't align your life to your sense of purpose, where would you end up? Or if you continue to dominate in your interactions with people, what is your life going to look like?

From experience, I know that some people "get" this right away; others need to take it home as a practice for a few weeks and pay attention to it before they really feel it in their body, before the consequences of their actions migrate from their abstract thoughts to their gut and their soul. But once it hits home, behavior starts to change. So if you don't get it right away, I urge you to keep at it for a week or two.

Building Commitment entails crafting a vision of the future based on an authentic understanding of who we are, where we stand, and where we want to go. James Collins and Jerry Porras spoke about vision as "knowing 'in your bones' what can or must be done. . . . It isn't forecasting the future, it is creating the future by taking action in the present." *Building Commitment is the path of vision.*

———

Building Practice is the process of consistently engaging in new behaviors to enrich our lives. It is the application phase of growth. While it is crucial to build awareness and to build commitment, they are not sufficient for transformation; *consistent action* is required.

Admiring our great insights and feeling proud of our new commitments will not, in themselves, get us to our desired destination. Lao Tzu wrote in the Tao Te Ching, "A Sage will practice the Tao. A fool will only admire it."

Practice makes possibilities practical. Or, as Esalen founder Michael Murphy put it, "Practice is the seedbed of miracles." Sometimes the "seedbed of miracles" will be *inner disciplines* such as meditation, to help us connect with Essence, that calm center within us that holds infinite potential for dynamism. Another helpful inner discipline is to examine our beliefs from moment to moment, to see if they are opening us up or closing us down.

Sometimes practices will be *outer disciplines* like starting the day half an hour earlier for more effective planning; showing more appreciation of employees or family members; making dietary changes; or exercising on a regular schedule. Regardless of whether it's an inner or outer discipline, we have to *do it*—consistently. "To keep the lamp burning," Mother Teresa said, "we have to put oil in it." To keep growing, we have to put practice into it.

Building Practice entails devising new, disciplined ways of behaving to enrich our life and the lives of others. *Building Practice is the path of discipline.* Discipline brings us the benefits, and the benefits self-generate continued practice.

Creating Your Growth Plan

Now let's get to work creating your personal growth plan. To build upon your discoveries and reflections from the book, I suggest that we construct the plan around the Six Seeds of Growth:

The Seed of Authenticity: Embrace the Flower, Embrace the Thorn
The Seed of Purpose: Play the Music in Your Heart
The Seed of Essence: Engage Essence as the Master, Employ Ego as the Servant
The Seed of Relationship: Always Connect
The Seed of Value Creation: Serving Parts and Whole
The Seed of Coaching: Drawing Forth Potential

One by one, we will take up each Seed, exploring its meaning and importance. Then we'll identify the most important priorities for you to focus on in order to sprout that Seed and help it blossom and bear fruit in your life. To make the plan most effective, each of these six powerful seed principles will be tied to the Three Paths of Coaching: Building Awareness, Building Commitment, and Building Practice. For example, when we take up the Seed of Purpose, we will look at how to build *awareness* of your core purpose, how to strengthen your *commitment* to living each day in a more purposeful and meaningful manner, and what *practices* you can undertake, right now, to help you honor that commitment.

As you go through this process, remember that transformation often does not require us to do many new things. It may only involve doing one or two that are fundamental enough to change our entire life. Pay attention to recurring themes—in your responses to the Wake-Up Call reflections and in the following exercises—and be aware of the most emotionally charged moments of insight or commitment. Be alert: They may not come as lightning flashes; they may appear as a "still small voice within." These clues may provide all you need to awaken profound changes in yourself and your life.

The Seed of Authenticity:
Embrace the Flower, Embrace the Thorn

The highest courage is to dare to appear to be what one is.
—Bishop John Lancaster Spalding

Of all the Six Seeds of Growth, authenticity may be the most important for effective, sustainable leadership. It can also be the most challenging. Most people never realize that it's an area of their lives that needs attention. In more than two decades of interacting with thousands of leaders, I've yet to meet an executive for coaching who comes to me lamenting, "I'm having real trouble being authentic." If it is so important, why don't we recognize it as an issue?

I think the answer is both simple and profound: *We are always authentic to our present state of development.* We all behave in perfect synchrony with our current level of emotional, psychological, and spiritual evolution or unfoldment. All our actions and relationships, and the quality and power of our leadership, accurately express the person we have grown to be. Therefore, doing the best we can with who we are and what we've got, we appropriately conclude that we are authentic.

There's a big hitch, however. While we are true and authentic to our current state of development, *we are inauthentic to our potential state of development.* As Shakespeare wrote so eloquently in *Hamlet,* "We know what we are, but not what we may be." As humans and as leaders, we have an infinite ability to grow, to be more, and to become more. Our horizons are unlimited. If there is an end point to growing in authenticity, I certainly haven't seen it.

To deepen authenticity, to nourish the Seeds of Growth within us, takes time and attention. In this world, the amount of distraction and busyness we all experience keeps us from undertaking the inward journey and engaging in the quiet reflection required to become more authentic human beings. John Gardner writes in his book, *Self-Renewal:*

> Human beings have always employed an enormous variety of clever devices
> for running away from themselves. We can keep ourselves so busy, fill our lives
> with so many diversions, stuff our heads with so much knowledge, involve

ourselves with so many people and cover so much ground that we never have
time to probe the fearful and wonderful world within. . . . By middle life most
of us are accomplished fugitives from ourselves.

Penetrating the commotion and distraction of our lives to explore the depths
of ourselves is the prerequisite for authenticity.

So what is authenticity? Judging by the leaders my colleagues at Leader-
Source and I have studied and coached over the years, authenticity appears to
be, more than anything, an alignment, a congruence of the inner and outer person. More often than not, the authentic person's beliefs, values, principles, and
behavior tend to line up. Commonly referred to as *walking your talk,* it is also *being* your talk at a very deep level.

Another prominent feature of highly authentic individuals is *awareness.*
Whether they have come to it naturally or have worked hard to attain it, the
most real, genuine, sincere people tend to be aware of both their gifts and their
vulnerabilities. This awareness manifests as an inner openness with themselves
about their strengths as well as their limitations—they know who they are and
don't apologize for their capabilities—and an outer openness with others about
their whole selves. They neither try to cover up their weaknesses nor hide their
light under a bushel. As Malcolm Forbes put it, "Too many people over-value
what they are not and under-value what they are."

Authentic people value all of who they are. "To be authentic you have to
be everything that you are, omitting nothing," Deepak Chopra wrote. "Within
everyone there is light and shadow, good and evil, love and hate. The play of
these opposites is what constantly moves life forward; the river of life expresses
itself in all its changes from one opposite to another. If you can truly embrace
these opposites within yourself, you will be authentic."

What happens to us when we are around people who are real and open
about themselves, warts and all? We trust them. Their authenticity and vulnerability have made them trustworthy, and we rush to their side.

Authenticity is crucial to leadership. It is far more important and fundamental than a person's leadership style. Leaders who know who they really are
usually outperform leaders who are unwilling to admit their flaws. Although I
believe the world is headed toward a time when top-down, authoritarian leadership will be outmoded, I have seen authoritarian leaders with substantial authenticity outperform leaders who strove to be collaborative yet lacked authenticity. I've seen leaders low in charisma and polish get in front of a group

and stumble around a bit, but their personal authenticity and substance were so tangibly established that they inspired the group members and moved them to a new level of excellence. Could such leaders benefit from working on their style of presentation? Certainly. But how much would it really matter, compared with their trust-inspiring authenticity? "The individual who does not embody her messages will eventually be found out," warns Howard Gardner in *Leading Minds,* "even as the inarticulate individual who leads the exemplary life may eventually come to be appreciated."

Many so-called leadership programs—as well as some leadership coaches—train clients or group participants in skills to support "desirable" leadership styles. This is more of a "charm school" approach, versus something of lasting substance. From my perspective, deeper work to foster growth, integrity, and authenticity yields a much better return on investment.

Bensen Quinn, in our story, possessed all the necessary prerequisites for leadership in the corporate world. He was intelligent, dynamic, and ambitious. Wanting to make something of himself, as his mother had urged him to do, he worked his way up from the city streets to the CEO's suite, from the walk-up apartment and the subway to a large estate and the corporate jet. But in the process he left something crucial behind. Bensen was authentic to his present level of development and understanding, doing his best to grow the company, maximize profits, and at the same time to provide for his family. But he was *inauthentic* to values that once meant a great deal to him, and to the kind of leader he had the potential to become: visionary, humane, motivating his employees with a sense of shared purpose.

Like most of us, Bensen was charging full-speed ahead, rarely if ever considering exactly where he was going and the ultimate consequences of his actions—on the wife who rarely saw him, the daughter whose awakening social conscience he shrugged off (largely because it stirred an awareness of what he was suppressing), and on the workers who labored in sweatshop conditions in his company's factories. It took a crisis to stop Bensen in his tracks, and a skilled coach to help him gain a deeper authenticity, aligning his actions with what he truly valued deep down. A crisis is not required, but it often seems as though life concocts one for us if we don't pay attention to our deep need for authenticity and growth.

The Seed of Authenticity:
Awakening Principles

As you commit to further developing your authenticity, pay attention to the following principles:

- Embrace the lifelong process of unfolding your strengths and acknowledging your vulnerabilities.

- Constantly attempt to be more real and honest with yourself and others.

- Move from being right to being real.

- Admit your mistakes and have a sense of humor about it.

- Go beyond perfectionism to being human; we are such perfectly gifted and perfectly imperfect beings!

- Pay attention to how your openness fosters openness and trust in others.

- Have the courage to practice the strength of vulnerability.

The Seed of Authenticity:
Growth Guide

Now work through the following questions. Go slowly and be sure to reflect on the most meaningful insights that surface for you. Again, take plenty of time to look honestly and deeply at yourself.

Building Awareness

If you were to survey a large group of your friends and associates, what would they say are your strengths and gifts? _____

_____

_____

If you were to survey the same group, what would they say are your weaknesses or vulnerabilities? _____

_____

_____

Are there strengths, gifts, or values that you held to be important earlier in your life, that you may have left behind? _____ *What are they?* _____

_____

How would your life be affected if you revisited or revived them? _____

_____

Do you feel able to look at yourself courageously, warts and all? _____
How can you foster the courage to look at, accept, and embrace all of who you are?

_____

_____

Building Commitment

What are the consequences of not applying your gifts? _____

_____

_____

Are there any behaviors in your life that you know you should change, such as self-destructive habits, neglect of your health, or insensitivity to others' needs? What are the long-term consequences of continuing in these behaviors? _____

_____

_____

What are the consequences of not being more open and vulnerable? _____

_____

_____

What is your new vision of how you will show up as a person or leader?

_____

_____

_____

Building Practices

What daily practices can you do to enhance your authenticity? (Try to include both inner practices to increase self-awareness and outer practices to act and relate to others more authentically.) _____

_____

_____

*What discipline(s) will you employ to sustain these practices? (For example: reflect on your progress twice a day; block out time in your calendar daily; ask colleagues for feedback weekly)*_____

_____

_____

The Seed of Purpose:
Play the Music in Your Heart

With stammering lips and insufficient sounds,
I strive and struggle to deliver right
The music of my nature.
                    —Elizabeth Barrett Browning

Purpose is the voice of authentic leadership. When a leader's voice lacks its intended power and impact, it's often a symptom of disconnection from personal purpose. When a leader's voice is strong, it often represents a personal connection to the leader's unique life experience and can be tangibly felt by all. However, for our voice to be strong, the melody of the music in our heart must be clearly heard.

A true leadership guru, Warren Bennis, contends that the purpose of leadership is to "remind people what is important." Reminding others what is important certainly penetrates the essence of leadership, doesn't it? In all parts of our lives—whether with ourselves, our loved ones, or our colleagues—contributing to their welfare by bringing clarity and focus to what's important is certainly a great contribution. However, before we can *remind others* what is important, we first need to *know ourselves* what is important. Sound easy? It's not. We all like to think we know where we stand and what we value, but authentically knowing our true values—the standards and guiding principles rooted deep in our guts—is one of the most challenging aspects of self-discovery.

When Kenji asked Bensen what was important to him, he started rattling off typical ideas: family, working hard, making a difference, serving others. Like Bensen, many of us would casually recite: "My family is the most important thing in my life. . . . Contributing to the welfare of the less fortunate is crucial. . . . Mentoring my employees. . . ." Well, they all sound good, and they are all values we should hold in high regard, but are they really your most important values?

Often what we say is important merely echoes the values we have unconsciously adopted from our environment. Although we'd be reluctant to admit it, what it often boils down to is, my family has always believed in . . . our organization says this is important . . . the latest business book says. . . . However, our truest values and sense of meaning are deeper than this.

We import our authentic values from our unique life experiences. *What have the hard times in your life—the struggles, tragedies, and traumas—taught you about what is important? What have the blessings of your life taught you about what is important? What has life taught you that you know for sure?* These are your real values—not the ones that were conveniently or unconsciously adopted. When we consciously embrace these rich and unique life experiences, we connect to the music in our heart, and our leadership voice takes on force and influence. "Follow that will and way which experience confirms to be your own," the great psychologist Carl Jung said.

A while ago, I was coaching a highly effective leader. On the surface he was a great communicator: He was articulate, direct, and clear. If anything, he was a bit too polished. One day, to his surprise, he got feedback that people didn't trust him . . . and not just a couple of people, but several key colleagues and staff members—people crucial to his success. It was a complete shock to him. Reeling from the feedback, he said, "I work hard on my communication skills and tell it like it is. My intentions are good. So what's wrong?" To get to the bottom of the story, we began examining how people perceived him and how he perceived himself.

Eventually the dynamic boiled down to the fact that under stress or crisis, he didn't inspire and move people by personally coming forward with more of himself. The more a crisis heated up, the more polished and detached his communication. People couldn't feel him. They couldn't sense where he was coming from, what he considered important and compelling. They felt he was smooth, slick, and calm but he wasn't real; he wasn't inspiring something meaningful from within himself.

He quickly realized that he couldn't set things straight by further refining his presentation skills; he had to look deeply and honestly at what was important to him. After some intensive work unearthing his most relevant and impactful career and life learning experiences, he began to connect to his deeper values. He started to share real stories to emphasize his message. In a crisis he shared a story about his first career failure and what he had learned about overcoming obstacles. He related his father's sage advice about running the family business, unexpectedly choking up in the middle of the tale. He began to show up as a whole person and people responded. Slowly but surely, he rebuilt trust.

We also helped him to uncover his *core purpose*—how his gifts serve the needs of others. At first this was a foreign idea. "I just do my job and get results!" he insisted.

"But *how* do you bring your whole self into doing your job and getting results?" I pressed. "What is your unique, meaningful contribution?"

After having him chart out five fantasy lives he would most like to live, we debriefed the common characteristic of these lives and uncovered his core purpose: *applying creativity and vision to realize new possibilities.* When he made his core purpose conscious, the realization was stunning. You could feel it in the room—a deep, reverent clarity about who he really was. With this heightened awareness, we then looked at each part of his life—family, career, community involvement, himself—and analyzed how aligned or misaligned his core purpose was with each of these.

To his surprise, his core purpose had the lowest alignment or application to himself! So the real work was to strengthen the connection of his core purpose to himself. How could he be more creative and visionary in developing himself? How could he realize new possibilities in the ways he showed up in his own life? As he did this personal alignment work, a foundation was built to bring his core purpose into all facets of his life. Later he commented in a coaching session, "core purpose is now my compass. It gives me the context from which to evaluate all my behaviors and decisions."

Core purpose *is* the compass that keeps our career and life decisions in harmony with our authentic talents, values, and meaningful contribution. As Shigenori Kameoka so beautifully wrote, "Find the seed at the bottom of your heart and bring forth a flower." Find the music in the bottom of your heart and compose a symphony of living and leading.

When considering purpose in our lives, we often confuse the *what* with the *how.* We ask ourselves, "*What* am I going to be when I grow up?" The answer we're looking for is a job description—doctor, lawyer, business owner—not a state of being—wise, energetic, compassionate, at peace. Later, we wonder what we'll do with ourselves when we retire. Always focusing on the external manifestation, we may miss the essence of purpose.

To find that essence, we need to ask, "*How* am I going to be when I grow up, or when I retire?" A short while ago I learned a valuable lesson on this dynamic in an unexpected setting. In our building, our offices and restrooms were cleaned daily by a young black woman, recently arrived from Africa, who was always gloriously dressed in the colorful garb of her native country. I was repeatedly struck by the delight with which she approached her mundane duties.

One evening she was joyously singing a beautiful song as she worked away. Approaching her in the hallway, I commented,

"You really love your work, don't you?"

Her demeanor stiffened and she became very serious. She set down her mop, looked piercingly into me and with a penetrating, instructive tone said, "Sir, I do not *love* to clean bathrooms!" Then with a soft, warm heart she shared, "I love *while* I clean bathrooms!" At that moment, I felt blessed to be coached by such a wise being.

Throughout the story, Kenji instructs Bensen as much by his example as by his more explicit or direct teachings. Early in the story Bensen observes, "The peace of the garden and the peace of the gardener are one; look how he moves," and as the story unfolds he repeatedly notes that Kenji's words and actions are aligned with the inner core of his being, with what he believes and values. This personal integrity creates a presence that is communicated and felt whether Kenji is peeling an apple, sculpting a corner of the garden, or attending to the needs of others. Bensen is inspired by this seamless integration of inner and outer purpose, and he begins to yearn for the same harmony and coherence in his own life.

Purpose is about how we show up to enrich whatever we may be doing. As leaders, most of us get lost in the "power of what," focusing only on outcomes and results. Shifting our attention from what to how is crucial to purposeful leadership. Learning to ask ourselves in real time, "How can I make a life-enriching difference?" is a valuable practice for leading with purpose.

The Seed of Purpose:
Awakening Principles

- Remind yourself of what is important to you, based on the lessons your life experiences have taught you.

- Practice reminding others what is important; when your behaviors open up possibilities and relationships then you are on purpose.

- Bring meaning and purpose to situations and concepts by sharing real life and real career stories.

- Connect with your core purpose—how your gifts serve the needs of others; measure success by your congruence with core purpose in all parts of your life.

- Shifting from "what to do" to "how to make a life-enriching difference" is key to leading with purpose.

- Pay attention to your energy. Finding our way to purpose is guided by following that which enriches and renews our vitality. As Ralph Waldo Emerson put it, "The world belongs to the energetic."

- Purpose is about living our lives from a perspective that is bigger than our immediate life concerns, and it is focused on giving versus taking.

- Find the meaning in your current life and career situation: "Bloom where you are planted," Nancy Reader Campion wrote.

- Purpose is the path of service; find meaning in service and serve that which is meaningful.

The Seed of Purpose:
Growth Guide

Take your time and reflect on key learnings that have surfaced for you.

Building Awareness

What have the traumas and blessings of your life taught you about what is really important? _____

_____

_____

What courage will it take for you to integrate and bring forth these values and life experiences into your life? _____

_____

_____

What is your core purpose? What are your gifts that serve others in all parts of your life? _____

_____

_____

Building Commitment

What are the consequences if you do not bring forth your deepest values into your life and into your leadership? _____

_____

_____

What are the consequences if you do bring forth these values into your life and into your leadership? _____

_____

_____

What is your vision of how you will show up in new ways if you do become more purpose-filled? _____

_____

_____

Building Practices

What daily practices *can you do to ensure that you keep your core purpose conscious? (For example: journaling daily to monitor the presence or absence of purpose; paying attention to the relationship of high and low energy when purpose is present or absent; in challenging circumstances, reminding yourself and others of what is important)*

_____

_____

_____

What discipline(s) *will be required of you to live more aligned with your purpose?*

_____

_____

_____

The Seed of Essence:
Engage Essence as the Master,
Employ Ego as the Servant

The leader beyond the millennium will not be the leader who has learned the lessons of how to do it . . . The leader for today and the future will be focused on how to be—how to develop quality, character, mind-set, values, principles, and courage.
—Frances Hesselbein, CEO of Girl Scouts USA

Essence is the soul of leadership; it is spirit expressing itself through the leader. If you have had the good fortune to be in the presence of spirit-led, life-enriching leaders such as Nelson Mandela or the Dalai Lama, you have probably walked away deeply moved by their aura of peacefulness and joy. The transcendental quality of their silence makes everything they say resound more deeply and clearly in our hearts. This palpable sense of tranquility that is untouched even by very stressful or life-threatening circumstances is the essence of effective leadership.

One of the Dalai Lama's monks, who had been imprisoned and tortured for years by the Chinese after their takeover of Tibet, was interviewed during a visit to Minneapolis. The reporter asked the calm, peaceful monk what he had most feared during his years of abuse. He responded in a deep, authentic, humble voice, "I was most afraid that I would lose my compassion for the Chinese." It was a stunning moment, rich with heart, spirit, and learning for everyone present; this is Essence in action.

Individuals who have taken the journey to this level of personhood are not only leaders of people and causes, but leaders of life. They are the ones committed to leading our world to a more enriching future, and they are the ones who, by virtue of who they are, can truly honor that commitment. Attaining this level of development, however, need not be the exclusive domain of a few. It is waiting for us all; it is the Essence of who we are. The ancient philosopher Plotinus affirmed this when he wrote that the spiritual dimension of life, which he referred to as *the Oneness,* "is gently and graciously present to anyone who wishes it."

If leadership is the act of going beyond what is—a definition I find useful—it begins by going beyond what is, *within ourselves.* The inward journey to the center, to the silent experience of Essence, is really the only pilgrimage in life. It is purpose with a capital P—the ultimate spiritual unfoldment we are all seeking. Far from being an esoteric thing, it may be the most practical grounding we can have as people and as leaders. This is certainly not a new or exotic idea. "In returning and rest you shall be saved," said the Prophet Isaiah; "In quietness and in trust shall be your strength."

Essence may be the easiest of all the Seeds to put into practice. You can cultivate it by engaging in a few minutes of daily meditation to quiet your mind. And you can catch hold of it in the midst of a tough situation, by taking a moment to stop and connect mentally to that calm center of creativity within, or by inwardly stepping back from the action and checking in with what's truly important to you before making a decision and moving forward. Most of us have had such moments, either consciously or inadvertently.

All too often, however, we are too caught up in the fast pace of our lives to awaken to Essence. As Joe Eastman, my colleague at LeaderSource and author of *What is Becoming Clearer to Me,* has written, "Speed and intensity are about being alive. Reflection is about being *awake.*"

Recently, I was coaching a CEO who was exceptionally effective in getting results year after year. The idea of going to a deeper level of life by building more silence into his routine was very foreign. "I don't need to pause more, I need to *do more!*" was his initial reaction to my coaching suggestions. One day he came in for coaching with a reflective, somewhat perplexed demeanor. When I asked how he was feeling he responded, "I don't know what happened today. I was completely stumped by some very challenging business issues. Instead of fighting through them, I took a walk through the trails behind our headquarters. I wasn't even thinking about the issues; I was just enjoying the walk, the gardens, and the break. Suddenly in a flash, the solution came to me. I was shocked. Where did this come from?!"

Like flashes of intuitive insight, the awareness of Essence, peace, spirit—or whatever we may wish to call it—comes to us through the practice of pause. It appears in the silence between our thoughts, the space between the problems and analysis. In physics, this is called the third law of thermodynamics: "As activity lessens, order increases." When we pause, the mind settles, expands, and becomes more powerful and orderly. As a result, we are able to go beyond the individual issues, combine seemingly unrelated variables, and come up with new solutions or perspectives. Maharishi Mahesh Yogi, the founder of Transcendental Meditation, has said that "The genius of man is hidden in the silence of his awareness, in that settled state of mind, from where every thought emerges. . . . This is not the inert silence of a stone, but creative silence."

Blaise Pascal, the French philosopher and mathematician, wrote that "All men's miseries derive from not being able to sit quietly in a room alone." With no pause, there is no reflection. With no reflection, there is no vision. With no vision, there is no leadership. Pause and reflection are the pathways to more expanded vision and more effective leadership.

So how do we access Essence more? To begin to answer this question, we need to make some distinctions between Essence, the transformative force in our lives, and Ego, the coping force in our lives. In chapter 14, "Awakening to Essence," Kenji introduces Bensen to both the principles and the direct experience of Essence. Essence, he teaches him, is "the life force within all things . . . the mysterious intelligence that guides and supports the growth of all." Because Essence is within us, as it is within everything, we can attune our lives to its silent power and gain its support for all that we do.

Ego, on the other hand, is the sense of limited individuality, the feeling of separateness and vulnerability. It is the individual coping mechanism that seeks security in the vast universe and tries to grab what it can of life's fleeting pleasures and treasures. In a central moment in the chapter and the book, Kenji explains this to Bensen:

> "Problems arise when we are not in touch with the depths of our being, our Essence. Not knowing about that inner richness, not experiencing it, we think we are only our body, our profession, our thoughts and ideas, our fears and desires. 'I am Kenji. I am a gardener, a father. I like rice.' Well, I *am* Kenji and all the rest—but that is not *all* that I am."
>
> "So the problem is *not* the ego?"
>
> "No, the problem is our belief that we are nothing more than our bodies and our limited, bounded personalities. So long as this belief colors our experience, we will continue to live on the surface of life, in the shallowest levels of awareness, while our true greatness lies within, untapped, unlived."

While all of us operate from both Ego and Essence, often we are overdeveloped in our identification with Ego—the sense of being an isolated, limited individual—and underdeveloped in our identification with Essence—our felt connection to the whole of life. It's important to recognize which mode we are in at any point in time, and to learn to shift to Essence more and more.

It's also vital not to characterize Essence as good and Ego as bad. Both are necessary and part of life. We need Ego in order to cope, adapt, and get things done; we need Essence to be our guide and our center. Psychologist and author David Richo put it like this: "Ego is not meant to be destroyed but, paradoxically, to be expanded so that it can extend its creative possibilities to all our psyche. It is liberated by being relieved of its arrogance and then opened to its potential for power *for* rather than power *over* others."

Ego is a muscle that needs to be exerted in order to get things done. But like most muscles, Ego is best used occasionally and in short bursts. If you try to use it all the time, like a muscle it will collapse and be of no use to you or others. Therefore, Ego is a better servant than master; effective at serving specific purposes, it is not great for running the whole show. Making Essence the master and Ego the servant is the key to life-enriching, sustainable leadership.

When Ego is primarily operating, certain qualities tend to be present:

- Preoccupation with image
- Fear
- Safety and security
- Control
- Focus on self
- Withdrawal
- Denial
- Distraction
- Anger
- Exclusion
- Winning at all costs
- Uneasy presence

When Essence is primarily operating, these qualities tend to come forward:

- Authenticity or genuineness
- Courage
- Compassion
- Balanced focus on self and others
- Creation of value and contribution
- Purpose or meaning
- Trust
- Service
- Connection
- Openness
- Inclusion
- Peaceful presence

When Bensen was operating primarily from his Ego, he was afraid to commit to change. He was in denial about how much he had distanced himself from his wife and daughter and about his company's wrongdoing. He was self-absorbed and easily irritated. When, partly through Kenji's teaching and his own meditation experiences, he opened up to Essence, all this changed. He began closing the gaps at home; he acknowledged HighQuest's failings and his own part in them; he began genuinely caring about others. Inner equanimity gradually began to replace his on-the-edge, Ego-driven mode of relating.

In order to more often make Essence the master and Ego the servant, try some of the following:

- Learn to notice when the qualities of Ego and the qualities of Essence are manifesting themselves in your life and leadership.
- Pay attention to how much more restricted and tense your body feels when you are in Ego.
- Pay attention to how much more expanded and at-ease your body feels when you are in Essence, leading in a more centered, life-giving way.
- Look at your impact on others when you are primarily in Ego mode and in Essence mode.
- Start to shift out of the more constricted Ego state into the more expansive Essence state as often as possible.

The Seed of Essence:
Awakening Principles

- Learn new practices to connect with Essence, or dust off old ones you once found effective and put them back into play. Practices may include meditation, prayer, listening to inspirational music, and leisurely walks in nature. Many people have also found dancing, running, and creative artistic activities such as painting or playing a musical instrument helpful in getting centered and connected to Essence. Whatever you choose, *practice daily.* These practices will enliven your awareness of Essence and help you recognize and shift to the Essence mode more easily. Remember, whatever you put your attention on grows stronger in your life.

- Train yourself to make decisions from a place of calm and peace versus a place of coping and distraction.

- When facing your most challenging times, learn to pause more to find solutions at a deeper level. Albert Einstein once said, "Problems can never be solved at the level at which they were created." Go to a new level through the power of pause.

- Begin your pilgrimage to Essence—the real pilgrimage of life.

- Prayer is connecting with Essence; Intuition is Essence connecting with us; Transcendence is Essence connected with Essence.

- Pay attention to how Ego and Essence are showing up in your life; seek to make Essence the master and Ego the servant.

The Seed of Essence:
Growth Guide

Take your time and reflect on the key learnings that have surfaced for you.

Building Awareness

Where in your life has the power of pause benefited you? _____

_____

_____

What courage will it take for you to find more pause in your life . . . in your work?

_____

_____

_____

Building Commitment

What are the long-term consequences if you do not lead from Essence more? _____

_____

What are the consequences if you do lead from Essence more? _____

_____

_____

What is your vision of how you will "show up" in new ways once Essence is the master? _____

_____

_____

Building Practices

What are the daily practices you can do to ensure your ability to live and lead from Essence more and from Ego less? (For example: prayer, meditation, journaling, mindfulness, nature walks, etc.) _____

_____

_____

What discipline(s) will be required to live and lead more from Essence and less from Ego? _____

_____

_____

The Seed of Relationship: Always Connect

Love alone is capable of uniting human beings in such a way as to complete and fulfill them, for it alone takes them and joins them by what is deepest inside themselves.
—Teilhard de Chardin

Connection is the glue of leadership, bonding parts and revealing wholeness. Recently I was speaking to a large group of leaders on the "Essence of Leadership." As part of the session, we brainstormed a model of leadership. In the process of doing this, one of the CEOs in attendance somewhat sheepishly volunteered "love" as a leadership quality. I was simultaneously impressed and intrigued by his suggestion. When I asked him to elaborate on what he meant, he responded,

> We all know what it's like when we love what we do . . . when we love the company we're connected to . . . when we love the products or services we represent . . . when we love the team of people we work with. This powerful *connection* drives us to higher performance and more effective, enlightened leadership. We are usually embarrassed to say it, but love, leadership and high performance are intimately connected. In fact, love is what connects them all.

At moments like this, I must say I feel hope for the world. For a CEO to have the insight and courage to express these deep principles is extremely encouraging. It sets a new paradigm of where effectiveness comes from, and reminds leaders of our core responsibility to overcome any difficulty by creating cultures that nourish as well as excel.

A while ago, I led a group of 90 executives at Pillsbury through a day of learning on the connection of their personal growth to their leadership effectiveness. Part of the process was an experiential exercise that illustrated the value of going beyond what is. At the conclusion of the session, Paul Walsh, then CEO of Pillsbury (and now CEO of Diageo), addressed his team with some interesting perspectives. "While it is true that the reality of business today requires that we 'go beyond what is' and enter new arenas we are less than prepared to deal with," he told them, "it is just as important that we are equally committed to the interpersonal connections with one another to bridge us to the future."

Real power emanates from our ability to connect to ourselves and those around us as we help people to go beyond what they thought possible. Gita Bellin wrote, "The impossible is possible when people align with you. When you do things with people, not against them, the amazing resources of the Higher Self within are mobilized." Bensen Quinn discovered this truth in dealing with the doctors treating his daughter: When he was aggressive and demanding, they closed down; when he switched gears and treated them with honest warmth and respect, they rallied to his side.

Too often, when we think of the word *connection,* we think of being connected *with something*—outside of ourselves. But outer connection rests on inner connection. The Seed of Relationship begins with self and extends outward to others and the context in which we are operating. It rests upon the inner self-relationship work of the Seed of Essence, the Seed of Purpose, and the Seed of Authenticity.

Before we can *connect,* we need *to be connected,* deep within ourselves. Henriette Anne Klauser wrote, "Being you is all about connection, about being real. When you are you, you connect with others." As leaders, when we have difficulty connecting with individuals or with any of our various constituencies, it may mean that we need to connect with self first, by focusing on these three Seeds.

Kenji helped Bensen move through these levels and stages of connection. He first helped him to connect more authentically to who he was and to what he valued and stood for. From that more centered, inwardly integrated standpoint, Bensen was able to more effectively connect to Emily, Katie, his assistants, his team, and, ultimately, to the higher purpose of business.

Bensen also had good models. Mick Callahan, the building materials magnate, demonstrated the quality of enlightened stewardship in the way he conducted his business, and Kenji repeatedly displayed it in his caring engagement with his students. Bensen, learning from them, gradually shifted away from an aloof, impersonal relationship to his business ("I thought of the employees more as numbers than as people," he confessed at one point) toward a more personal, caring connection. By the story's end, his decisions and actions demonstrated how connectedness and long-term value creation go hand in hand.

———

To genuinely connect with self, others, and the whole requires two essential practices: Authentic Listening and Authentic Voice. This too begins within. "The more faithfully you listen to the voice within you, the better you hear what is sounding outside of you," wrote former United Nations Secretary General Dag Hammarskjold.

Jill, like most business people I have coached, considered herself a good listener. Able to comprehend and reconstruct the facts, data, and content of even very complex meetings, she was confident in her listenership. However, although she took in the explicit messages present, she missed the fears, beliefs, and unspoken messages. *Good listeners hear what is said; great listeners hear the unsaid.* To become a great listener, she needed to learn Authentic Listening. In *Finding Your Voice,* Larraine Matusak, citing leadership expert Perry Smith, wrote, "When we want to see something better, we sometimes squint. Therefore, if we want to hear something better, perhaps we should squint with our ears."

"Squinting with our ears" requires having empathy to the underlying, often unrevealed concerns of the other person or constituency. Daniel Goleman, speaking from his groundbreaking work on emotional intelligence, affirms, "At the very least, empathy requires being able to read another's emotions; at a higher level, it entails sensing and responding to a person's unspoken concerns and feelings. At the highest levels, empathy is understanding the issues or concerns that lie behind another's feelings." Authentic Listening requires the leadership quality of *going beyond what is* to penetrate the deeper reality present. The result is genuine connection and relationship.

To begin practicing more Authentic Listening, consider the following guiding principles:

- Honor what the person has to say as being important, even if you may not agree with it.
- Honor the unique contribution and self-expression of every human being.
- Be open to the possibility that every situation and every person around you is your teacher.
- Give the gift of presence. Practice the discipline of giving your undivided attention.
- "Squint with your ears" to hear the fears, concerns, and beliefs present. "Hear what a person wants to say, what he doesn't want to say, and what

he is unable to say without help," B. Fittipaldi said in *New Listening: Key to Organizational Transformation.*

- As Stephen Covey teaches (echoing the words of St. Francis), Seek not to be understood, but to understand.
- Ask questions to go to a deeper level to clarify, open up possibilities, and uncover unspoken messages. As you ask questions, stay open as opposed to being judgmental.
- Express appreciation. One of the most convincing arguments for this attitude came from Voltaire, who wrote, "Appreciation is a wonderful thing. It makes what is excellent in others belong to us as well." Or as J. Allen Boone put it in *Kinship with All of Life,* "The most effective way to achieve right relations with every living thing is to look for the best in it, and then help that best into fullest expression."

Don was a very accomplished speaker. He had the gift of being able to master a topic, get in front of a group, and deliver his message with precision. Audiences were typically impressed by his brilliant analysis, depth of detail, and command of data. However, something was missing. Without even being able to articulate it, people leaving his sessions felt informed, but not particularly inspired.

Good leaders master the art of communicating with their heads; great leaders master the art of communicating with heart *and* head. Don needed to develop more Authentic Voice by balancing his analytical competence with more emotional competence. John Kotter from Harvard Business School has said that "Motivation and inspiration energize people, not by pushing them in the right direction as control mechanisms, but by satisfying basic human needs for achievement, a sense of belonging, a feeling of control over one's life and the ability to live up to one's ideals. Such feelings touch us deeply and elicit a powerful response."

Authentic Voice that genuinely connects people can be defined in eight words: *shared feeling, shared meaning, shared understanding, shared mission.* These eight words capture the entire process of being a leader for life and leading from the inside out. Living these eight words is not easy; it requires an ongoing life-long commitment to personal development *and* emotional engagement with others.

To begin the process of developing a more Authentic Voice, consider the following guiding principles:

- Risk more openness, vulnerability, and emotion in your relationships. If you think you are offering enough of these qualities, then offer more.
- Explore the traumas and privileges of your life in order to connect to what is truly important to you. Practice the leadership art of reminding others what is important, to help them rise above immediate circumstances.
- Share real-life personal or career stories to *inspire* people, rather than sharing only concepts, facts, and data to *inform* people. "To communicate is not just a matter of pushing information at another person," Daniel Goleman said. "It's creating an experience, to engage their emotional gut and that's an emotional craft."
- Exhibit genuine energy and passion for what you care about.
- Balance the head and the heart, analysis and emotions, in your communication.
- Be the mouthpiece for that still, quiet voice resonating in your heart.
- Always remember that the heart can leap over barriers built by the mind.

The Seed of Relationship:
Awakening Principles

- All effective, fulfilling outer relationships begin with our inner relationship to our self. Begin to enhance that relationship by cultivating the Seeds of Essence, Purpose, and Authenticity.

- Seek to connect love and leadership to enhance sustainable high performance.

- Practice Authentic Listening. Get to the heart of what's being said and what's not being said.

- Express your Authentic Voice by sharing heartfelt career and life stories that illustrate your real values.

- Measure the true value of your legacy by how much connection you have brought into the world.

The Seed of Relationship:
Growth Guide

Take your time and reflect on the key learnings that have surfaced for you.

Building Awareness

*How well is your leadership bonding people together to go beyond what is?*_____

_____

_____

How well are you authentically listening to the deeper needs of people? _____

_____

_____

_____

How well developed is your authentic voice in expressing values, emotions, and vulner-abilities? _____

_____

_____

What courage *will it take to improve in these areas?* _____

_____

_____

Building Commitment

What are the consequences if you do not *more openly connect with people?* _____

_____

_____

What are the consequences if you do *more openly connect with people?* _____

_____

_____

What is your vision *of how you will show up in new ways as you become more open and connected with people?*_____

_____

_____

Building Practices

What are the daily practices *you can do to ensure that you continually strive to connect with people more? (For example: daily journaling on your experiences of connection or lack of connection; asking for feedback regarding your relationships; looking for the meaning, beliefs, and fears beneath people's words)* _____

_____

_____

What discipline *will be required of you to more authentically listen and to more authentically express your voice?* _____

_____

_____

The Seed of Value Creation: Serving Parts and Whole

There is that which scattereth, and yet increaseth, and there is that that witholdeth more than is meet, but it tendeth to poverty. The liberal soul shall be made fat and he that watereth shall be watered also himself.

—Prov. 11:24

The Seed of Value Creation is germinated through enlightened, sustainable leadership. Value Creation goes beyond getting financial results. From the vantage point of Value Creation, getting results is not enough; this is *not* what the magic of leadership is all about.

Even mediocre leaders get results, and all too often at unacceptable costs. We can achieve our goals and unintentionally harm our health in the process; we can get results and unknowingly damage employee morale or commitment; we can squeeze out earnings and jeopardize customer relationships; we can push for cost savings and diminish quality or harm the environment; we can advance our career and destroy our family relationships.

Taiichi Ohno, the father of the Toyota Production System, defined waste as "any human activity which absorbs resources but creates no value." Good leaders get results; great leaders get sustainable results by serving multiple constituencies. Service is the purpose of leadership; it is the rent we pay for the privilege of being a leader.

Recently I was speaking at a conference where Dee Hock was featured. As you may know, Dee Hock was the founder and chairman of Visa and was named one of the eight people who most changed the world through business in the last 50 years. Emphasizing the connection between service and leadership, he said, "As leaders, when we get in the bad habit of thinking that others are there to serve us, we are not leaders, we are tyrants. However, when we go through the emotional, psychological and spiritual transformation and realize that our job is *to serve everyone else,* then we deserve to be called a leader."

This is a powerful re-frame of leadership, isn't it? It's so easy, as we advance through leadership roles, to get caught up in the bad habit of thinking that others are there principally to serve our needs. But at some point, this shift to service needs to happen if we are going to move from leadership that is self-serving and short-term to leadership that is constituency-serving and sustainable. In Winston Churchill's often-quoted words, "We make a living by what we get. We make a life by what we give." We are measured as a manager by what we produce. We are judged as a leader by what we give. Or as Einstein said, "It is high time the ideal of success should be replaced with the ideal of service."

A while ago, I was coaching a highly driven, results-oriented senior executive from a high-tech firm. Although Greg wasn't aware of it, the belief system driving him was *I achieve, therefore I am*. Everything in his field of view needed to serve his ego mission. To feed this self-serving belief system, he developed a leadership approach requiring ever higher doses of control in order to deliver his results high. Unaware of his underlying drivers, he prided himself on being a "results-oriented guy."

As time passed and his career advanced, his relationships were suffering—particularly downward in the organization. Because he was producing results, his bosses loved him. But they were as unaware as he was of the heavy costs being paid. One day a very comprehensive 360-degree assessment, with comments and feedback on his personality and performance from coworkers and people above and below him in the organization, revealed how others were really viewing his leadership. At first he resisted the input. "I'm so results-driven, sometimes I drive people too hard and they just can't take it," he said. "Maybe I need more high-achievement people like me in the organization. Then the assessment would be different."

Over time in the coaching process, Greg began to see how his leadership approach was getting results but not creating sustainable value. At one particularly poignant moment he confided, "The truth is I've been controlling everyone else to serve my need to succeed and avoid my fear of failure. My real failure—which I couldn't see—has been not serving my people."

This is the watershed moment for all leaders who move from tyranny to stewardship. It is also the moment when leadership moves from being burdensome to being purposeful and more fulfilling. Albert Schweitzer wrote, "Every person I have known who has been truly happy, has learned how to serve others." Rabbi Harold Kushner came to a similar conclusion. "I doubt there has been one recorded case of deep and lasting fulfillment reported by a person whose basic mindset and only question was: what am I getting out of this?"

The path of leadership transformation is a journey from control and domination to one of inspiration and service. If we don't make this transformative leap, what behaviors will we justify on the altar of financial results? Destroying the environment? Producing substandard products that are unsafe for customers? Providing working conditions unfit for employees? It's chilling to think what we as humans can justify as we strive to achieve our lofty goals. As Robert Fulgham so aptly said, "It's just that fame and fortune ought to add up to more than just fame and fortune."

Am I saying that financial results are not important? Certainly not. Financial results are the fuel of organizations. But what are the financial results for? If only for the shareholders, are they sustainable? Can they continue into the future if the needs of the employee, the customer, and the environment are not being served? Certainly not. The way of the new leader in the 21st century will be to create more balanced measures and thus to achieve financial results while serving the needs of self, others, and the whole. Finding the creative, life-enriching ways to serve these three main constituencies is the challenge for authentic leadership today.

In our story, we witnessed the gradual awakening of Bensen Quinn to a broader range of constituencies. At first, he was passionate about one and only one constituency: the shareholders. As he started to wake up, he also became passionate about serving the interests of his employees and contributing to the broader community. This is the natural process of leadership from inside out: as leaders wake up to a deeper level of themselves, their kinship to broader constituencies, and their desire to serve, also wakes up.

Laurence Bouldt expressed this beautifully in *Zen and the Art of Making a Living:* "One can take either the view that life is sacred or that life is a commodity," he writes. The commodity view of life "is interested in profit, domination, and control" over nature and other people. On the other hand, "A sacred view gives birth to feelings of duty, protection, and . . . caring and sets up *internal* constraints against the exploitation of other individuals, groups or species."

The contrast between narrow, self-serving leadership and a more open constituency-serving leadership was made crystal clear to me at a recent conference in Mexico City, at which I was a speaker. This conference, sponsored by the Caux Roundtable, a group dedicated to transforming business through ethical principles, featured Sherron Watkins, the courageous whistle-blower from Enron. She recounted the now familiar story of the company's collapse, adding a chilling detail: four days before the evident and impending bankruptcy, the senior executives paid themselves a $50+ million "retention bonus" for a three-month stint! And this was at the very moment that thousands of employees were losing their jobs and watching their hard-earned pensions evaporate, and shareholders were seeing their investments disappear.

At the same conference, Isao Uchida, president and CEO of Yokogawa Electric Corporation, shared the strikingly contrasting story of how his company handled a recent severe downturn in business. Determined not to be the first CEO in their more than 80-year history to lay off an employee, Mr. Uchida first cut his own salary, then the executives' salaries, and later the salaries of the management group. Still facing financial difficulties, he addressed the entire organization, asked for their forgiveness, and proposed a salary cut to avoid layoffs. He went on to say if they accepted, he was committed to making it up to them when the company's fortunes turned around. The 19,000 employees unanimously accepted.

Enron's leadership had one constituency: the most senior executives. Yokogawa had 19,000 constituents as well as the broader community it impacted. One leader sustained value creation, whereas another group of "leaders" destroyed it.

Moving from a self-serving focus to a constituency-serving focus requires making a fundamental shift in awareness. As Wendell Berry explained in his *Recollected Essays,*

> We have lived by the assumption that what was good for us would be good for the world. We have been wrong. We must change our lives, so that it will be possible to live by the contrary assumption that what is good for the world will be good for us. And that requires that we make the effort to know the world and to learn what is good for it. We must learn to cooperate in its processes, and to yield to its limits.

Later in the Caux Roundtable conference, Mr. Uchida shared the essence of his constituency-serving philosophy, which he continually imparts to his employees: "The sun is always watching you." When we know in our soul that a higher reality sees all, our inner moral compass more often points us in the direction of serving the whole.

One of the most powerful leadership tools for serving all our constituencies is to foster a compelling vision of our organization's unique Value Creation proposition. What life-enriching vision does this organization serve? When I visit organizations, I like to ask people at all levels, "What do you do?" It seems like a very basic question, but actually it is a type of *Value Creation Audit*. Most people in most organizations respond with a very factual, mundane description of their job. But some people and organizations see their role and contribution on a deeper level.

While at a very purpose-driven health care organization, I asked the receptionist of a senior executive what her job was really about. She paused, looked at me with great pride and conviction, and said, "We heal people, Mr. Cashman. That's what we do here. We bring people to wholeness. Our work won't be done until every person in the area is well." The individuals in this organization, top to bottom, understood their reason for being and their unique Value Creation vision.

The Seed of Value Creation:
Awakening Principles

- Good leaders get results; great leaders get *sustainable* results by serving the interests of multiple constituencies: shareholders, employees, customers, the community, the environment, the world.

- Financial results are only one measure of Value Creation. Henry Ford said, "A business that makes nothing but money is a poor kind of business." True Value Creation requires that we also measure how the lives of people, the organization, the environment, and the world have been enriched.

- Great leaders at some point in their career go through a personal transformation and realize that their role is to serve, not to be served.

- Moving from tyranny to stewardship is the path of sustainable, value-creating leadership.

- As leaders we need to bring our self-serving behaviors into conscious awareness to avoid unknowingly sabotaging genuine Value Creation.

- To build a compelling platform for a value-creating culture, insure that people on all levels of the organization have a heartfelt understanding of the life-enriching vision the organization serves.

The Seeds of Value Creation: Growth Guide

Take your time and reflect on the key learnings that have surfaced for you.

Building Awareness

Take a calm, open-eyed look at your leadership at work and in your family. Is it more about serving others and their needs, or about serving yourself? _____

How do you feel about this? _____

_____

_____

What growth (emotional, psychological, spiritual) do you need to go through to move from being served to serving others? _____

_____

_____

When you are more of a tyrant than a steward, what behaviors show up?

_____

_____

What self-limiting beliefs or fears do you have that may get in the way of serving others? (For example: fear of failure, need for image enhancement or recognition, need for financial security, etc.) _____

_____

_____

What courage will it take for you to control less and serve more? _____

_____

_____

Building Commitment

What are the consequences for you if you do not bring forth more service-oriented leadership? _____

_____

_____

What are the consequences for your organization if it does not have a clearer, more meaningful Value Creation vision? _____

_____

_____

What are the consequences for you *if you* do *bring forth more service-oriented leadership?* _____

_____

_____

What are the consequences for your organization *if it* does *have a clearer, more meaningful Value Creation vision?* _____

_____

_____

What is your vision *of how you will show up in new ways to serve others and create more value?* _____

_____

Building Practices

What are the daily practices *you can do to ensure you serve more and control less? (For example: focus on and measure employee and customer satisfaction, be a more authentic listener, solicit feedback from key people)* _____

_____

_____

What are the daily practices *you can do to ensure your self-limiting beliefs or fears don't get in the way of Value Creation?* _____

_____

_____

What discipline *will be required for you to create more value in* your life? _____

_____

_____

What discipline(s) *will be required for you to create more value in* your organization? _____

_____

_____

Please note: While this section of the Growth Guide has focused on Value Creation in a business and organizational context, it is important to note that the principles of serving self, other, and the whole are relevant to all domains of our lives. Whether in our family, our community, or our friendships, the practice of overcoming our self-serving tendencies by committing to serving the greater good equally applies.

The Seed of Coaching:
Drawing Forth Potential

We mark with light in the memory the few interviews we have had with souls that made our soul wiser, that spoke what we thought, that told us what we know, that gave us leave to be what we inly are.

—Ralph Waldo Emerson

The first five Seeds in this Growth Guide have focused on self-coaching to promote your transformation as a person and as a leader. The principles and practices introduced in the sixth Seed will prepare you to begin coaching others with greater confidence and skill.

Indeed, of all the skills of leadership, coaching may be the most important. Why? Helping to foster the growth of those around us gives sustainability to our leadership and perpetuates optimal, ongoing value creation.

Coaching is the art of drawing forth potential onto the canvas of value creation. It's the gentle yet firm hand of leadership guiding the way like a caring friend, helping the coachee to steer clear of danger or set a more positive course.

Leadership is more than just a job. The leader of a group of any size, from a family, club, congregation, or classroom to a multinational corporation or a nation, sets the tone for all the members of the group. When you are a leader, other people look to you, depend on you. Their lives and destinies are, to a significant extent, in your hands. That's why I believe that leadership is a sacred calling.

That calling is best honored when the leader sets the highest example of personal and professional behavior, then works to raise all others to the highest level as well. To accomplish both of these tasks, nothing is more vital than coaching.

Effective coaching to bring out the strengths and talents of all the people in the group or organization serves a dual role. It is a generous contribution to each individual's growth and fulfillment. At the same time, it is the most practical strategy for maximizing the effectiveness and success of the group. The more capable and fully developed each individual in your group, the stronger

the group. Each person in the group who is not living up to his or her capabilities is dragging the group down, dimming its full glory.

In the early years of a new century, it is becoming clear to everyone—as it
became clear to Bensen Quinn—that in business, the responsibility of leaders
for the lives and destinies of others extends far beyond maximizing financial
gain for shareholders and the management team. The repercussions of narrow
vision and shortsighted goals have been felt throughout the economy of the nation in recent times, and an effort is being made to replace the type of leadership that produced the Enron, Arthur Andersen, WorldCom, and other corporate scandals that are reverberating through the economy as I write these final
pages of the book, with a more visionary brand of leadership that serves a broad
spectrum of constituencies. As Bensen told his Board of Directors, leaders
ought to strive for a more *balanced scorecard,* where financial performance is accompanied by employee satisfaction and well-being; customer satisfaction; concern for human and labor rights, environmental impact, and community relations; and a sincere dedication to ethical behavior.

In this increasingly complex world of incessant change, technological advancement, globalization, and ever-present threats to our safety and security,
the need to focus on the importance and meaningfulness of where we are
headed as individuals, organizations, and as a nation has never been more critical. Today, survival and its rewards go not to the fittest, but to the *most purposeful.* A coach, by guiding us to step back from the fray to ascertain which
parts of the action are crucial and important and which parts are distracting,
nonessential, or downright damaging, can help us maintain our focus and direction.

For many of us, the word *coach* evokes images of a hulking figure in a sweatshirt, blowing a whistle and barking directions to a more or less compliant
group of youngsters. But a genuine coach has a far more interesting and refined
role than giving orders.

If you were on a mountain-climbing expedition, struggling with some difficult terrain, lost in a fog or snowstorm, unable to see the top of the mountain
or much of the path ahead, you would be grateful for a veteran guide, calling
down from above, "Go to the right. Dig in. Watch out for loose rocks. You're
doing fine." The guide has perspective, experience that you don't have, and crucial knowledge.

Similarly, the players on a sports team, caught up in the moment-to-moment action on the field, have little perspective. An effective coach rises above the playing field to get a more complete picture, from which to more effectively facilitate strategy.

A personal coach works in the same way. Using evaluation tools as well as in-depth interviews to gain an understanding of the client's present situation and life and career goals, the coach then combines knowledge and expertise with facilitation skills to draw forth potential and impart wisdom.

The coach's task is not to pontificate, not to take a stand, not even to teach—although at times sharing expertise may carry a flavor of teaching. The real task of the coach is to help the persons he or she is coaching to open up to their own gifts and their own inner guidance, so they can determine for themselves their best possible direction, bring forth their greatest abilities, and make their best contribution.

"Letting the self emerge is the essential task of leaders," Warren Bennis wrote. Helping the self of others emerge is the associated task that gives your leadership added power.

Imposing expertise ("this is how you do it") may bring results in the short run. However, facilitation—drawing out the person's own ideas, values, strengths, and skills—results in *growth* that will apply to this and all future situations.

Some coaches simply assert their expertise. *Great coaches blend expertise and facilitation to help the players go beyond their previous boundaries.* In *Masterful Coaching,* Robert Hargrove notes, "When most people think of learning they don't think in terms of having to change themselves. They tend to think of learning as . . . acquiring ideas, tips, techniques, and so on. Seldom does it occur to them that the problems they are facing are inseparable from who they are or the way they think and interact with other people."

In our story, Bensen's unsatisfying relationship with his daughter was based on who he was as the narrative begins: inattentive to her, self-absorbed, critical of her idealism, and thus unwilling to be supportive of her life. Once he dealt with his own shadows, he became able to truly love, support, and listen to her.

It was the same at work. Perceived as a gruff and arrogant tiger, a know-it-all who was good at giving orders but who never listened, he was feared by his employees, even his executive team. When his heart and his communication skills opened up, they gradually—and with some amazement—reciprocated, becoming more forthcoming with suggestions.

In short, as he changed inside, his life and leadership changed as well. "Change is a door that can only be opened from the inside," Terry Neil wrote. And yet, I know many leaders who, despite enormous competencies and skills, do not make the connection between their own growth and transformation and that of their organizations. Transformation is not an event but an ongoing process of unfolding all of who we are and expressing it in our actions. Transformational coaching creates a shift toward our deeply held purpose and sparks our desire to make a bigger difference in the world.

Athletes have coaches. Actors have coaches. Politicians have coaches. Increasingly, business people have coaches. Too often, business coaches aim for a charm school or image enhancement outcome. That is not enough. We need to develop a new breed of coaches who focus on *transformation* leading to exceptional, sustainable performance, whose aim is developing the whole person rather than merely tweaking the external facade.

Indeed, what would our world be like if all the Bensen Quinns had their Kenji, their transformational coach? From my work with many Bensen Quinns over the years, I am confident we would have a world of leaders more passionate about the high performance and across-the-board sustainability of their organizations, their communities, and their world.

To accomplish this, people who coach others need to move from a *transactive model* concerned primarily with competencies, learning skills, and techniques to a *transformative model* focused on fundamentally shifting people's view about themselves, their values, and their sense of purpose.

Influenced by the work of Robert Hargrove, I think most coaching today fits within one of three categories:

- *Transactive coaching* (building skills and competencies)
- *Pattern coaching* (revealing old patterns and building new patterns of belief and behavior)
- *Transformative coaching* (fostering a fundamental shift in point of view, values, and purpose)

In our story, Kenji did very little transactional coaching with Bensen, whose business skills and competencies were exceptionally developed. Rather, Kenji's questioning process helped Bensen first to discover his patterns of thought and behavior and then to create a shift in his self-understanding and his fundamental approach to leadership. From Kenji's very first questions—"Are you all right, Mr. Quinn?" and "What music will I be remembered for? Am I touching people's lives, right now, in a way they are going to remember?"—he began examining Bensen's way of life, shaking his comfortable sense of self, and awakening him to transformation.

———

So what are the core skills to help us move from being a transactional coach focused on skill building and imparting knowledge to being a transformational coach focused on revealing patterns and fundamentally shifting perspective? As we have seen from the Growth Guide thus far, three equally important processes are required:

- Building Awareness
- Building Commitment
- Building Practice

As leaders, we are constantly faced with the task of *Building Awareness:* Awareness of changing market conditions, emerging economic realities, new capital needs, cost concerns, and operational issues dominate our time and attention. But often the greatest task of Building Awareness is in the human, interpersonal domain. I would venture to say that most business problems today are of a human, interpersonal nature. People problems are typically quite complex, yet when individuals, teams, or managers in conflict come to us with their concerns, don't we all too often slip into a reactive, knee-jerk mode, looking for a simple fix?

Helping others to Build Awareness requires discipline on the part of the coach to stay out of the expert or fix-it approaches to coaching. If we don't, the awareness we build will be *our awareness*—that is, we will be imposing our awareness onto the coachee—as opposed to building the awareness of the person we are coaching *from the inside out.* St. Theresa of Lisieux stated it this way: "One of the most difficult things about being a spiritual director is to encourage people along paths you would not choose for yourself." Building Awareness requires openness to help the person we are coaching *to sort out their current reality for themselves and begin to chart out alternative future possibilities.*

To guide your ability to Build Awareness with people you coach, keep the following principles in mind:

- *Stay open and stay out of expert or fix-it mode.* The answers already lie within the person; your job is to help to clarify and reveal them. The one time Bensen approaches Kenji for advice (when he is hanging back on his de-

cision to confront the Board of Directors with his new plan), Kenji re-
fuses the role of expert and puts the ball back in Bensen's court: "Look
within to find your true conviction, what you believe, what you stand
for," he tells Bensen. "Feel the answer in your heart, have courage, and
take action—go the way of a true leader."

- *Use questions to help the person sort out his or her current situation.* Before we
  can move forward with power, we need to know where we stand, understanding both life-enriching and life-damaging behavior and beliefs.
  "I've found that I can only change how I act if I stay aware of my beliefs
  and assumptions," writes Margaret Wheatley, author of *Leadership and the
  New Science.* Very few people take the time or possess the necessary in-
  trospective skills to do this without the gentle prodding of a coach. Keep
  in mind the Native American saying, "the first people had questions and
  they were free. The second people had answers and they were forever en-
  slaved." Questions *are* the language of coaching. They are powerful tools
  for transformation because, as Bertrand Russell taught, "In all affairs it's
  a healthy thing now and then to hang a question mark on things you have
  long taken for granted." If you look back at the sequence of Kenji-
  Bensen dialogues, you will see how consistently Kenji used this method
  to facilitate Bensen's unfolding self-discovery.

- *Be courageous enough, as Robert Hargrove advises, "to discuss the undiscussable."*
  The coach's job is to shed light on dark regions previously unexplored.
  Recall how Kenji gently confronted Bensen with his hidden altruism and
  rekindled his latent impulse to serve.

- *Speak directly but with concern.* Help the person *compassionately* to see his or
  her limitations, misattributions, limiting beliefs, and damaging behaviors.
  Keep in mind: directness without compassion will create resistance, directness with compassion will create openness. Confront in a caring manner.

- *Help the person to explore the differences between his or her intentions and other
  people's perceptions.* Discrepancies between how people see themselves and
  how others perceive them often hold the key to growing in self-
  knowledge and overcoming blind spots. Helping people to see aspects of
  themselves through the eyes of others can be challenging, but effective.
  Use feedback tools like 360-degree assessment to assist in this ongoing
  process.

- *Build awareness by example.* The greatest teachers and coaches teach more
  by their being than by their doing. Kenji gave Bensen a vision of living

by *how he lived* as much as by what he said. If you strive for authenticity, open up to Essence, align with your life purpose, and connect to other people, you will spontaneously create more value in everything you do; those you coach will model their lives upon what you are living. The Bhagavad Gita, an invaluable ancient handbook on leadership development, guides us: "Whatsoever a great man does, the very same is also done by other men. Whatever standard he sets, the world follows it." Or as Anne Sophie Swetchine so beautifully put it, "There is a transcendent power in example. We reform others unconsciously when we walk uprightly."

- *Help people to uncover and align with what is meaningful and important to them.* As coachees discovers the core principles that guide their meaningful contributions in the world, help them to explore how aligned or misaligned the various part of their lives—personal, family, community, career, spiritual—are with these values. An effective transformational coach is both an archeologist who helps to unearth the important structures—that is, the core meaningful contributions—supporting our past, and a builder who helps us construct a future based on these principles and values.

Building Commitment is the second stage of transformational coaching. Having awareness without emotional engagement and commitment is an empty promise to ourselves. We want to exercise, we just don't feel compelled to do it. . . . We want to spend more time at home, but we never seem to leave the office before 7:30. . . . We say our spiritual life is important, but we rarely reflect on it beyond Sunday services. . . . So what makes us committed to actually do something?

Commitment comes from *emotional engagement* with the life-enriching and life-damaging consequences of our current behavior. Thinking about it—building awareness—is a good beginning, but it's not enough. We have to truly feel it. This is why trauma is such a superb teacher. Lying in a hospital bed after a heart attack, we can see the ramifications of our behavior in no uncertain terms.

To elicit commitment, we must help people to envision the positive and negative outcomes—what they will gain and what they will lose—if they continue on their current path. When the emotions deeply register both the compelling reasons to change and the damaging consequences of the behaviors to leave behind, transformation begins. In the words of Margaret Wheatley, "The greatest source of courage is to realize that if we don't act, nothing will change for the better."

To guide your ability to Build Commitment with people you coach, keep the following principles in mind:

- *Help people to sort out consequences.* By guiding people to fully grasp the life-enriching and life-damaging consequences of their current behavior or path, you will help them to feel the creative tension between where they want to end up and where they are actually headed as a result of their actions. Helping people to envision these alternative futures and to make new life choices is the essence of coaching and building commitment. Remember, the person has to *see* and *feel* these consequences for himself or herself—not just see your version of the consequences.

- *Allow your commitment to catalyze their commitment.* Often it is the emotional engagement of the coach that serves as the impetus for the transformation to begin. It was Kenji's unwavering commitment to Bensen's growth that lit the fire for his transformation. "There comes that mysterious meeting in life when someone acknowledges who we are and what we can be, igniting the circuits of our highest potential," writes Rusty Berkus.

- *Look for openings.* Commitment is far more likely to take place when vulnerability (i.e., the likelihood of undesirable or challenging future scenarios' coming to fruition) is sufficiently high. Look for these openings and leverage their growth potential. Situations that might make people more open to commitment include less-than-positive performance reviews, disturbing 360-degree feedback, life traumas, career setbacks, relational breakdowns, broken commitments by others, new or exceptional challenges, need for new skills, lack of preparedness, fear of failure, and new career or life responsibilities. Look for these openings as an opportunity to accelerate progress.

- *Make sure commitment leads to practice.* If commitment does not lead to practice, then it is your responsibility as the coach to help the person do one of two things: explore more deeply the consequences of staying on his or her current track, in order to achieve a more genuine emotional engagement leading to actual practice, or find new practices that are more suited to the person. Not everything works for everyone.

- *Be patient.* As coaches we are motivated to help people grow—now. However, each flower needs to unfold at its own pace. If you must be impatient, be impatient with developing your own enhanced skills as a coach.
- *Remember the why.* Coaches remind people what is at stake and why they are doing something in the first place. Use the "Power of Why" to uncover the person's underlying fears, assumptions, beliefs, and motivators. Wait for the right moment of opening to ask in a caring manner, "Why?" If one "why?" doesn't get to the heart of things, you may ask it two or three times in a row in order to dive deeply under the surface conversation.

Building Practice is the third stage of transformational coaching. Without practice, there is no transformation. Practice breathes life into our new awareness and commitment. We can be fully aware and committed to noble goals, but if we fail to practice them, it is like someone who lights a lamp and then closes his eyes. "In the end," said Max De Pree, "it is important to remember that we cannot become what we need to be by remaining where we were."

Beginning practice makes the possible probable; advanced, enduring practice makes the possible real.

Practices involve the consistent repetition of new behaviors that transform our lives. Exercise is a practice to build health. Meditation is a practice to unfold our spiritual life. Reflecting at the end of each day on how our interpersonal interactions went is a practice that builds relational effectiveness. Not letting fears or limiting beliefs sabotage our goals can be a lifelong practice for most of us, helping us to move forward when the easier or lazier way would be to remain where we are, locked in our limiting belief systems.

For a practice to become a habit, often it needs to be *consistently engaged* for at least 40 days. A day here and a day there will not effect transformation. At first our practice requires discipline, that is, doing something we may not be inclined to do. Over time, however, the discipline is replaced by the life-enriching benefits we are gaining; then the practice becomes more self-sustaining and requires less effort. Discipline carries us to the benefits, and the benefits sustain the new behavior.

To guide your ability to Build Practice with people you coach, keep the following principles in mind:

- *Co-create the practice with the person.* A practice must push boundaries but also be suitable to the person. Ask the person you are coaching, "What new behavior could you practice that over time would move you forward?" Then take time to brainstorm together to co-create a meaningful practice. Keep the practices simple and defined. Make sure the person wants to give the practice a try.

- *Hold the person accountable.* Define how often the person will do the practice (daily, twice a day, etc.) and over what duration (a week, a month, etc.). Meet with the person to audit progress and lack of progress. Hold him or her accountable, set new goals, and create new practices as needed.

- *Avoid Intellectualizing.* Thinking about doing something is not the same as doing something, so make sure your practices are *behaviors that engage the person in a new way* rather than encouraging him or her only to *think about* behaving in a new way without actually taking the leap into action.

- *Just do it. . . . or do something else.* While some practices are more dynamic (exercise, asserting our viewpoint, expressing our values) and others are more reflective (pausing to connect with Essence, reflecting on our day), the key to practice is taking action. An initial practice may not be the one that revolutionizes the person's life, but it is the beginning of a process that will lead to a practice that does have an impact. Sometimes the most important contribution a coach can make is to keep people trying new practices and then helping them struggle through the challenges that come up until they settle on an enduring practice and improvement takes place.

The Seed of Coaching:
Growth Guide

To help you prepare yourself to build your coaching skills, take some time to reflect on the following questions:

What qualities do you have that already make you an effective coach? _____

_____

_____

_____

What qualities or behaviors do you feel you need to develop? _____

_____

_____

_____

How would being a more effective coach result in positive changes in your organization?

_____

_____

_____

The next time you coach someone, how can you keep from being Mr. or Ms. Fix-it and instead guide the person to his or her own solution? _____

_____

_____

_____

What do you need to practice in order to be a more effective coach? _____

_____

_____

_____

Awakening the Leader Within:
The Journey Begins

Well, it seems we have arrived at the end of our present journey together. I hope this moment finds you with a deeper sense of purpose and fulfillment than the moment you first picked up the book. I also hope the process of reading the tale of Bensen's transformation, and your own reflections and inner work, both during the story and through the Growth Guide, have served as a catalyst to spark your own growth, and that you will now light the torch of everyone you touch.

May we all have the courage to grow like Bensen, and the wisdom to inspire others like Kenji. If we do, we can accomplish great things for our organizations, our families, and our planet.

My wish to you as you continue your own journey is: *be authentic, be purposeful, transform your life, transform our world.* In the inspiring, prophetic words of the Native American leader Chief Seattle, words that remind us of our great responsibilities as leaders, as coaches, and as human beings:

> The earth does not belong to man, man belongs to the earth.
> All things are connected like the blood that unites us all.
> Man did not weave the web of life, he is merely a strand in it.
> Whatever he does to the web, he does to himself.

May your strand of leadership be strong and your contribution to the web of life be rich with authenticity and purpose.

About the Author

Kevin Cashman is founder and CEO of Leader-Source®, a leadership development and executive coaching consultancy with a global clientele and offices across the United States. Referred to as "the Mayo Clinic of Leadership Development" by *Fast Company* magazine, LeaderSource takes a whole-person approach to leadership effectiveness.

Over the past 20 years, Kevin and his team have coached thousands of senior executives and senior teams to enhance performance. He is the founder of the *Executive to Leader Institute*®, which has been recognized for its interdisciplinary approach to executive coaching. His clients span a variety of Fortune 500, global, and fast-growth companies in the consumer products, health care, medical products, high technology, manufacturing, service, and food industries.

Kevin is the author of four books on leadership and career development. His book *Leadership from the Inside Out* was named the best-selling business book of 2000 and was also named one of the top 20 best-selling business books of the decade by CEO-READ. Kevin has been featured as a contributing author along with Warren Bennis, Stephen Covey, and Marshall Goldsmith in the books A *New Paradigm of Leadership* (1997) and *Partnering: The New Face of Leadership* (2002). He is also a contributing editor to *Executive Excellence* magazine along with Peter Senge, Charles Garfield, and Ken Blanchard. He has written numerous articles on leadership and career management, and he has been featured in the *Wall Street Journal, Chief Executive, Human Resource Executive, San Francisco Examiner, Fast Company, Strategy & Leadership, Oprah, CNN* and other national media.

A frequent keynote speaker at major conferences and corporate events,

Kevin was formerly the cohost of the CareerTalk radio program. He has been chapter president, board member, and fellow of the International Association of Career Management Professionals.

Kevin's educational background includes a psychology degree from St. John's University. A believer in dynamic life balance, he has participated in more than 50 triathlons and has practiced and taught meditation for over three decades. He lives in Minneapolis on the Mississippi riverfront overlooking the historic St. Anthony Falls.

About the Collaborator

Jack Forem is a freelance writer living in Westminster, California, specializing in books on human development and life enhancement.

About
LeaderSource®

LeaderSource is a leadership development and executive coaching consultancy serving as a catalyst in the transformation of leaders and organizations.

With offices across the United States, LeaderSource® serves the needs of leaders and organizations nationally and internationally. Referred to as "the Mayo Clinic of Leadership Development" by *Fast Company* magazine, LeaderSource takes a whole-person approach to leadership effectiveness. LeaderSource's clients span a variety of Fortune 500, global, and fast-growth companies in the consumer products, health care, medical products, high technology, manufacturing, service, and food industries.

Offering an entire continuum of leadership development programs, LeaderSource seeks to awaken leadership at all levels of organizations and at all stages of career and life development. Key LeaderSource offerings include: *Executive to Leader Institute*®, an intensive, interdisciplinary, one-on-one coaching program for senior executives; *LeaderSynergy*®, a comprehensive team-coaching experience to optimize senior team effectiveness; *LeaderCatalyst*®, a transformational learning experience (in groups) that fosters leadership development and coaching; *Manager to Leader*®, a one-on-one coaching program for key managers; *LeaderConnect*®, an intensive, whole-life executive career transition coaching program; and *LifePlan Institute*SM, a whole-life retirement coaching program for executives and their spouses.

LeaderSource Headquarters
The Crown Plaza Building
100 Portland Avenue
Minneapolis, MN 55401
Phone: 612-375-9277
Fax: 612-334-5727
www.leadersource.com

Bibliography

The following list of books combines resources used and recommended reading.

Albom, Mitch. *Tuesdays with Morrie.* New York, NY: Doubleday, 1997.

Bennis, Warren. *On Becoming a Leader.* Reading, MA: Addison-Wesley, 1990.

Block, Peter. *Stewardship: Choosing Service over Self Interest.* San Francisco, CA: Berrett-Koehler, 1996.

Boldt, Laurence G. *Zen and the Art of Making a Living: A Practical Guide to Creative Career Design.* New York, NY: Arkana Penguin, 1993.

Branden, Nathanial. *Six Pillars of Self-Esteem.* New York, NY: Bantam Books, 1995.

Campbell, Joseph. *The Power of Myth.* New York, NY: Doubleday, 1988.

Cashman, Kevin. *Leadership from the Inside Out.* Provo, UT: Executive Excellence, 1998.

Champy, James, and Nitin Nohria. *The Arc of Ambition: Defining the Leadership Journey.* Cambridge, MA: Perseus Books, 1999.

Collins, Jim. *Good to Great: Why Some Companies Make the Leap . . . and Others Don't.* New York, NY: Harper Business, 2001.

Dreher, Diane. *The Tao of Personal Leadership.* New York, NY: Harper Collins, 1996.

Eastman, Joseph Maynard. *What Is Becoming Clearer to Me.* Littleton, CO: Profitable Publishing, 2002.

Emerson, Ralph Waldo. *The Collected Works of Ralph Waldo Emerson.* Cambridge, MA: Belkoop, 1984.

Flaherty, James. *Coaching: Evoking Excellence in Others.* Woburn, MA: Butterworth-Heinemann, 1999.

Frankl, Viktor E., and Gordon W. Allport. *Man's Search for Meaning.* Washington Square Press, December 1977.

Gardner, Howard, with the collaboration of Emma Laskin. *Leading Minds: An Anatomy of Leadership.* New York, NY: BasicBooks, Perseus Books Group, 1995.

Goleman, Daniel. *Working with Emotional Intelligence.* New York: Bantam Doubleday Dell, 1998.

Goleman, Daniel, Richard Boyatzis, and Annie McKee. *Primal Leadership: Realizing the Power of Emotional Intelligence.* Boston, MA: Harvard Business School Press, 2002.

Hargrove, Robert. *Masterful Coaching.* San Francisco, CA: Jossey-Bass/Pfeiffer, 1995.

Hawken, Paul, Amory Lovins, and L. Hunter Lovins. *Natural Capitalism: Creating the Next Industrial Revolution.* Little, Brown and Company, 1999.

Hendricks, Gay, and Kate Ludeman. *The Corporate Mystic: A Guidebook for Visionaries with Their Feet on the Ground.* Bantam Books, 1996.

Jaworski, Joseph. *Synchronicity: The Inner Path of Leadership.* San Francisco, CA: Berrett-Koehler, 1996.

Kouzes, James M., and Barry Z. Posner. *Credibility: How Leaders Gain and Lose It; Why People Demand It.* San Francisco, CA: Jossey-Bass, 1993.

Leider, Richard J., and David A. Shapiro. *Whistle While You Work: Heeding Your Life's Calling.* Berrett-Koehler, 2001.

Leonard, George. *Mastery: The Keys to Success and Long-Term Fulfillment.* E. P. Dutton, 1991.

Levoy, Gregg. *Callings: Finding and Following an Authentic Life.* New York, NY: Three Rivers, 1997.

Mahesh, Maharishi, Yogi. *Science of Being and Art of Living.* New York, NY: Penguin, 1995.

Maslow, Abraham. *Toward a Psychology of Being.* New York, NY: Van Nostrand Reinhold, 1968.

Matusak, Larraine R. *Finding Your Voice: Learning to Lead . . . Anywhere You Want to Make a Difference.* San Francisco, CA: Jossey-Bass, 1997.

Percy, Ian. *Going Deep: Exploring Spirituality in Life and Leadership.* Toronto, Canada: Macmillan Canada, 1997.

Richo, David. *When Love Meets Fear: How to Become Defense-less and Resource-full.* Mahwah, NJ: Paulist Press, 1997.

Segal, Jeanne. *Raising Your Emotional Intelligence: A Practical Guide.* New York, NY: Henry Holt, 1997.

Seligman, Martin E. P. *Learned Optimism: How to Change Your Mind and Your Life*. New York, NY: Pocket Books, 1998.

Senge, Peter. *The Fifth Discipline: The Act and Practice of the Learning Organization*. New York, NY: Doubleday Currency, 1994.

Terry, Robert. *The Seven Zones of Leadership*. Palo Alto, CA: Davies-Black, 2001.

Tzu, Lao. *Tao Te Ching of Lao Tzu*. New York, NY: St. Martin's, 1996.

Wheatley, Margaret J. *Leadership and the New Science: Discovering Order in a Choatic World*. San Francisco, CA: Berrett-Koehler, 1999.

Whyte, David. *The Heart Aroused: Poetry and the Preservation of the Soul in Corporate America*. New York, NY: Doubleday Currency, 1994.

Wilber, Ken. *No Boundary: Eastern and Western Approaches to Personal Growth*. Boston, MA: Shambhala, 1978.

Acknowledgments

The first and foremost person to acknowledge for this book is Jack Forem, my collaborator. When I think of all the partnering and teaming experiences in my career, this one is the best. We laughed our guts out and cried our eyes out, never once experiencing anything but complementary flow. I can't wait until our next project, and we both know what it is, don't we? Also, the warmest of thanks to Roberta Forem for supporting Jack and me with your sage counsel and for adding so much at crucial decision points.

Next, I'd like to thank Christiane Francois. What can I say that I haven't said to you before? I'm a very fortunate man to be blessed with a woman so intelligent, so wise, and so beautiful. If you, the reader, enjoyed the quotes in the Growth Guide, you can thank Christiane for her amazing research. Christiane, do you think we have enough quotes left over to guide us through the rest of our lives together?

I'm dedicating this book to the memory of one of my real-life Kenjis: Sidney Reisberg. Sidney was my business partner, mentor, and friend for more than 20 years. Like Kenji, Sidney guided me, nurtured me, challenged me, and helped me become a more complete human being. Like Kenji, Sidney's body passed on toward the end of the book. Like Kenji, Sidney passed on his precious wisdom and love of life to me. I love you, Sidney, and hope to carry forward some of your wisdom and legacy.

I have been blessed to have been mentored from a young age by a real-life master teacher, Maharishi Mahesh Yogi; his wisdom, inspiration, and knowledge have transformed my life.

Without my clients, this book could not exist; it captures *their* wisdom and *their* career-life stories. As my clients demonstrate daily, the coach always grows more than the coachee. Special thanks go to all of the clients and supporters of LeaderSource who have given such valuable input into this project:

Margie Adler, Ann Bancroft, Jim and Deena Behnke, Warren Bennis, Dean Buresh, Dan Carr, Judy Corson, Tom Debrowski, James Ehlen, M.D., Cliff Eslinger, Chuck Feltz, Janet and Doug Fiola, Sarah and Fred Haberman, John Haines, Dan Harding, Rob Hawthorne, Mike Howe, Paul Howes, Dianne Hranicky, Richard Hynes, Ron James, David Koch, Peggy Lauritsen, Richard Leider, Greg LeVoy, John Lilly, Kate Ludeman, David McNally, Marti Morfitt, Robert Morgan, Kurt Mueller, Craig Neal, Liz Otto, Linda Page, Mike Peel, Scott Peterson, Br. Deitrich Reinhart, Cindy Rodahl, Bill Scheurer, Jim Secord, David Shadovitz, Steve Shank, David Smart, Linda Sorrell, Marchita Stanton, David Strand, Gregg Vandesteeg, David Wessner, David Whyte, Kevin Wilde, and Steve Young.

This book would also not exist without LeaderSource. Unless you have been through one of our coaching programs, you just can't know what an amazing, talented group of people they are. Often people tell me, "Kevin, your books, speaking and coaching are great, but what's really fantastic is your *team!*" I'm so appreciative of all of you and I hope you all know that. Thanks to Cecile Burzynski, our COO, for keeping the business together as I ventured into the writing wilderness . . . again! Special thanks to Sherri Rogalski for your work on the manuscript and your constant enthusiasm, support and encouragement about the book. Thanks to Faye Way for keeping me sane and organized, as usual. What would I do without you? Thanks to Mary Orysen and Karla Lindblad for tolerating me when I would show up like the "old" Bensen Quinn, at times! Most importantly, thanks to the team of Leader-Source coaches who shared their wisdom and input on the manuscript: Janet Feldman, Joe Eastman, Katie Cooney, Bill McCarthy, Pat Mulvehill, Renée Garpestad, Sarah Flynn, Anne Tessien, Jody Thone, Karen Dobbins, Mary Ann Donahue, Paul Strickland, Steve Ruff, and Al Watts. Thanks for your presence in my life.

Not many authors can say this, but I do have the best literary agent in the world: Laureen Rowland at the David Black Agency. Even if you weren't my agent, I'd still want to hang out with you. Your encouragement, wisdom, and tenacity are wonderful.

Deep, heartfelt thanks to Airié Stuart at John Wiley & Sons, my publisher. Airié, I knew from our first meeting that you were the right choice for this book! Thanks also to Michelle Patterson, Laurie Frank Harting, and Emily Conway at Wiley for your tremendous support.

The greatest acknowledgment goes to you, the reader. Thank you for the opportunity to live my purpose and hopefully be an instrument of essence to enrich your life.